ALEXANDER DALLIN *is Adlai E. Stevenson Professor of International Relations at Columbia University. He is the author of* German Rule in Russia, 1941-45, *and several other books.*

THOMAS B. LARSON *is a Senior Fellow at the Russian Institute at Columbia University, where he also teaches courses on Soviet politics. He has written numerous articles on Soviet affairs. As a former Foreign Service officer he served in Moscow and Paris. He was also Chief of Research on the USSR and Eastern Europe in the Department of State.*

Soviet Politics
Since Khrushchev

Edited by
ALEXANDER DALLIN
and
THOMAS B. LARSON

PRENTICE-HALL, INC. A SPECTRUM BOOK   Englewood Cliffs, N. J.

Preface

A colleague, recently back from the Soviet Union after an absence of several years, summed up his experiences by reporting that he brought with him three distinct impressions, for each of which he could offer some evidence: (1) things have not changed; (2) things have gotten worse; (3) things have improved. Other observers of the Soviet scene, whether on the spot or from afar, have been similarly struck by the simultaneity of contradictory trends since the retirement of Nikita Khrushchev in October, 1964. While at all other "turning points" of Soviet politics, over the past half-century, it was relatively easy to determine the general direction of the change and the political orientation of the leadership, no such simple answers have emerged with regard to the post-Khrushchev era. Indeed, the very fact that we refer to it in this fashion, with no name of its own, is indicative of the problem.

Some part of the difficulty may well be due to the external observer and his tools and to the handicaps of communication (including the strikingly greater reticence of the Kosygin-Brezhnev regime to make public pronouncements than was true of the ebullient Khrushchev, who was always prepared to argue and improvise). But when all possible allowance is made for these extraneous considerations, there remains a vast area of uncertainty in the interpretation of the present Soviet policies and purposes, which must be assumed to reflect uncertainties in Soviet reality itself. In other words, the contradictions, ambiguities, and lack of simple or single answers are among the major characteristics of the present phase of Soviet development.

Given the search—and need—for an understanding of these trends, it has seemed desirable to make available in this fashion a series of papers initially prepared for another purpose. Under contract with the United States Arms Control and Disarmament Agency and under the auspices of the Russian Institute at Columbia University, a group of specialists in Soviet affairs undertook to reassess the conclusions reached in an earlier study essentially concerned with Soviet attitudes and conduct with regard to arms control and disarmament, produced under a similar arrangement. The earlier study examined this problem

v

in the setting of the Khrushchev era.[1] The follow-up inquiry addressed itself to the same range of questions for the period following Khrushchev's ouster.[2] It was as background for that study that the papers included in this volume were originally solicited. They provided so excellent a basis for an extended series of discussions by a group of scholars that all those connected with the project readily agreed on the utility of their separate publication.[3]

The essays in this volume discuss the major areas of Soviet policy and politics; by design, they do not spotlight arms control policies directly—these are treated in the separate volume cited above—but rather seek to analyze and interpret relevant trends in Soviet domestic and foreign affairs. They do not claim to provide definitive answers and assessments. In fact, it might be said that they provide several assessments: the careful reader will detect some significant differences of interpretation among the contributors; the editors would probably have others to add. Such a diversity of approaches and interpretations is, we believe, both healthy and particularly appropriate in this instance; it will, we hope, be instructive to the reader too. We have been interested to discover that, in spite of these variations, there emerges from these essays a common core of insights and perceptions.

Thomas B. Larson, as the author of the final report of this project, was also responsible for coordinating and reviewing the contributions here presented, working with the authors on such revisions as were called for and on bringing the essays up to date. Alexander Dallin, as chairman of the study, initiated the definition of the topics and the scope of the papers with the authors and reviewed the final product. Constance A. Bezer was an invaluable administrative assistant who handled all tasks, possible and impossible, with equal dispatch. Our thanks go also to those other colleagues who, at various stages, commented on individual papers or participated in our discussions: Abram Bergson, Severyn Bialer, Urie Bronfenbrenner, Zbigniew Brzezinski, Loren R. Graham, Harland Moulton, Kent K. Parrot, Warner R. Schilling, Marshall D. Shulman, Helmut Sonnenfeldt, Robert C. Tucker, and Lyman Wooster.

ALEXANDER DALLIN
THOMAS B. LARSON

[1] Alexander Dallin *et al., The Soviet Union and Disarmament* (New York: Frederick A. Praeger, Inc., 1965).

[2] Thomas B. Larson, *Disarmament and Soviet Policy: 1964-1968* (Englewood Cliffs, N.J.: Prentice-Hall, Inc., 1968).

[3] Needless to say, the judgments expressed in this volume are those of the author and do not necessarily reflect the views of the U.S. Arms Control and Disarmament Agency or of Columbia University.

Contents

vii

Chapter 6

Chapter 7

*Soviet Politics
Since Kruschchev*

The Soviet Union in the
Post-Revolutionary Era: An Overview

1

RICHARD LOWENTHAL

Three years have passed since N. S. Khrushchev was deposed as leader of the CPSU and the Soviet government by a bloodless and "legal" coup by his immediate colleagues and subordinates—the controlling group of the bureaucratic oligarchy. The colorful, impulsive individualist who raved against the "cult of the individual," the bold, iconoclastic reformer who was also an ardent ideological believer, the ambitious adventurer who challenged the power of the United States with his missiles and then sought a dialogue with that chief opponent, was replaced by a tight-lipped collective of faceless, cautious, and pragmatic men—agnostic in everything but their commitment to the greatness of Russia and to the need for orderly procedures. Compared with the giants of the revolutionary age and the period of transition, with Lenin and Stalin and even with Khrushchev, this grey *directoire* of post-revolutionary administrators appeared at first sight incapable of governing a world power: their inability to make great decisions would either lead to their being overthrown in renewed internal struggles or to the decline of their country. Overnight, the spreading conviction that the Soviet Union was no longer a serious threat to

RICHARD LOWENTHAL (Ph.D. Heidelberg, 1931) is Professor of International Relations at the Free University of Berlin. His career has spanned many countries and included public service, political action, academic instruction and research, journalism, and administration. He left Germany in 1935 for England, where he became political journalist for Reuters and foreign affairs commentator for *The Observer*. He is the author of many widely-known articles on Soviet and Communist affairs and (under pseudonyms) the author of various books, the latest of which (under his own name) is *World Communism*. He has been associated with the Russian Research Center at Harvard (1960-61) and the Research Institute on Communist Affairs at Columbia (1963-64), and has taught at Columbia and the University of California at Berkeley.

1

Western interests gained a new foundation in a kind of psychological impressionism: those "clerks" were simply too boring to be dangerous.

Yet if we compare the state of the Soviet Union today with what it was at the time of Khrushchev's fall, those early, complacent expectations are by no means confirmed. At home, the collective leadership has maintained its division of labor and has stabilized its rule without major purges. It has overcome the crisis of confidence within the Party apparatus caused by Khrushchev's reorganization of 1962, even though the underlying problems remain unresolved. It has managed to combine an effective liberation of the sciences from *doctrinaire* interference with a tightening of *political* control over non-conformist writers and artists, and to maintain the official strictures on Stalin's arbitrary rule while containing the flow of literary exposures. Finally it has achieved marked improvements in the rate of economic growth and, above all, in the income of the peasant population, by a combination of investment shifts and planning reforms carried out despite the continued bureaucratic resistance against both, and so far without a major visible political showdown.

Abroad, the improvement has been far more dramatic. In the East, the challenge of Chinese hostility has been contained, in part, by a limited re-engagement in Vietnam and persistent offers of a united front, which have virtually isolated Peking from its former Asian supporters without any serious risk of a clash with the United States, and in part by a steady improvement of relations with the great non-Communist nations of Asia. In Europe, the loosening of the Warsaw Pact has been halted at the point reached after Rumania's "declaration of independence" and has given way to some degree of military and political consolidation among the other partners. At the same time, the growing disintegration of NATO has permitted Moscow to stimulate competition for its favors among the Western powers and to regain the diplomatic initiative in this theater. Paradoxically, the Soviet Union thus faces the United States in a stronger political position than before China turned from an ally into an enemy. After a period of humiliating and frightening American military superiority, the development of ABM defenses has now given Moscow a new asset for military bargaining as well. Even in the ideological field, the abandonment of all public claims to doctrinal authority or intervention in the affairs of other parties has enabled Khrushchev's successors to overcome the decline of international influence and regain a more respected position in a number of independent-minded Communist Parties, while the influence of pro-Soviet Communists in the ruling nationalist parties of progressive Arab countries has increased at the same time.

Of course, not all these successes can be attributed to the skill and wisdom of the collective leadership alone. Their economic policies in particular have greatly benefited from the bumper harvest granted them in 1966 by an act of God, while their foreign policies have been favored no less effectively by the actions of Messrs. Mao Tse-tung, de Gaulle, and Johnson. Yet it is well-known that the gods help only those who help themselves, and even windfalls cannot be exploited successfully without policy decisions. What the above record suggests is precisely that the post-Khrushchev oligarchs have made a number of important new decisions, both at home and abroad, even though they may have refrained from announcing them by the familiar ideological fanfares. In a number of cases, their seeming indecisiveness may rather have been a reluctance to use big words and dramatic gestures, which seems characteristic for post-revolutionary regimes, combined with a desire to keep the real issues in the inner circle and out of sight of the masses, which is typical of oligarchies. I do not intend to deny that in dealing with Russia's problems in this pragmatic, cautious, and even secretive new style, they may have tried to sweep some truly vital issues under the carpet, and that history may yet catch up with them. But on the whole, they have simply followed the economic principle of seeking to achieve big effects with the smallest possible means and, in particular, have sought to rationalize Soviet policies by eliminating the "waste" due to the need for public, ideological justification. The results suggest that, in the present phase of Soviet history, bureaucratic rationality has distinct advantages over inspirational leadership.

THE POST-REVOLUTIONARY REGIME

The present phase is post-revolutionary in the sense that the process of planned transformation of Soviet society, imposed on it from above by the dictatorial Party, has spent itself. To that extent the regime may also be described as post-totalitarian, even though the formal institutions of single-party rule are still intact. The dynamics of planned transformation had run into increasing resistance as the growth of an industrial society began to bring forth a dynamic process of a different kind—that of spontaneous economic development—and as Khrushchev's efforts to continue pursuing the goals of the revolution from above by changing its methods ended in failure. The new Party Program adopted at the XXII Congress in 1961 may be said to have marked the end of the revolutionary era and the first victory of the new dynamics of spontaneous social growth over the old dynamics of ideologically guided transformation—the beginnings of the emancipation of Soviet society from the strait jacket of the totalitarian state. Khrushchev understood the historic significance of the turning point well enough to wish to adjust the organization of the Party to its new, post-revolutionary role, which he conceived as revolving chiefly around economic administration. What he failed to understand in time was the fact that the primary concern of the Party would henceforth be to maintain its power by keeping the evolution of society within acceptable bounds, and that such a post-revolutionary regime did not require the unforeseeable initiatives of his type of dynamic leadership, but the calculable routine of stable, bureaucratic institutions.

The new regime, then, neither seeks to return to the utopian goals and the violent methods of Stalin's revolution from above, nor does it see itself in a liberal spirit as the mere representative of society and of the pressures for reform arising from it. It still wishes to control society, not in the totalitarian sense of imposing a preconceived pattern on it, but rather as an enlightened autocracy seeking to balance the need for reform with its own instinct of self-preservation, and to act as an arbiter between the various institutional groups within the bureaucratic elite that reflect the different tendencies within society. It thus holds on to the Party leadership's monopoly of political decision while permitting a growing pluralism of interests and opinions within the oligarchic structure. Hence, while it is true that the Party is no longer the driving force of society but rather is reacting to impulses resulting from its spontaneous growth, this is not the same as to claim that it has given up its policy-making role. The actual character of the regime, as radically different from the Stalinist model of the totalitarian *demiurgos* of society as from the liberal model of a political market in which the representatives of the social forces freely negotiate their compromises, is more reminiscent of tsarism during one of its moderately reformist periods, when the bureaucracy tried to keep society under tutelage by seeking to canalize its evolution.

The present essay aims not at a comprehensive description of the domestic policies of this regime, but merely at an outline of some characteristic features of its power structure, its attitude to "ideological" problems, and its relation to the pressures for economic reform.

The Bureaucratic Oligarchy

The present leadership has its origin in a collective revolt of the bureaucratic oligarchy of Party and state against the persistent efforts of N. S. Khrushchev to extend his personal power by appealing over their heads to wider strata of the Soviet public. In the institutional field, its policies have therefore turned around the dual effort to defend the privileges of the oligarchy against "democratic" instrusions and against any return to one-man rule.

The first and basic measure for restoring the oligarchy's sense of security has been the undoing of Khrushchev's "Party reform" of 1962. This has restored the Party machine's unity on the regional level and its ability to exert over-all control. At the same time it has given greater security and responsibility to the economic bureaucracy. The public criticism of Khrushchev's frequent and arbitrary reorganizations has also been intended to give the upper and middle ranks of the bureaucracy a greater sense of stability; at the XXIII Congress, this was underlined in principle by the revocation of Khrushchev's "rotation rule" and in practice by the small number of changes in the composition of the Central Committee. The reintroduction of Party conferences that are to meet in the intervals between congresses also serves to strengthen the *esprit de corps* of the oligarchy. It is characteristic of this political climate that Soviet criticism of the Chinese "cultural revolution" has focused from the start on the mobilization of young, inexperienced outsiders against the tried and proven Party cadres which form the true backbone of any Communist state. Equally typical is the recent *Pravda* attack on the Yugoslav Party reform for its tendency to dispense with the directing role of a disciplined Party.[1]

Closely linked with this oligarchic attitude is the new style of Party life as demonstrated at the XXIII Congress—the tendency not to explain the Party's problems in public, and to announce its policies not as if they were the result of difficult choices, but as if they were matters of course. This has indeed misled a number of observers into assuming that no new decisions were made. In fact, as will be discussed below, decisions had been made on such diverse topics as a reappraisal of the world relation of forces, the tactics for dealing with the Chinese ideological challenge, the treatment of Stalin and the Stalinist period, and the dropping of the utopian aspects of the 1961 Party Program—but they were applied rather than announced. Discussion and explanation were left to internal circulars and elite periodicals; the Party Congress was treated as a public demonstration that had to present a smooth façade to the non-initiated.

This applies in particular to the measures taken to prevent a return to one-man rule. Besides the decision to maintain a division of powers between the heads of Party and government and the dissolution of all of Khrushchev's hybrid Party-state bodies, these include above

[1] I. Pomelov in *Pravda*, February 20, 1967.

all the new relation between the renamed Politburo and the Secretariat, as well as the abolition of the Bureau for the RSFSR. The point is that the Central Committee secretaries are, and the members of the RSFSR Bureau were, subordinates of the First or General Secretary in an executive body. Stalin, however, in 1952 had made all the secretaries members or candidates of the Party Presidium, and Khrushchev repeated the practice at the height of his power from 1957 to the spring of 1960 and later varied it only by introducing some RSFSR Bureau members in the place of some secretaries—thus swamping the collegiate, policy-making body with people who were his subordinates in their executive function. Now only four secretaries are members[2] and two are candidates of the Politburo, and it seems likely that the reintroduction of this name is precisely intended to underline the political primacy of the Politburo over the Secretariat just as the return to the title of General Secretary underlines subordination within the Secretariat. Thus, Brezhnev, while recognized as the leading or senior member of the collective, will not have an automatic majority in the policy-making body and therefore, to use the words of *Pravda* (July 20, 1966), will not be in a position to act as its commander!

The temporary lack of a Second Secretary in charge of organization and personnel—as Khrushchev was under Malenkov and Kozlov was under Khrushchev—appeared as another precaution against the concentration of power in the Secretariat. For almost three years after Khrushchev's fall, all senior appointments seem to have remained matters for collective decision; only by mid-1967 were there indications that Suslov, the ranking Secretariat member under Brezhnev, was taking over the traditional duties of a chief of cadres. Finally, the redivision of Shelepin's "Party-state control" and the successive demotions both he and his close associates have suffered are evidence of the same preoccupation.

The effort to retain ultimate policy-making power in the hands of the Party's Politburo would be hopeless unless the leadership was willing to grant some freedom of expression to other sections of the bureaucratic oligarchy—to the military and the secret police, and the economic administrators and the managers. In fact, the public expression of different opinions by spokesmen for various elite groups, which began during the Khrushchev era, has become a generally accepted practice under the new regime. At the same time, the Party, i.e., the Politburo, is reserving the right of decision and pretending to be "above the battle." The appearance of differences of opinion *within* the Party leadership is to be avoided as far as possible; individ-

---

[2] Since Shelepin's transfer to trade union work, there are only three.

uals and institutions may differ publicly on important issues until the Party has spoken—but when it speaks, it is supposed to speak with a single voice.

The New Role of "Ideology"

The post-Khrushchevian Soviet leadership has puzzled a great many observers by the contrast between its emphasis on "ideological control" and the ideological hollowness of its utterances. On one side, it has blamed Khrushchev's 1962 reorganization for weakening the ideological role of the Party and has increasingly tried to impose ideological restrictions on the literary criticism of the Soviet scene and even of the Stalinist past. On the other hand, it has been more consistent than Khrushchev in liberating the natural, and to some extent even the social, sciences from doctrinaire shackles and has taken a strikingly agnostic attitude to the ideological goal of "communism" itself.

The apparent contradiction resolves itself as soon as we grasp the changed function of "ideology" in a post-revolutionary, bureaucratic regime. The leaders of that regime no longer believe in the possibility of forcibly transforming society in accordance with an ideological blueprint. Hence they no longer need a concept of a utopian goal— belief in the indefinite progress of productivity and the standard of living, of science and general education is sufficient to them as a guide for action, and "communism" is now no more than the limiting concept for this indefinite progress. Neither do they need a coherent doctrinaire system to inspire faith and self-sacrifice in the service of the revolution: for what is now required of the Soviet citizen, the combination of material incentives and patriotic pride is enough. (The Agitprop official Stepakov has beautifully illustrated the relation between material and moral incentives by the example of a ruble note, which states the cash value on one side but bears the emblem of the Soviet Union on the other!) But they do need controls to stop the spread of unpatriotic and antisocial ideas—hence they do need "ideological guidance" as an instrument of national and social discipline. Thus a marked decline in the revolutionary ideological motivation of the regime and in its interest in the cohesion of Marxist-Leninist doctrine is accompanied by a growing concern to suppress dangerous thoughts; we are faced not with a return to the totalitarian transformation of minds, but with the use of bureaucratic censorship as a weapon against dissent.

In Khrushchev's Party Program of 1961, the changes in the social structure required for attaining the higher stage of communism were no longer pictured as objectives for direct political action, but as the eventual automatic results of a steady growth in productivity and in the standards of living and of education. But if the vision of the future society had no relevance for present action, it was dangerous to promise its advent within a definite period; hence the present leaders have dispensed with the time-table for the journey to Utopia. Moreover, as Khrushchev's "polytechnic" reform of education proved to be an obstacle to effective, specialized learning, they have scrapped this piece of applied utopianism as well.

Again, if Marxist-Leninist doctrine could no longer be used to define valid policy goals, it was dangerous to allow the ex officio defenders of that doctrine to interfere with the sciences required for the operative goal of economic progress. If Party and state could no longer shape society at will but had to react to its spontaneous and often unforeseen development, empirical, undoctrinaire sociology was needed to study that development. Hence the emancipation of the sciences from doctrinaire interference has proceeded steadily under the new regime, quite undisturbed by the occasional laments of Agitprop functionaries, and scholarship is increasingly developing into an autonomous sphere of Soviet society.

On the other hand, the campaign to bring the literary intelligentsia under "ideological" control has been motivated not by a concern for doctrinaire uniformity but for practical respect for authority. The writers have been attacked for exposing one-sidedly the seamy sides of Soviet life, for undermining the younger generation's respect for their bureaucratic elders who served Stalin, and for destroying patriotic legends by their unvarnished descriptions of the last war. Even in the case of Siniavsky and Daniel, the central charge was not ideological anti-communism, but an unpatriotic "fouling of their own nest." The whole campaign has not been linked with any serious and concerted attempt to reinforce compliance with the formal canons of "socialist realism" but has turned on the Party's interest in banishing the treatment of subjects considered detrimental to national and social discipline. The Fourth Writers' Congress, in 1967, was notable not only for its suppression of Solzhenitsyn's complaint against the censorship, but also for its avoidance of literary controversy from either conservatives or innovators.

The so-called end to destalinization belongs in the same context. Apart from a few statements by individual "neo-Stalinists," there has been no attempt to whitewash Stalin's arbitrary rule. Memoirs containing instances of it have continued to be printed, and the general criticism of his purges has been repeated, though not officially stressed, in the jubilee year of 1967. What has been rejected, however, has been the concept of "the *period* of the personality cult" with its implication that the whole generation of bureaucrats who rose in the later thirties is tainted, and the tendency to dwell on this period and to use it for discrediting that generation. The meaning of this change, decided on the eve of the XXIII Congress, was not a general attempt to stop reform in the ideological sphere, but an effort to protect the Stalinist generation from the consequences of reform. It was thus part of the consolidation of the bureaucratic oligarchy.

Finally, this development has been linked with the growing effort to intensify the military-patriotic education of the younger generation and to raise the prestige of the army, and with the increasing prominence of army leaders and political officers in public life, which has been clearly promoted by Brezhnev himself.

Economic Reforms and Economic Priorities

Like Khrushchev in his final years, the new collective regards economic progress as the principal test of its own performance. Also like Khrushchev, it is more seriously exposed to the pulls and pressures of contradictory interests in this field than in any other. More clearly than elsewhere, we can thus see here which decisions have been taken and which have been evaded.

The most important decisions have been the massive increase of agricultural investments, announced in March, 1965, for the next five-year period, and the commitment to introduce promptly the minimum wage for collective farm (*kolkhoz*) peasants announced at the XXIII Party Congress. Aided by the 1966 record harvest, these policies have led to a remarkable rise in agricultural incomes and have created a favorable climate for further productive progress in the country-side after a period of stagnation. Politically, their adoption has clearly been facilitated by Brezhnev's inclination to treat agriculture as his and the Party machine's special domain, and therefore to align himself with the more "liberal" members of the collective on this subject.

Nevertheless, some further agricultural reforms have so far been postponed, indicating persistent conservative resistance. This applies in particular to the proposal, sponsored by the Komsomol and at times supported by *Pravda,* for permanently assigning to mechanized working teams within the *kolkhoz* responsibility for separate plots and to the project for creating *kolkhoz* associations on all levels with considerable autonomous powers, which Brezhnev himself sponsored at the Party Congress. Deadlock on these issues appears to be the reason for the repeated postponement of the *kolkhoz* congress that was to revise the model statute for collective farms. There have also been indications of attempts, so far unsuccessful, to use the 1966 record harvest as a pretext for scaling down agricultural investments.

In the field of industrial planning, the basic decisions have been the undoing of Khrushchev's 1957 reorganization—the dissolution of the economic councils (*sovnarkhozy*) and the restoration of the central industrial ministries—and the accelerated, though still very gradual, introduction of "Liberman-type" reforms increasing the managerial autonomy of successive groups of enterprises. There is no contradiction between these two aspects, as the "recentralization" of the planning machinery is not a retrograde measure but the correction of an unsuccessful experiment and is compatible with increased managerial autonomy. But quite apart from that alleged contradiction, there is evidence that bureaucratic resistance against the policy of increasing the scope for the manager and the forces of the market is still considerable; in particular, the vital issue of price reform is likely to have to be fought for at every step. Yet as the development of growth rates and productivity indicates, the balance-sheet of the compromises within the oligarchy has so far been one of clear, if moderate progress.

Continuation of that progress is likely to depend most of all on the shifting balance of priorities among armaments, heavy industry, consumer goods industry, and agriculture. The earlier tendency to reduce the arms budget has clearly been reversed under the combined impact of the Cuban defeat and the Vietnam war; the military leaders have achieved a definite condemnation of Khrushchev's excessive reliance on rocketry and obtained funds for a major effort to modernize Soviet conventional forces. But up to the Middle Eastern crisis of the summer of 1967, at any rate, the exponents of the need for a steady rise in the standard of living seem to have succeeded in keeping the arms drive within bounds and maintaining investment proportions that ensure a reasonable parallel development of the different sectors of the economy. The net effect of the struggle of interest groups, in this as in other fields, has up to now not been indecision and paralysis, but moderate, if still insecure progress.

Conflicts and Question Marks

So far, this paper has deliberately concentrated on the short-term achievements of the post-Khrushchevian oligarchy, while leaving the problem of its long-term viability to one side. The justification for this procedure lies in the need to correct, in the light of experience, the somewhat facile assumption that such a regime, because it must tend to paralysis or instability, could not decide a number of urgent issues successfully. Nevertheless, the contradictions perceived by the critics of the regime are real and from the viewpoint of long-term viability are significant.

There seem to be two such contradictions of central importance for the future of the oligarchic regime. The first is that even an oligarchic leadership needs a single leader if it is to maintain some cohesion and independence from the institutional power groups between which it is seeking to arbitrate. The role of the prime minister in oligarchic, eighteenth-century England is a good example of that. But the leader of a stable oligarchy must be replaceable, and his powers limited in institutional terms. I therefore agree with Zbigniew Brzezinski's view that the Soviet oligarchs will have to find an institutional solution for the problem of leadership if they wish to avoid the re-emergence of a leader with uncontrolled powers after a period of factional struggles or paralysis.

The other, more fundamental contradiction concerns the problem of popular participation. In a period of post-revolutionary fatigue, the people may be willing to accept for a time that decisions are made within a limited stratum of bureaucrats and are scarcely explained to them. They are grateful for being left alone to live their own lives and think their own thoughts after decades of forcible "mobilization." But even non-revolutionary progress requires some sort of communication between government and people, and thus the present secretive style will be increasingly difficult to maintain. As the areas of free discussion multiply, popular interest in the disputed issues will revive, and the temptation for rival groups and factions to appeal to "public opinion" in a wider sense will grow. This is a problem that cannot be solved within the confines of an oligarchic-bureaucratic system: it points to its eventual supersession with the further maturing of Russian society.

THE GUARDIANS OF THE NATIONAL INTEREST

The rise of the post-revolutionary, bureaucratic oligarchy has also marked an important shift in the balance of the forces motivating Soviet foreign policy. Brezhnev and Kosygin have come to power on a wave of sobering disappointments with Khrushchev's grandiose experiments abroad as well as at home. The dualism between the "normal" objectives of national power politics and the specific worldwide goals arising from the ideology of the ruling Communist Party may be traced in Soviet foreign policy as late as Khrushchev's attempt at a world-wide political breakthrough, which started with his Berlin ultimatum in November, 1958, and ended only in the Cuban missile crisis four years later. During the final years of Khrushchev's reign, however, the defeat of that grand offensive coincided with the final disappointment of his belief in a natural harmony of interests between independent Communist states and with the final change of the domestic role of the Party from a driving force of permanent revolution to an administrator of economic construction. These developments served to weaken decisively the role of "world revolution" as a motivating force for the Soviet leadership. The success of Western containment had proved that a world-wide breakthrough could not be achieved without risking world war. The growing conflict with China, and its exploitation by such lesser allies as Cuba and Rumania, had proved that the rise of new Communist regimes was not necessarily relevant to the power and greatness of the Soviet Union. The turn toward the primacy of economic construction at home was in part justified by the argument that the example of rising prosperity at home was also the best contribution the Soviet state could make to the cause of communism abroad—that henceforth domestic improvement was their foremost international duty.

The new leaders may still perceive the world scene in sufficiently ideological terms to believe in the ultimate world-wide victory of the Communist system. They no longer, however, regard the achievement of that victory as a task of Soviet foreign policy; they may be relied upon to define the objectives of that policy strictly in terms of the national interest. But we are dealing here with the national interest of a world power; and while it is true that the Soviet Union has acquired many characteristics of a satisfied power, it is also inevitably involved in world-wide rivalry with the United States and is still smarting from the humiliation of its Cuban defeat. Among the new leaders, concentration on the national interest is thus accompanied by an acute concern with national dignity, and increased realism in appraising the international relation of forces with a dogged determination to change that relation to their own advantage. In the reticent style of the new regime, the reappraisal—and the implied critique of Khrushchev's self-deception about Soviet strength—was conveyed, on the eve of the XXIII Congress, in an article by Alexei Rumiantsev[3] which, under the pretext of commenting on the thesis that "the socialist world system" had already become "the decisive factor in the development of human society," reinterpreted it as referring to a process that would fill an entire historical epoch. He warned of the dangers that might flow from regarding as already solved the

[3] *Mirovaia Ekonomika i Mezhdunarodnye Otnosheniia*, No. 1, 1966.

tasks still confronting "progressive humanity" and thus losing touch with reality. Through the veil of his abstractions, we may perceive the new leaders blaming Khrushchev for exposing Soviet relative weakness by his Cuban adventure, taking note of the dangers of a period of clear American military superiority, but also pledging a serious, long-term effort to catch up with American strength.

The decline of the world-revolutionary commitment and the realistic concentration on the national interest have been accompanied by closer ties between its political and military leadership, symbolized by Brezhnev's own military-political past, by increased publicity and prestige granted to the military leaders, and by an intensification of military patriotic propaganda of a strongly nationalist hue. It must indeed be regarded as natural that within a bureaucratic oligarchy the influence of the military should rise with the decline of the doctrinaire ideological element. But there exists also a specific affinity, which is too often overlooked, between the nature of a bureaucratic regime and the consciousness of the continuity of the national interest; the very concept dates from the age of the absolute monarchies, and for centuries the bureaucrats of the foreign service have acted as guardians of the "national interest" tradition in all the old European powers, defending it against the onslaughts of democratic opinion and its changing ideologies. It may be argued that, carried on through the person of Chicherin and favored by the instincts of Stalin, elements of this tradition in the foreign service have survived all the upheavals of the Russian revolution. Their influence is naturally increasing under the present post-revolutionary, bureaucratic regime.

Soviet Perception of the World Scene

While the fact that the foreign policies of the new regime have so far served the national interest well is fairly obvious, an understanding of those policies will be facilitated if we first seek to outline the context in which that interest is perceived by the Soviet leaders.

We may start from the assumption that the Soviet leaders are fully conscious of having moved into a triangular constellation of world affairs, in which they will have to ensure their long-term security and to compete for influence against Communist China as well as against the United States and its West European allies. Despite their persistent offers of a "united front" to Peking and their public backing of Mao Tse-tung's domestic opponents, we may also assume that they are under no illusions that the former close ties with Peking could be restored in any foreseeable circumstances; even if a new Chinese leadership should change from Mao's rigid and fanatic hostility to a more pragmatic attitude toward the Soviet Union, it would never surrender its basic independence but merely regain the option of working now with, now against the Soviet Union on specific issues. In other words, China would remain a potentially hostile power, and Soviet actions suggest a thorough awareness of this long-term threat— a threat they must see as likely to grow with the growth of Chinese power.

Moreover the Soviet leaders, like many Western observers, are inclined to regard this growth as inevitable, because they take it for granted that despite all the present upheavals and setbacks, "socialist" China will eventually solve her problem of industrialization, just as "socialist" Russia solved hers despite the errors of Stalin. As China's power potential is regarded to an increasing degree in these ideological terms, its eventual threat must appear ever more formidable to Soviet eyes.

On the other hand, the Soviet leaders have reason to hope that the danger from the West will progressively diminish. That hope is not nowadays based on a belief in the growing prevalence of "reason" and peaceful intentions among the American leaders; any such belief is now regarded, in the light of recent American behavior, as a Khrushchevian illusion, and the unceremonious manner in which the ageing Mikoyan was dropped from the Politburo may well have been due to his share of responsibility for it. But the same developments in the West which have undermined the belief in growing capitalist "reasonableness" have strengthened the Soviet leaders' reliance on the "internal contradictions" of the capitalist world, as shown by the conflicts within the Western alliance.

It is the progressive disintegration of that alliance, as expressed first in the initiatives of General de Gaulle, then in the *de facto* withdrawal of American leadership, and lately in the rise of an anti-American current in West Germany, that is now the main foundation for Soviet hopes that the danger in the West is bound to decline and may even decline fairly rapidly.

Between the prospects of increasing Chinese and declining Western power, the Soviet leaders probably now regard their own East European power sphere as broadly stable. They have accepted the emancipation of most of the East European regimes from satellite status, brought about by their growing internal stability and national identification as well as by the decline of Soviet ideological authority due to the effects of destalinization and to the Chinese challenge and the consequent limitation of their own power to command. But they rely on the fact that the broad similarity in the outlook of the regimes, combined with Soviet military and economic preponderence in the region and in part with an awareness of common dangers, will suffice to maintain the cohesion of the bloc on a new basis, closer to the classical type of hegemonial alliance than to the Stalinist empire, and to ensure a measure of cooperation under this new type of Soviet leadership, even if further changes of form should prove necessary.

Proceeding from this kind of analysis, the Soviet leaders have apparently concluded that the conflict with China presents long-term dangers against which limited, preparatory measures must be taken in the present, while the conflict with the West presents short-term opportunities for weakening the strongest opponent, which justify major immediate diplomatic initiatives. At any rate, that has been the proportion of their activity in the past two years. Soviet policies toward other parts of the world have developed as a function of those two major conflicts.

The Long-term Containment of China

Soviet precautions against the Chinese threat have proceeded along three main lines, which may be described as frontier protection, diplomatic encirclement, and competitive re-engagement in Vietnam.

Despite the combination of Chinese propaganda claims and local harassing tactics in the frontier regions with the working-up of a general atmosphere of anti-Soviet hysteria, the Soviet leaders have not let themselves be pushed into the kind of reaction appropriate to an imminent threat of war. They have made the judgment that the Chinese wish to maintain an atmosphere of general hostility and frontier tension but are fully aware of their present military inferiority and do not therefore consider war at this time. Accordingly, the Soviet Union has responded with measures of domestic propaganda and with the mobilization of a kind of territorial militia in the frontier regions, but so far with only minor reinforcements of the regular forces there.

The most important Soviet precaution from a long-term point of view has been the systematic effort to consolidate good diplomatic relations with the major non-Communist nations of Asia. In the case of Japan, that effort has been particularly striking in the improvement of economic relations in a deliberate race against the Chinese and has been notably successful. In the case of India, where Soviet relations have long been good, the Soviet Union has first helped to prevent a concerted Pakistani-Chinese attack and then brought India and Pakistan to the negotiating table on conditions which cost India nothing yet convinced Pakistan that it could not achieve its objectives by relying on Chinese help. Tashkent has not brought the Kashmir issue closer to a solution, but China closer to isolation. Even in Indonesia, where close cooperation among Sukarno, Peking, and the

Indonesian Communists had virtually eliminated Soviet influence for a time, the failure of the pro-Communist coup of September 30, 1965, gave Moscow the opportunity to recover some lost ground, even while the Soviet press protested against the anti-Communist massacres. Everywhere, Soviet diplomatic influence has increased, while Chinese influence has decreased.

Finally, the new leadership quickly decided to reverse Khrushchev's policy of quiet disengagement from the Vietnam conflict so as not to leave to China a monopoly of its exploitation among Communist and national-revolutionary movements. Re-engagement began in a situation in which South Vietnam appeared to be on the eve of collapse, and the Soviet leadership believed that the main task was to offer to the Vietnamese Communists their good offices for consummating their victory in the form of negotiations which would leave the Americans an acceptable road to withdrawal. But after the American decision to bomb the North, beginning during Kosygin's visit in February, 1965, and to step up intervention in the South, the Soviet leaders continued their active material as well as propagandist support for the Vietnamese Communists. They associated this support with persistent proposals for a common front of all "socialist states" in this cause and for a truce in Sino-Soviet polemics. The rigid refusal of the Maoist leadership to cooperate or to stop polemics, on the grounds that the Russian leaders were "really" plotting with the Americans against the Vietnamese people, forced the Vietnamese Communists into an attitude of ideological neutrality between Moscow and Peking. It has also resulted in a similar detachment of the formerly pro-Chinese Communist Parties of North Korea and Japan and has probably contributed to making the conflicts within the Chinese leadership more acute. The Chinese have thus lost their chance of leading an Asian Communist bloc and have been isolated even among the Communists of the region.

The Soviet leaders have achieved all this while avoiding the risk of a direct clash with American power, without allowing the lines of communication to Washington to become blocked despite the inevitable cooling of relations, and without renouncing the option of resuming mediation efforts if conditions should either become more favorable or if the risk of escalation should become too serious for them.

The Soviet leaders have been even more successful in their competition with China for influence in the third world, owing not only to their superior economic and military resources, but largely also to their concentration on governments in power in preference to aspiring revolutionary movements. Thus the Chinese bid to turn a "Second

Bandung" conference of Afro-Asian governments into an anti-American demonstration while excluding the Soviet Union from participation failed in 1965 because most of the governments concerned would not commit themselves to policies that would have deprived them simultaneously of American and Soviet aid. Also in 1965, the demonstrated inability of Peking to give Pakistan effective help against India enabled the USSR to pose in Tashkent as a mediator between the ex-belligerents, thus excluding China from further influence on the issue, while the catastrophic defeat of the pro-Communist coup in Indonesia destroyed Peking's but not Moscow's influence in that country. Among the nationalist Arab regimes, the readiness of the new Soviet leaders to continue the policy of Communist cooperation within the ruling Parties, initiated by Khrushchev during his last year in power, and to supplement it since the spring of 1965 by diplomatic support for a "progressive" version of Pan-arabism has enabled them greatly to consolidate Russian influence in the region. Only in Latin America has Soviet willingness to improve relations and offer economic aid to all governments had to be paid for by the growing alienation of Castro and of the Cuban-oriented guerilla movements and by a widening split between the latter and the Moscow-oriented Communist Parties; it remains to be seen whether Moscow's or Havana's calculations will prove more realistic.

New Initiatives in Europe

This freedom of movement has been used by the new Soviet leadership above all in Europe, where the political disarray of the Western alliance and the preoccupation of the United States with the Pacific theater has offered the Soviet Union an apparent chance to obtain a major shift in power relations to its own advantage before the power conflict with China assumes major dimensions. What it hopes to achieve is apparently nothing less than what Khrushchev hoped to achieve during *his* grand offensive—an end of the confrontation with American power in Europe by an American withdrawal on the basis of the status quo, leaving the Soviet Union as the preponderant power on the old continent. In contrast to Khrushchev, his successors are seeking to achieve this not by a combination of nuclear blackmail with bilateral negotiations with the United States, but by the exploitation of the differences among the Western powers and by the offer of replacing the military alliances with a "European Security System."

The new mobility of Soviet diplomacy in Europe began with the deliberate encouragement of the French desire for better relations with Moscow, for which Khrushchev had shown only a very limited interest. The rapprochement with Paris bore immediate fruits within the European Soviet bloc, where it enabled the Soviet Union to direct the desire of the East European states for increased Western contacts primarily to Paris and thus to contain its dangers without applying serious pressure. It has reaped a spectacular result in de Gaulle's secession from the NATO military organization, creating a number of difficulties for the maintenance of American forces in Europe on the present scale. Finally, it has put West Germany under substantial pressure by threatening it with isolation in Europe. At the same time, the Soviet leaders have been careful not to grant de Gaulle a monopoly of this rapprochement, but rather to foster a competition for their favors among the Western powers, from which the United States has been unable to exclude itself. Apart from the steps taken to improve relations with Italy and with the Vatican, the use of Kosygin's London visit to suggest a British mediating role and to demonstrate the possibility of a multiplication of direct wires is characteristic of these tactics.

The political framework for all these moves has been formulated in the concept of a "European Security System" which should eventually supersede the present military alliances. In the Soviet view, as endorsed by the member states of the Warsaw Pact at the Bucharest conference of 1966, such a system would center around a peace treaty with the two German states, in which both East and West would guarantee the frontiers and the permanent denuclearization of Germany. The attraction of this proposal for European opinion, in the West and among the neutrals as well as in Eastern Europe, lies in the stabilization of Germany's eastern frontier and of her non-nuclear status as well as in the prospect of a parallel withdrawal of American and Soviet forces. The implied catch is the demand for the international legitimation of the present East German regime, which is the last Soviet satellite in the sense that it could not be maintained without either the presence of Soviet troops or, at any rate, a continued Soviet right to unilateral intervention. The Soviet leaders themselves have implicitly recognized this by sponsoring a series of bilateral treaties of assistance, intended to perpetuate the ties between East Germany and the states of the Soviet bloc for another twenty years—regardless of any possible dissolution of the Warsaw Pact. But in a situation where American forces went home while Soviet forces remained actually or potentially on the Elbe, the Soviet Union would become the preponderant power on the European continent. Although it is unlikely that the present Soviet leadership would wish to use this preponderant position either to overrun Western Europe militarily at the risk of making the American guarantee operative or to promote its forcible sovietization, the effect would nevertheless be that the West European states would have to adjust to living within the orbit of Soviet preponderance just as Finland has long adjusted to this fact. The results for the world balance of power can easily be imagined.

In this form, the Soviet concept of a "European Security System" has therefore not been accepted by any Western power. General de Gaulle in particular, while favoring the principle of a supersession of the military alliances in Europe by a system of all-round guarantees, has repeatedly rejected the idea that the present East German regime could form part of such a system. Yet by refusing to coordinate his diplomacy toward the USSR with that of the United States and talking as if a European settlement "among Europeans" were possible, he has prevented himself from using the only effective answer to that proposal—i.e., that the Americans will not leave Europe on such a basis. The United States, on the other hand, has so far not offered to the Europeans any concept of its own for a settlement but has talked as if a military détente between the present NATO and Warsaw Pact alliances, developed gradually by the Americans and Russians on behalf of their respective wards, would eventually solve the political problem more or less by itself. Indeed, in suggesting a gradual and reciprocal reduction of American and Soviet forces in Europe as a major element of this process of détente, the United States may have given the impression to the Soviet leaders that the confrontation with American power in Europe could be whittled down to zero level *without* a settlement. For the Soviet leadership, this would be equivalent to a settlement on their terms. It would also amount to an ending of the confrontation on the basis of the status quo. Such a whittling down of the American presence without a negotiated settlement would sooner or later leave the West Germans with no alternative but to recognize the present East German regime and to renounce their American ties.

In fact, alongside the Soviet initiatives for a rapprochement with various West European powers and for discussions about a "European Security System," the refusal to improve relations with West Germany was until 1968 the third characteristic of Soviet European policy under Khrushchev's successors. This refusal was maintained in the face of growing West German efforts to join the détente and, in particular, to establish diplomatic relations with the East European states. It was obviously based on the Soviet leaders' belief that if only the West Germans were consistently kept out in the cold during a general improvement of East-West relations in Europe, they would eventually have to accept Soviet terms for a settlement, including recognition of the legitimacy of the present East German regime. In the absence of coordinated Western counterproposals the question remained open as to what alternative options Moscow could perceive.

Parallel with these diplomatic initiatives, the post-Khrushchev leaders have endeavored to improve their military posture in Europe. They have not allowed talk about a possible dissolution of the Warsaw Pact to interfere with the steady efforts to improve its military performance, including regular joint maneuvers of its northern member states. At the same time, they have considerably increased their naval forces in the Eastern Mediterranean and their military cooperation with the national-revolutionary regimes of the Arab world, thus developing a growing threat to NATO's southern flank and the physical backing for a propaganda campaign against the presence of the American Sixth Fleet in the Mediterranean.

The initiatives just described were geared toward improving the Soviet diplomatic position in Europe without involving them either in major negotiations with the United States or in a serious crisis, and eventually toward obtaining by a variety of indirect moves the American withdrawal and the Soviet preponderance in Europe, which both Stalin and Khrushchev had failed to achieve by frontal pressure. But the Mediterranean and Middle Eastern activities of Khrushchev's successors do constitute a form of such pressure; and in the summer of 1967, they did lead to an international crisis which was bound to alarm large sections of Western opinion, and which damaged Soviet prestige by exposing both the extent of Soviet arms deliveries to the Arab states and the miscalculations on which this policy was based. The damage appears, however, to have been more than compensated for by the further consolidation of Soviet influence in the region, following the Arab military defeat. But the contradiction between a diplomacy of détente and a practice of regional pressure remains unresolved.

The Dialogue with the United States

The dialogue with the leading world power, which Khrushchev was always seeking, both during his grand offensive and after its failure, has not been abandoned by his successors; but so far it has played a far less central role in their policies. This is not only because of the war in Vietnam or the Soviet desire not to give ammunition to Chinese accusations of Russo-American complicity. Whenever the present leaders regard direct negotiations with Washington as useful and important, they engage in them without allowing themselves to be seriously inhibited by those considerations. A more important temporary obstacle is probably that they have been impressed with the superiority of American military strength and do not wish to negotiate on major issues from a position of weakness. Hence they have given priority to the weakening of the American diplomatic position by indirect moves on one side and to the strengthening of their own military potential on the other. For the sake of that strengthening, they have even been ready, in the eastern Mediterranean and Middle East, to run some risk of a Russo-American crisis, while taking care to keep it under control. But they have carefully refrained from provoking such a crisis at points known to be considered vital by the United States—be it in Berlin or in Latin America.

The one issue on which the dialogue has been successfully continued has been the treaty to ban nuclear proliferation. This is hardly due to an overwhelming interest in the substance of the treaty on the part of the Soviet leaders, who have been reasonably sure of American unwillingness to proliferate even without it. In fact, their behavior suggests that their principal interest may have been the hope to drive a political wedge between the United States and West Germany, thus further contributing to the disintegration of NATO. It must be said that a considerable sector of West German opinion, though not the responsible leaders of the Bonn government, has enthusiastically leaped into the trap.

The other major issue on which a dialogue has apparently been weighed is also in the field of arms control—the possible limitation of ABMs and other rocket weapons. Here, they have clearly waited until their advance in the introduction of ABMs has given them a bargaining weapon, and there has been evidence of differences within the Soviet leadership as to when and on what terms negotiation should be joined. As far as can be judged at this point, the decision seems to have been to use the American interest in avoiding a large-scale ABM-race in order to press for a reduction in the American superiority in offensive rockets. If it should turn out that this is not to be obtained, Soviet willingness to continue the dialogue on the subject must appear doubtful.

Apart from the field of arms control, the Soviet Union under Khrushchev's successors remains as ready as in the past to seek a dialogue in a crisis situation so as to reduce its risks; the use of the "hot line" during the Middle Eastern war and the subsequent meeting between Prime Minister Kosygin and President Johnson have illustrated this once again. All this implies, of course, that the new Soviet leadership continues to perceive the United States both as a major antagonist in a power conflict and as a partner in efforts for limiting the forms of that conflict. But the decline in Soviet ideological fervor and the rise in the importance of the new conflict with China are posing the larger question of whether the present leadership might also be ready to see the United States as an eventual partner for ending the conflict, for power conflicts, however large and vital, are distinguished from primarily ideological conflicts by the fact that a settlement is conceivable in principle. There is nothing in the conduct of Khrushchev's heirs to indicate that they are envisaging such a settlement at the present time; but it is perhaps more remarkable that there is nothing in their conduct that would necessarily exclude an effort to attempt it in the future.

Concluding Remarks

Much more clearly even than in the domestic field, the record of the present oligarchic leadership in world affairs appears to be characterized not by indecision and paralysis, but by caution, skill, and considerable success. That success appears all the more remarkable if we bear in mind that the leaders had to absorb the repercussions of the break with China and to deal with the United States from a position of visible military inferiority. The fact that the collective leadership has been conspicuously helped by the mistakes of their foreign opponents does not diminish their achievement in exploiting these windfalls while avoiding major blunders of their own. Yet it is true that these mistakes, by easing the tasks of Soviet foreign policy, have spared them the agony of really hard and bitter decisions, which might have severely tested the cohesion of the Politburo. The period since Khrushchev has proven that an oligarchy can govern well as long as events beyond its control do not force it to the wall; how it would function in a real crisis remains to be seen.

2 Reforms in Government and Administration

JERRY F. HOUGH

In the wake of the removal of Khrushchev, the new Soviet leadership sharply criticized the frequent and drastic reorganizations of Party and state which had marked the previous decade. Yet, paradoxically, the reorganizations undertaken by the new leadership have proved as sweeping as those of the former First Secretary—and they have been compressed into a shorter period of time. While to a large extent the Party and administrative structures which emerged in 1965 and 1966 represented a return to those which had existed prior to 1957, significant differences are observable. And continually one observes signs of the leadership trying to decide whether to launch a type of reorganization whose scope and significance would far outweigh anything undertaken by Khrushchev.

THE GOVERNMENTAL APPARATUS

The Soviets

Less than six weeks after Khrushchev's removal, the Central Committee met briefly to undo the last and most drastic of the Khrushchev reorganizations—the bifurcation of the Party apparatus and the local soviets. At most territorial levels the responsibilities and powers of the soviets were little affected by this action. However, in the oblasts (or at least in 85 of the oblasts) there had been both an industrial soviet and executive committee (*oblispolkom*) and a rural soviet and execu-

JERRY F. HOUGH (Ph.D. Harvard, 1961) is Associate Professor of Political Science at the University of Illinois. He has contributed to various journals, primarily in the field of public administration and Soviet politics, and is the author of the forthcoming book, *The Soviet Prefects: The Local Party Organs in Industrial Decision-Making.*

tive committee, the former supervising the city soviets and the latter the soviets in the rural districts (raions). Now there was a return to unified oblast soviets and executive committees, which were said to have been given additional powers.[1]

While Brezhnev asserted at the XXIII Party Congress that "local soviets must be given a larger measure of independence in dealing with economic, financial, and land questions," [2] there is little evidence of substantial change in this respect. Soviet scholars and officials all assert that the role of the soviets had been significantly reduced during the period 1960-1964. Yet, this policy was only partially reversed after 1964. In the industrial realm, for example, the abolition of the *sovnarkhozy* resulted in the return of many "local industry" enterprises to the soviets, but their number and importance were much less than in the 1950's.

The most striking example of the continuing limitations on the role of the soviets can be found in the relationship of the raion soviet to agricultural administration. When the *kolkhoz-sovkhoz* territorial-production administrations had been formed, the district Executive committees (*raiispolkomy*) had been relieved of responsibility for administering agriculture and had been limited primarily to such functions as education, culture, road maintenance, and communal services. In 1964 the raion agriculture organs once more were placed under the supervision of the district Party committees (*raikomy*) (as well as the oblast agriculture administration), but they were not resubordinated to the raion soviets. The *raiispolkom* continued to perform certain agricultural functions in the realm of planning, land use, and legality of *kolkhoz* actions,[3] but its lack of authority over the raion production administration has meant that its role in agriculture usually has been of a "purely formal" nature.[4] There has been considerable agitation for returning the production administration to its former position of "dual subordination" to the raion soviet and the oblast agriculture administration, but in vain.[5]

[1] *Sovety deputatov trudiashchikhsia,* No. 6 (June, 1966), p. 9.

[2] *Pravda,* March 30, 1966, p. 8.

[3] *Sovety deputatov trudiashchikhsia,* No. 2 (February, 1966), pp. 68-69.

[4] *Ibid.,* No. 7 (July, 1966), p. 68. In some districts the *raiispolkomy* still try to integrate the agricultural plan into the raion plan, but these soviets "can't realize their mission openly and legally . . . because of an absence of powers." *Ibid.,* No. 1 (January, 1966), p. 68. In the agricultural sphere they can do little more than attempt to persuade either the production administration, the Party *raikom,* or higher officials to take action.

[5] Hardly an issue of *Sovety deputatov trudiashchikhsia* has appeared without such appeals. See that of the Director of the USSR Institute of State and Law, in No. 8 (August, 1965), pp. 9-18; that of the Chairman of the Leningrad *oblispolkom,*

Although the position of the soviets remains quite restricted, the historian of the future may decide that the most interesting change made in the role of the soviets between 1964 and 1966 was the expansion in the number of commissions (committees) of the USSR Supreme Soviet. Formerly each house had four commissions (credentials, legislative proposals, budget, and foreign affairs), while the Council of Nationalities had a fifth commission—the economic commission.[6] In 1966 the economic commission of the Council of Nationalities was abolished, and the other four were supplemented in both houses by six commissions dealing with different realms of the economy:

1. Industry, transportation, and communications;
2. Construction and building materials;
3. Agriculture;
4. Health and social security;
5. Education, science, and culture; and
6. Trade and services.[7]

The immediate significance of this action seems slight. The budget commission already had had branch sub-commissions with 30 to 40 members, and there is little evidence that the new commissions have assumed a vital role.[8] Thirteen of the 20 commission chairmen are Party officials, and the most recent published accounts of the work of the commissions suggest that the discussions in them are dominated by members of the Party Central Committee.[9] Yet, if the Supreme Soviet is ever to become a significant factor in the policy-making process, it will be because the commissions begin to play a greater role in shaping legislation, the budget, and the plan. It is possible that the expansion in the number of commissions will gradually be followed by an increase in the length and meaningfulness of their sessions. However, while every spring has its harbingers, every harbinger in human affairs is not followed by its spring.

Agricultural Administration

Although the fall of Khrushchev brought few changes in the governmental apparatus supervising agriculture at the local level, the administrative organs at higher territorial levels were not left unchanged. In

---

in No. 1 (January, 1966), pp. 66-72; and that of the Chairman of the Presidium of the Supreme Soviet of Turkmenia, in No. 3 (March, 1966), pp. 20-26. An interesting collection of letters on the subject can be found in No. 7 (July, 1966), pp. 67-72.
[6] *Ibid.,* No. 5 (May, 1966), p. 20.
[7] *Pravda,* August 3, 1966, p. 3; August 4, 1966, p. 6.
[8] *Sovety deputatov trudiashchikhsia,* No. 5 (May, 1966), p. 21.
[9] *Izvestiia,* December 11, 1966, p. 2.

particular, the new leadership partially reversed the 1961-1962 policy of dividing the Ministry of Agriculture into three separate agencies —a Ministry of Production and Procurement of Agricultural Products, a Ministry of Agriculture limited to the functions of "a research and extension service," and an All-Union Farm Machinery Agency (*Soiuzselkhoztekhnika*).[10] The Farm Machinery Agency was retained after 1964, but the Ministry of Production and Procurement of Agricultural Products was abolished and its functions returned to the Ministry of Agriculture. The continuity with the earlier organizational forms was emphasized by the reappointment of V. V. Matskevich as Minister of Agriculture.[11]

Industrial Administration

The new Soviet leaders took almost a year to come to a decision about the basic organization of the industrial hierarchy,[12] but the decision, when it did come, involved a basic repudiation of the Khrushchev structural innovations and the re-creation of an administrative system which bore considerable resemblance to that which existed prior to 1957. The all-Union, republic, and regional *sovnarkhozy* were all abolished as also was the coordinating Supreme Economic Council. The industrial state committees were replaced by ministries with direct administrative authority both over the industrial enterprises and the major industrial research institutes.[13] In all, 17 all-Union and 12 Union-republic ministries were established in the industrial realm, compared with 16 all-Union ministries and 11 Union-republic ministries in 1957.[14]

The major structural differences between the ministerial system of 1965 and that of 1957 lies in the creation of a separate system in the

[10] Merle Fainsod, *How Russia is Ruled* (Cambridge, Mass.: Harvard University Press, 1963), pp. 555-57, 565-69. The phrase, "a research and extension service," is Fainsod's.

[11] *Pravda*, February 18, 1966, p. 1. A list of the administrations and departments of the Ministry can be found in *Kolkhozno-sovkhoznoe proizvodstvo*, No. 8 (August, 1965), pp. 47-48. For an article by Matskevich on the structure of the ministry, see *Selskaia zhizn*, June 24, 1965, p. 2. See also Roy D. Laird, "New Trends and Old Realities," *Problems of Communism*, XV, No. 2 (March-April, 1966), 21-28.

[12] Actually the industrial reorganization took place in two stages. In March, 1965, the state committees in the defense field were transformed into ministries. *Pravda*, March 4, 1965, p. 2. The abolition of the *sovnarkhozy* and the creation of the other ministries did not occur until October.

[13] The decisions effecting the industrial reorganization and the speeches justifying them can be found in *Pravda* and *Izvestiia*, September 28, 1965, to October 3, 1965, and October 10, 1965, p. 1.

[14] The new ministries are listed in the Supreme Soviet law making the necessary change in the Constitution. *Pravda*, October 3, 1965, p. 1.

realm of supplies procurement. In the center there was formed a Union-republic State Committee for Material-Technical Supply (headed by a deputy chairman of the Council of Ministers), while Chief Administrations for Material-Technical Supply were created in the republics. The RSFSR also was divided into 24 regions, each with its own office of supply.

The actual role of the Committee for Supply and its relations with the ministries remain somewhat unclear, but the decree establishing the committee emphasized its responsibilities for timely deliveries rather than planning of supplies.[15] Retention of the republican and regional supply offices seems to be an attempt to retain some of the advantages of the *sovnarkhozy* by creating an institution with some capability of maneuvering supplies on a regional basis and organizationally inclined to struggle against uneconomic procurement decisions reflecting departmental pressures.

People's Control

Formally at least, the new Soviet leadership also abolished another Khrushchev innovation—the Committee of Party-State Control under a chairman who (at least at the oblast level and above) was both a Party secretary and a deputy chairman of the council of ministers or executive committee (*ispolkom*). In its place was established a Committee of People's Control.

The abolition of the Committee of Party-State Control is easy to explain in terms of a political struggle for power.[16] However, the

[15] See *Pravda*, October 10, 1965, p. 1; December 15, 1965, pp. 2-3. A Council of Ministers decree of January 27, 1967 is said to have strengthened the role of the territorial administrations vis-à-vis the ministries.

[16] The power of the Chairman of the Committee of Party-State Control resided in the combination of his ability to acquire information about the performance of key political and administrative personnel and his access to the three most important policy-making committees—the Politburo, the Secretariat, and the Council of Ministers. He had the potential opportunity to discredit other officials with his investigations and a number of forums at which he could subtly use the information which had been gathered against them. Moreover, he was one of the few Politburo members who had extensive information about candidates for vacancies in such posts as *obkom* First Secretary and was in a position to challenge candidates suggested by the General Secretary and to suggest alternatives. Since the Chairman (Alexander Shelepin) was a man who had made a particularly wide range of contacts in his earlier career, he inevitably posed a potential threat to the General Secretary.

The reorganization of the Committee—and especially the removal of its Chairman from the Secretariat—provided a graceful way to ease Shelepin out of this strategic post, for, in retaining his seat on the Secretariat, he automatically had to give up the chairmanship of the Committee of People's Control. He then could be assigned much less sensitive work, apparently supervision of light indus-

impact of this reorganization on provincial administration is much less apparent. In several respects the Committee of People's Control resembles the Committee of Party-State Control more than previous state or soviet control organizations. Thus, the chairmen of the people's control committees in the republics, oblasts, cities, and raions (unlike the officials of state or soviet control) are nearly always members or candidate members of the bureaus of the Party committees.[17] In addition, Party spokesmen continue to emphasize the particularly close relationship of the new committee to the local Party organs.

Below the highest level at least, the work of the Committee of People's Control seems little different from that of its predecessor. It continues such functions of the old Ministry of State Control as the investigation of specific complaints of mismanagement and the conducting of general surveys of general managerial practices or problems (e.g., the way "control by the ruble" is being handled throughout the area). While the local committees participate in the nation-wide investigations, their primary function is to relieve the departments of the Party committee of some of the burdensome duty of investigating specific complaints and to assist the local first secretary and bureau in obtaining information on questions of current interest. If this image of the work of the Committee of People's Control is correct, then the placing of the provincial chairmen on the Party bureaus should not be seen as an indicator of the committee's power in Soviet society, but more as an administrative convenience to keep the chairmen informed about the current interests of the bureau.[18]

---

try and trade. His successor (Pavel Kovanov), a man who had probably developed few contacts in a decade of Party work in Georgia and who sat neither on the Secretariat or the Politburo, was in a much less influential position than Shelepin had been.

[17] Eight of the fourteen republican bureaus elected in the spring of 1966 contained the republican chairmen of the Committee of People's Control among their full members. In the other six republics the chairman was a candidate member of the bureau. An examination of oblast newspapers in Krasnodar, Rostov, Volgograd, Ulianovsk, and Yaroslavl reveals that three of the chairmen are full members of the *obkom* bureau and two are candidate members. See also *Pravda vostoka*, July 27, 1966, p. 3.

[18] For a different interpretation of the Party-State Control Committee, see Grey Hodnett, "Khrushchev and Party-State Control," in *Politics in the Soviet Union: 7 Cases,* eds., Alexander Dallin and Alan F. Westin (New York: Harcourt, Brace, & World, Inc., 1966), pp. 113-64.

THE PARTY APPARATUS

The Central Party Organs

Of all the changes in the post-Khrushchev period, few have received more publicity in the West than the changing of the name of the Presidium back to Politburo and that of First Secretary back to General Secretary. However, whatever the "Kremlinological" significance of these steps, the most interesting developments within the central Party organs have taken place within the Central Committee and the Secretariat.

One important change has been the removal from the Party Rules of the requirements that a certain percentage of the members of the Party committees (25 per cent in the case of the central organs) be "renewed" at each Party election and that, except in special cases, a man not be re-elected more than a specified number of times. This rule had had a major impact on the turnover rate of secretaries of primary Party organizations (their tenure was set at two years). At higher levels the abolition of this rule has less immediate impact, for the newly elected Party committees did meet the old "renewal" requirements if these are defined generously. 25.1 per cent of the present voting members of the Central Committee were newly elected at the XXIII Congress; in the republics the prescribed rate of turnover seems to have been easily exceeded.[19]

Nevertheless, the abolition of the renewal rule did reflect a tendency to maintain substantial continuity in the membership of the central Party organs. At the two previous Party Congresses a large percentage of the members of the existing Central Committee had not been named to the new one. Less than 50 per cent of the living full members of the 1956 Central Committee were re-elected in 1961; in turn, only two-thirds of the 1952 full members had been re-elected in 1956. (The 1952-56 rate of turnover is very similar to that of 1956-61 if we take into account the shorter time gap.) However, of the 166 full members of the 1961 Central Committee who were still alive in 1966, 83 per cent were named to the 1966 Central Committee. The basic continuity in Central Committee membership is reflected in a significant aging of this body. The average age of the voting members of the Central Committee increased from 49 in 1952 to 51 in 1956, 52 in 1961, and 56 in 1966.[20]

[19] See Jerry F. Hough, "In Whose Hands the Future?" *Problems of Communism,* XVI, No. 2 (March-April, 1967), 21.
[20] *Ibid.,* pp. 19-21.

In terms of personnel, the Secretariat of the Central Committee does not show nearly the same degree of continuity as the Central Committee itself. Even leaving aside Khrushchev, only one-third of the dozen secretaries of 1964 still hold this post three years later, and the duties of all posts but one have been at least partially re-defined.[21] Yet, there has been continuity in the sense that the Secretariat remains quite large and still is composed of men who specialize in a variety of policy spheres.

Indeed, the policy of creating a specialized Secretariat has been carried out more systematically than had been the case previously, as many of the secretaries have been placed in direct charge of one of the major Central Committee departments. Thus, it is certain that the Central Committee secretaries, I. V. Kapitonov, M. S. Solomentsev, and F. D. Kulakov, head the organization-Party work department (the new name of the Party organs department), the heavy industry department, and the agriculture department, respectively. It also is highly probable that M. A. Suslov and B. N. Ponomarev head the administrative organs department and the international department respectively.[22]

The changes with respect to the secretaries handling economic questions are particularly interesting, for they illustrate very well the dangers of making hasty generalizations about trends in Party work. In 1964 the new leadership abolished the Central Committee bureaus for agriculture, for heavy industry and construction, and for the chemical and light industries.[23] Moreover, a number of articles appeared

[21] Of the 1964 secretaries, only Brezhnev, Demichev, Ponomarev, and Suslov remained on the Secretariat in January, 1968. Of these, Demichev has been shifted from the Bureau for the Chemical and Light Industry to work in the agitation-propaganda field, and Brezhnev, of course, has become the General Secretary. Moreover, as shall be discussed in Footnote 33, the responsibilities of Suslov also, have probably changed.

[22] In the case of the administrative organs department and the international department, it is clear that some secretary heads the department. In both cases a deputy head of the department was named to the Central Committee or the Auditing Commission at the XXIII Party Congress in 1966, but the 1966 yearbook of the *Bolshaia sovetskaia entsiklopediia,* which includes biographies of all the members of these bodies, does not list any man specifically as head of the department. It is most improbable that a deputy head would be elected to one of these bodies and the head of the department not elected, and when this occurs in other cases, a secretary is found to head the department. When a conference of heads of administrative organs departments of republican and lower Party organs was, held, Suslov was the only Central Committee secretary to attend, and presumably he is the department head.

[23] I cannot find any official decree on the abolition, but the republican bureaus, were officially abolished at the Central Committee Plenums in late December, and the changes in the central Secretariat had presumably taken place by that time.

in the press, warning against excessive Party involvement in detailed economic administration. From these two developments, one might conclude that the role of the Secretariat in the economic sphere has been significantly reduced in the last two years.

However, an examination of the biographies of the Party secretaries involved indicates that such a conclusion surely is wrong insofar as the central Secretariat is concerned. Although Khrushchev frequently spoke of concentrating the attention of the Party on production questions, the men who were placed in charge of the economic bureaus of the Central Committee actually had little administrative experience in economic work. One (A. P. Rudakov) had been a staff official in the Party apparatus for two decades; the second (V. I. Poliakov) was a professional newspaperman; the third (P. N. Demichev) had been in political work in the army and in civilian ideological work for over two decades. Their background strongly suggests that, in staffing the bureau chairmanships, Khrushchev was looking for men with an ability with words, men whose primary responsibilities would lie in the writing, drafting, and information-collecting realms.

After 1964 these three men were removed from responsibility for economic affairs. Poliakov was dismissed immediately, Demichev was transferred to ideological work, and Rudakov died. They have been replaced by men with far greater experience in economic administration. At the present time, the three secretaries handling economic questions include a former RSFSR Minister of Grain Products (F. D. Kulakov), a former plant director and *sovnarkhoz* chairman (M. S. Solomentsev), and the country's top defense industry administrator since 1941 (D. F. Ustinov).

Such a concentration of managerial talent in the Secretariat surely is not a coincidence. The most plausible explanation for it is that the Party leader no longer holds the post of Chairman of the Council of Ministers and that he wants men with great technical authority directly within his immediate office. Because of the background of these secretaries and because of the logic of the situation, it would stretch credulity to assume that they are not having a significant impact on substantive economic decisions.

The Local Party Organs

Since 1964 there has been even more change in the lower reaches of the Party apparatus than in the center, but even at this level it would be wrong to speak of any transformation in the basic role of the apparatus.

In the republican Party organs the major post-Khrushchev innovation—indeed almost the only innovation—has been the abolition of the bureaus for industry and agriculture. However, in a large majority of the cases the chairmen of these bureaus have continued as republican Party secretaries, and they still handle industrial and agricultural questions respectively. It is not at all clear that their role has changed, or, in fact, that it was significantly different in 1962-64 than it had been earlier.

At the oblast level the post-1964 changes have been much more important. In 85 of the oblasts there had been both an industrial (or urban) *obkom* and an agricultural (or rural) one, but this arrangement has now been abolished. The Party leadership explicitly recognized that the unified Party organs had played a key coordinating role prior to 1962. In the words of a *Partiinaia zhizn* editorial:[24]

> [Prior to 1962] the administrative divisions of the country had been changed. The names of the organizations had been changed. But always within the boundaries of this or that administrative unit, there had been a single Party organization which had embraced all of the given area. The Party organ in this area united and coordinated the activity of all the Soviet, economic, and public organizations. It led and bore complete responsibility for all aspects of political, economic, and cultural life.

With the re-unification of the *obkomy*, the leadership re-established an institution which, they hoped, could serve these functions once more.

The Party organizations of the city and the urban raions had been only marginally affected by the reorganization of 1962, and the 1964 decisions had a correspondingly minor impact upon them. The impact of the 1964 reorganization upon the rural Party organs was, however, much more dramatic. After 1962 there had been two Party institutions in the rural areas below the level of the oblast. The Party committee of the *kolkhoz-sovkhoz* territorial-production administration had served as the major Party organ at this level, supervising agriculture and also the institutions serving the rural population. A separate zonal industrial-production Party committee supervised the industrial enterprises and construction organizations in towns too small to have a Party *gorkom*. In 1964 the rural *raikom* was re-established, and its authority was restored over other administrators within the raion.

The reorganization of 1964 also unequivocally placed the agricultural production administration under the directing control of the *raikom*. Now, as prior to 1962, the *raikom*, "as a political organ, coordinates and directs the efforts of [all] the raion organizations"; its bureau once more decides such questions as "the development of

---

[24] *Partiinaia zhizn,* No. 23 (December, 1964), p. 4.

branches of [agricultural] production or [the development] of this or that farm as a whole." [25]

In a real sense, however, there may not have occurred a simple return to the status quo ante in the raion arrangements. While in the urban areas the local Party organs had long played a coordinative role, the rural *raikom* had also traditionally served as *the* district agriculture office. Or, using the analogy of the prefect, the rural *raikom* had in practice functioned primarily as a traditional prefect, concerned for the most part with law and order and with tax collections (although of a product rather than money nature). The other local Party organs, on the other hand, had evolved into the more modern type of prefect associated with a differentiated state structure and with a developmental situation.[26]

Since 1964 the preconditions have finally been created for a similar evolution in the role of the rural *raikom*. Unlike the head of the old district agricultural sections, the head of the production administration usually seems to have a sufficiently impressive background and staff that the *raikom* might be willing to rely more heavily upon him. Since the administration was able to function for two years in a setting in which neither its officials nor the local Party officials were accustomed to the Party officials occupying a completely dominant role, the psychological conditions for more meaningful delegation of authority also may thereby have been established.

Other developments also increased substantially the coordinating responsibilities of the *raikom*. The independence of the production administration from the district soviet means that the officials of the *raiispolkom* no longer are in a position to resolve conflicts between the agricultural officials and those supervising other sectors of the economy. At the present time only the *raikom* is in a position to perform these functions, and the pressure of these duties may inexorably reduce the time it can devote to detailed agricultural questions. The refusal to subordinate the production administration to the raion soviet suggests that the leadership may consciously be utilizing the pressure of time to modify the role of the *raikom* in the desired direction.

[25] *Pravda*, November 18, 1966, p. 2.
[26] See Brian Chapman, *The Profession of Government* (London: Allen & Unwin, 1959), pp. 72-73; Henry Maddick, *Democracy, Decentralization, and Development* (London: Asia Publishing House, 1963), pp. 51-52; M. P. Pai, "The Emerging Role of the Collector," *Indian Journal of Public Administration*, VIII, No. 4 (October-December, 1962), 478-88. The relevance of the prefectoral model for understanding the role of the local Party organs will be discussed in a forthcoming book of mine.

Conclusions

An administrative system is not simply a conglomeration of organizations but a network of subtle relationships which exist within and among these organizations. Clearly, some attempt must be made to evaluate changes in these relationships which have occurred since Khrushchev's removal.

Unfortunately, in Western discussions of the Soviet administrative system, statements about the changing role of the Party or state apparatus may be accepted uncritically or interpreted in a sweeping manner, the Soviet qualifying remarks being treated as ritual. In the process, words like "decentralization" or "recentralization" are often used with an abandon which students of American federalism and organizations have long since learned to avoid.

Degree of Centralization

Consider, for example, the question of whether the administrative hierarchy, particularly the industrial hierarchy, has become more centralized in the last few years. Certainly the abolition of the *sovnarkhozy* has meant that a number of decisions which formerly were made in the provinces are now made in Moscow. Local authorities now find it more difficult to induce heavy industry plants to produce a number of types of consumers' goods which the local population needs.[27]

Yet, to what extent can we speak of a real recentralization within the industrial realm? The answer to this question is not clear, for there is no such thing as "recentralization" in general or "decentralization" in general. More decisions may now be made in Moscow, but this does not mean that the plant manager has less autonomy. On the contrary, the enterprise director now is able to make some decisions which formerly required the approval of higher agencies. It seems likely that in the future his role will become even greater.

The simultaneous "recentralization" and "decentralization" in the industrial sphere may be intrinsically related. If a country is to have any economic planning, certain decisions about the economy must be made on a national basis (as, indeed, they are even in the United States). In some respects real decentralization to the plant level is more compatible with a network of ministries than with a network of *sovnarkhozy*. This is not to deny that the ministries still retain a very detailed involvement in plant decision-making, nor that some of

[27] *Izvestiia*, January 10, 1967, p. 3.

them (and the financial and banking institutions as well) have been undermining reforms already introduced.

Meaningful generalizations about the degree of centralization must be based not on a cursory examination of the structure established, but on a study of the relationships within the structure. These generalizations require information that only very detailed studies (or in many cases, field observations) can provide. What, for example, is the maximum expenditure or investment which a lower official is permitted to make without seeking the approval of his superiors? If—as is now said to be the case with the construction of administrative buildings in the rural areas—the maximum is raised from 50,000 to 100,000 rubles, then a significant change may have occurred, particularly if such changes are a general phenomenon in the system.

But even this information is not enough. We also need to know the extent to which higher approval may be given automatically to certain types of proposals and the extent to which lower officials are motivated to take independent action or to make proposals. We need to know the extent to which superiors are willing to wink at innovative actions of a formally illegal nature. If, for example, officials of the lower soviets "often" resort to contrivances to divert funds intended for captial repair to the reconstruction and expansion of school buildings and clubs,[28] one could easily exaggerate the significance of a decision which officially authorized such diversion.

Whatever the changes, the Soviet administrative system remains extremely centralized in comparison with Western systems—and this will continue to be the case as long as administrators in the various sectors of the economy are subordinated to ministries which are part of a unified system of public administration.

Within any organization truly major policy decisions—particularly those involving very large investments—almost invariably will require approval at higher levels in the hierarchy. Even though large organizations frequently are responsive to innovative suggestions from below, the probabilities that innovations will occur in a system are reduced if there is a severe restriction on the number of organizations with access to independent sources of large-scale capital.[29] Such a restriction

[28] *Sovety deputatov trudiashchikhsia,* No. 1 (January, 1966).

[29] As Marshall Goldman has pointed out: "Despite the growth of large corporate research laboratories, a large proportion of the basic discoveries in the United States continue to come from small firms, which sometimes succeed so well that they turn into large corporations themselves—like Polaroid, Itek or Xerox. . . . It is not enough to have inventors with ideas that are advanced for their day; there must also be a wide variety of financiers around to support them. The more sources of capital there are, the more likely it is that an investor will be found

also thereby reduces the extent to which the system is genuinely decentralized.

The Party-State Relationship

It is also difficult to assess the degree to which meaningful changes have occurred in the general relationship between Party and state. Certainly the reunification of the Party apparatus has increased the span of control of the First Secretaries below the republican level, and it has thereby reduced the frequency with which they and the bureau can involve themselves in detailed decisions concerning any one sphere of the economy. Moreover, the abandonment of the frequent practice of naming industrial managers directly to the post of *gorkom* First Secretary may mean that there is now less danger that these men will have a deep interest in industrial questions alone.[30]

On the other hand, it is also quite clear that (except in the rural *raion*) there have been no gross changes in the authority relationships between the Party officials and the governmental and economic officials within their territory. Party officials from the level of the central Secretariat down through the *raikom* continue to be responsible for economic results and continue to participate vigorously in economic decision-making.

The changes which have occurred in the Party-state relationship have been subtle and hard to define, except for those created by the reunification of the apparatus. The more important changes taking place have not, I think, been the product of the post-Khrushchev period, but rather are the continuation of long-term trends.

In surveying the history of the Party-state relationship over the last thirty years, one does not find any marked cyclical movement between Party involvement in economic affairs and Party disengagement from them. Rather one finds a number of slow, evolutionary developments along the lines suggested by Barrington Moore.[31] One finds an increased awareness that Bolshevik spirit cannot overcome all obstacles, that "objective conditions" can be a legitimate factor limiting administrative performance. There has been an increased tendency to defer on technical questions to those with specialized knowledge, an increased understanding of the need to use more sophisticated tools in analyzing and controlling the real world, an increased willingness to

---

who can appreciate the worth of a particular investment." *Foreign Affairs*, XIV, No. 2 (January, 1967), 330.

[30] This point is discussed a bit more fully in my article, "In Whose Hands the Future?" pp. 23-24.

[31] Barrington Moore, *Terror and Progress—USSR* (Cambridge, Mass.: Harvard University Press, 1954).

let the various governmental agencies function as pressure groups which are permitted to present their views not only in closed meetings but also before the public.

These developments were, of course, visible in the Khrushchev period (or even earlier), but they have accelerated somewhat since 1964. The bifurcation of the Party apparatus in 1962 essentially represented an attempt to maintain existing levels of local Party participation in specialized decision-making at a time when society was becoming more complex and differentiated. The failure of the 1962 reorganization should have convinced the Soviet leadership that the type of Party participation in decision-making which is possible and desirable is affected by a growth in the scale of organization and an increasing specialization of labor.

The frequent post-Khrushchev references to the need for "objective" political and administrative decisions are associated with such a growth in understanding, for they essentially constitute an appeal for increased reliance upon the advice of those with the requisite specialized knowledge and experience. Although administrative habits and attitudes on such questions can scarcely have changed drastically in three years, recent official statements may actually be a reflection of an attitude which had already become quite widespread among Party and governmental officials and which already had come to govern many aspects of the Party-state relationship.

To the extent that this is true, the most important fact about the present campaign may be that it signifies a further evolution in thinking at the highest levels of the Party. If so, we may see not only a reinforcing of administrative trends already in motion, but the adoption of central policies which would permit Party officials to behave more "objectively" than they sometimes could in the past. We may, for example, see agricultural policies which, for the first time, give the local Party officials the real possibility of deferring to local agricultural expertise on many questions.[32]

The question remains—*whose* specialized knowledge is to be the basis for policy? On economic planning, is it to be the economists who speak of increased reliance upon market mechanisms or is it to be the

[32] In my opinion much of the harmful intervention of the lower Party officials in agricultural questions has resulted not from ideological blinders nor from a compulsion to increase their power. Rather, it has resulted primarily from pressure from above—from demands that corn acreage be increased, from detailed delivery plans which leave little local leeway in the selection of crops to be planted, from delivery plans so large that land cannot be spared for necessary crop rotation plans, etc. Relieved of this type of demand, the *raikom* secretary would, I think, be much less intrusive in his intervention in agriculture—or at least his decisions would be much more reflective of advice from agricultural specialists.

ministerial officials who seem more dubious about these mechanisms? On legal questions, is it to be the lawyers who are pressing for added safeguards for the accused or is it to be the police whose perspectives on the requirements of "law and order" are rather different? On appropriations questions, should it be the military which calls for more defense expenditures or the automobile industry officials who advocate more private cars? On literary questions, should the leadership defer to the Voznesenskys or should it defer to the Surkovs, and no doubt many others (an American TV writer could probably compile a suggestive list) who are concerned lest "public morality" or "public morale" be undermined? On educational policy, should deference be given to the university professors who want to concentrate their attention on research problems which interest them or to other groups who demand that more of the university's time be spent on teaching or on research of more immediate practical benefit? Indeed, on almost any question, should policy reflect the bright ideas of younger specialists or those of experienced older men?

For such questions there seldom are rational-technical answers. Rather, these are prime examples of "the political question"—the question on which men with different specialized knowledge and different interests come into conflict. In the Soviet Union the Party leadership still attempts to ensure that such "political conflicts" are resolved within the Party organs at the different territorial levels.

Party spokesmen continue to insist that Party officials concentrate their attention on "political questions" (politicheskie voprosy), and this phrase is meant to refer not simply to ideological and organizational questions but also to political questions as defined here. The changes introduced since 1964 increase the probability that these "political questions" will be decided within the Party institutions. When the Party leader also holds the post of Chairman of the Council of Ministers, there may be a tendency for many important questions to be decided upon without consultation with the Politburo and for the role of the Secretariat in policy-making to be somewhat reduced, particularly in the economic sphere. When the General Secretary is not the head of government, he may well choose to rely much more heavily upon the Secretariat, and, in any case, any "political question" of significance must probably be brought to the Politburo for resolution.

Post-1964 developments have had similar consequences at lower territorial levels as well. The re-establishment of all-Union ministries to supervise a number of industries means that the republican councils of ministers no longer have responsibility for much of heavy industry. Consequently, only the republican Party organs remain in a position to resolve a series of problems arising between all-Union enterprises and republican institutions and to provide over-all coordination for the republic's industrial development program. At the oblast level the re-creation of united Party organs means that there is once more an institution at this level which can resolve many conflicts between local administrators in different sectors of the economy—conflicts which, from 1962 to 1964, had to be settled through negotiation or had to be referred to the republican level. And, of course, as we have seen, the return of the *raikom* to a position of primacy in the countryside has similar implications at the raion level.

The question of where "political decisions" are made is not the only crucial one. Of even greater concern is the question of whether the decisions reached within the Party organs reflect the results of bargaining among various groups in society or reflect the values of a small group of Party officials (or even of one man) standing largely above the group conflict. And if the pressures of "society" influence or shape Party decisions, to what extent are these the pressures arising from public aspirations or to what extent are they the pressures of the major institutional centers to prevent any attack upon their vested interests?

It is still too soon to judge whether there have been important, long-term changes in the way that political decisions as defined here are reached. Of course, one very important "subjective factor" has been removed from the policy-making process. By 1964 there were many major institutions whose vital interests had been adversely affected by Khrushchev's policies, and the great number of changes since his removal correspond rather closely to what one would expect from the creation of a bargaining situation among the major bureaucratic centers. Many of the post-1964 decisions (e.g., those on education and on genetics) satisfied the interest groups most directly involved, and none of the decisions has involved a total defeat or even a major threat to any of the important institutional competitors. (The change in this respect is a very good index of the extent of Khrushchev's power prior to his removal.)

While the process by which "political decisions" are made has obviously changed, it is not at all clear whether the changes are simply the natural—and temporary—product of a period of succession crisis or whether they represent a qualitative transformation in the basic political system. Some suggest that the Soviet Union is entering a stage of its history in which the Party leadership will be unable or unwilling to move against the vested interests of important institutional centers of power. They foresee an immobility in which these institutions are able to act as veto groups, effectively thwarting any major policy changes.

Such a development is certainly possible, but it would require major institutional changes designed to secure some independent base of power for Central Committee members. At the present time this independence is guarded to some extent by the practice of making Central Committee members virtually immune from serious demotion.[33] However, when the ageing of the top leadership begins to interfere with administrative performance, the ideological commitments to industrialization, military security, and higher living standards are likely to furnish all the legitimization necessary for a widespread "renewal of personnel." Unless there are major restrictions on the General Secretary's (and probably the Secretariat's) role in personnel selection, there almost surely will emerge a leader with the power and desire to launch a vigorous attack upon key elements of the status quo.

[33] In the two years since the XXIII Party Congress only two full members of the Central Committee (N. G. Yegorychev and A. D. Daniialov) seem to have been demoted to posts which would not warrant re-election to the Central Committee.

3 Politics and Ideology in the Post-Khrushchev Era

WOLFGANG LEONHARD

Political and ideological developments in the Soviet Union in the wake of Khrushchev's fall in October, 1964, have by no means been uniform. In the first months following Khrushchev's ouster, one could clearly see the striving to continue the destalinization reforms in internal affairs and to make changes only in the techniques of governing. However, since the spring of 1965, there has been a discernible change in policy, the aim of which has been to water down and delimit the destalinization (with the process varying greatly in different fields) and to shift to a tougher policy. This process occasioned many disagreements within the Soviet leadership. The XXIII Party Congress, held in March-April, 1966, reflected the steadily increasing conservative trend. It also gave evidence of the suppression of many fundamental political questions, which the decisive forces and the Party leadership could not agree upon. Nor have the developments since the XXIII Party Congress as yet provided an answer to the "suppressed issues."

The present paper will attempt to describe a few of the most important political and ideological changes in the Soviet Union subsequent to Khrushchev's ouster. Of these changes, the most important are, I believe: (1) the deceleration of the destalinization process and the

WOLFGANG LEONHARD has combined a career of free-lance writing, interpretive journalism, and public lecturing, with academic teaching and research, both in the United States and West Germany. His *Child of the Revolution* is widely acclaimed as an exceptionally interesting autobiographical account of his years in the Soviet Union and, from 1945 to 1949, in East Germany. After spending two years in Yugoslavia, he made his home in the West. He studied at Oxford University and has taught at the University of Michigan, Columbia University, and is now visiting professor at Yale University. He has been a regular contributor to *Die Zeit*, a leading German newspaper, and the author of several other books, including *The Kremlin Since Stalin*.

41

transition to a tougher policy; and (2) the transition from a utopian view of the future to a more realistic and sober outlook. There have been also delays and hesitations on important decisions, disagreements among various factions, and recognition of a "Party-free sphere." Individual problems confronting the Soviet Union (in such areas as economics, agriculture, culture, and foreign policy) are touched upon only insofar as they have a direct bearing on political and ideological changes. Finally, an attempt is made to summarize the political and ideological changes since Khrushchev's fall and to describe the present political and ideological situation in the Soviet Union.

THE WITHERING OF DESTALINIZATION

To a large extent, the same key problem occupies the spotlight in the political and ideological developments *since* the fall of Khrushchev as before his fall: how Soviet communism should adapt itself to changing internal and international conditions. Both the internal changes (the advent of a modern Soviet industrial society and the growing influence of social forces emerging from that society) and the multiplicity of new international problems (the atomic age, the self-assertion of other Communist countries, decolonization and the emergence of dozens of newly independent nations in Asia and Africa)—all these things have necessitated a change in the methods as well as in the general political line of Soviet communism.

Just as under Khrushchev (however, with completely different results), the leadership and the Party apparatus have been faced with the problem of whether to promote or decelerate these modernization processes; the problem of deciding in which areas of public life (national economy, agriculture, domestic policy, Party, ideology) certain reforms should be enacted or rescinded; and the problem—once the decisions are made to carry out these reforms in given areas—of what scope, at what rate, and under whose leadership these reforms should be enacted. It is in the attitude toward these problems that meaningful changes have taken place in the period following Khrushchev's fall. At the same time different factions have made themselves known, running the gamut from extreme liberals and reformers, on one side of the spectrum, through "moderate modernizers" and conservatives, to dogmatic, neo-Stalinist apparatchiks on the other.

With this as a point of departure, it is understandable that the "Stalin question" has been such an important issue since Khrushchev's fall. Attitudes toward Stalin and the Stalin era have often become a kind of yardstick of basic political posture. The more intense and substantial the criticism of Stalin and his system, the sooner and the easier it was to combat and ferret out what remained of Stalinism in all spheres of public life—in the economy, politics, ideology, culture, and the nationalities question. And the reverse is also true: the more the supposedly "positive sides" of the Stalin era were emphasized—as has unfortunately been the case since the spring of 1965—the more clearly could be seen the attempt either to block completely the necessary reforms or to keep the changes within narrow limits. Now as before, the attitude toward Stalin is generally the mirror of attitudes toward reform; it shows whether and to what extent the leadership and the Party apparatus are prepared, willing, and able to bring about necessary reforms in all areas of Soviet life.

Continuation of the Destalinization Process
(Autumn, 1964-Spring, 1965)

Immediately after Khrushchev's fall, the Soviet leadership made it clear that it would continue the basic line of the destalinization policy and promised to adhere to the decisions of the XX, XXI, and XXII Party Congresses as well as to the 1961 Party Program. Most importantly, the recognition of the XX and XXII Party Congresses was a clear indication that the new leadership (or at least a majority in the leadership) intended to continue the political destalinization and to set themselves apart from Khrushchev solely through the introduction of other forms, methods, and styles of operation. In so doing, the new Soviet leadership clearly gave the Party and population to understand: We have toppled Khrushchev, but we did not do so because we were in disagreement with his destalinization program. In essence, we want to accomplish the same things in a different, less hectic and hurried, more businesslike way. This line was immediately reinforced by clear-cut actions. At the December, 1964, session of the Supreme Soviet, Kosygin announced that the economic reform would be continued. At the same time, he placed the production of consumer goods sharply in the forefront, while the defense budget was reduced by 600 million rubles.[1] In agriculture, a more liberal and tolerant posture vis-à-vis private farmland and livestock was evident.

In cultural policies, hopeful signs of a somewhat more liberal course could be discerned. Iosif Brodsky, the Leningrad poet who had been arrested under Khrushchev, and Olga Ivinskaia, Boris Pasternak's life companion, were released from prison. Other authors and poets who had been sharply criticized under Khrushchev once more had a stronger voice in public life. In March, 1965, this tendency was also stressed in

---

[1] *Pravda,* December 10, 1964.

a policy-making article by A. M. Rumiantsev, then editor-in-chief of *Pravda*.[2] The article was distinguished by its conciliatory tone and hinted at a respite for intellectuals, provided they behaved responsibly.

In the sciences, with the fall of Lysenko (February 4, 1965), the way to serious research in the field of genetics was free. A tolerant attitude toward sociology, social psychology, cybernetics and econometrics was clearly visible. Rehabilitations of purged and forgotten leaders continued. Destalinization continued even in the important sector of Party history and reached a point where at least a partial rehabilitation of Nikolai Bukharin was reportedly planned.[3]

The Change in Direction (April-July, 1965)

This continuing destalinization and the relatively liberal course remained in force until about March, 1965. In the spring of 1965, however, a reaction against this began to become noticeable. It apparently stemmed from the escalation of the Vietnam war, particularly with the inauguration of the American bombings of North Vietnam in mid-February. After the failure of attempts by the Soviet leadership to promote a cease-fire in Vietnam—assuming the bombing of North Vietnam was stopped—the first signs of a tougher line became evident.

This development began with a thrust by conservative elements in the armed forces to rehabilitate the role of Stalin during the war; this was a kind of ideological buttress for a desired increase in the armaments budget. In April and May, 1965, there was a rapid succession of "positive" references to Stalin the war-leader by Marshal Bagramian, Marshal Konev, and Admiral Kuznetsov.[4] In Brezhnev's speech on May 8, 1965, in connection with the 20th anniversary of the victory in World War II, for the first time since Khrushchev's "destalinization," the First Secretary of the Party referred to Stalin's role in the war in a positive light.[5] This positive mention of Stalin (underscored by a televised film in which Stalin was similarly shown "positively") indicated that a halt had been called to destalinization. However, the fact that other Soviet leaders did not follow Brezhnev's example indicated uncertainty or disagreement in the leadership over the "Stalin question."

The second thrust, closely related to this, was the reassessment of

---

[2] *Pravda*, February 21, 1965.

[3] Edward Crankshaw, "The Last Word of Bukharin," *Observer*, May 23, 1965, and (with the full text of Bukharin's last letter) Wolfgang Leonhard, "Bucharins letzter Brief," *Die Zeit*, May 21, 1965.

[4] *Literaturnaia gazeta*, April 17, 1965; *Pravda*, April 21, 1965; *Neva*, No. 5 (1965). See also Erich Pruck, "Die Umwertung Stalins und Chruschtschows in Wehrkundlicher Sicht," *Osteuropa*, No. 11-12 (1965), pp. 807-12.

[5] *Pravda*, May 9, 1965.

the Soviet state security service. This was touched on in an article by Soviet state security chief Semichastny, published at the beginning of May, in which Cheka traditions were lengthily eulogized and praised, while Stalin's crimes were barely mentioned.[6] An extensive publicity campaign followed—considerably stronger than under Khrushchev—featuring certain Soviet "intelligence agents" such as Richard Sorge and Colonel Rudolf Abel.

This was followed, not without dissension, by an increased emphasis on heavy industry and defense needs, expressed, among others, in the speeches by Politburo member M.A. Suslov on June 2 and by General Secretary L. I. Brezhnev on July 3. Soviet Navy Day (July 24, 1965) was used to popularize the new line.

Economic problems occupied the limelight during the summer and autumn. In September, 1965, a harder and tougher course in cultural policies became apparent, connected with the halt on destalinization and with the partial rehabilitation of the Stalin tradition. The starting signal for this was the "Rumiantsev affair."

A Tougher Course Prevails

On September 9, *Pravda* editor-in-chief Alexei Rumiantsev (appointed in December, 1964) published an article openly criticizing two newspapers: *Selskaia zhizn* for its attacks on Vladimir Tendriakov and *Izvestiia* for its attacks on Vasili Aksenov. As Tendriakov and Aksenov are well-known liberal writers, Rumiantsev had once again identified himself as a defender of the liberal intelligentsia. But times had changed. Two weeks later, Rumiantsev was replaced by Mikhail Zimianin, a Foreign Ministry official.

At the same time, the entire Agitprop apparatus of the Party Central Committee was reorganized. In addition to Piotr Demichev, the Party Secretary responsible for ideology, three top ideological functionaries were appointed: Vladimir I. Stepakov (Agitation and Propaganda), Dimitri Polikarpov (Culture), and the "dogmatist" Sergei P. Trapeznikov (Science and Education). Former Belorussian partisan commander Vladimir Malin was appointed Rector of the Party's Academy of Social Sciences. The shakeup of the Agitprop apparatus and the change in editors-in-chief of two leading newspapers were clearly the prelude to a change in the general political line, in which Trapeznikov may have been assigned the role of a "little Zhdanov."

Trapeznikov had been Director of the Moldavian Party School in Kishinev in the early 1950s when Brezhnev was First Party Secretary of the Moldavian SSR. He later advanced to the post of Deputy Director

* *Pravda*, May 7, 1965.

of the Higher Party School in Moscow and published a dogmatic book in defense of the Stalinist collectivization.[7] In October 1965, Trapeznikov published an important article in which he warned against excessive criticism of the Stalin era (what he called "voluntarism" or "subjectivism"):

> Narrow-mindedness and subjectivism can also be found in a few works on the history of the Party and of the people in their struggle for industrialization, collectivization and the cultural revolution. Incorrect appraisals of the collectivization movement appear. . . . One cannot overlook the serious mistakes made in the appraisal of the Great Fatherland War. . . . A subjective judgment was also apparent in the appraisal of particular personalities and their roles in the great transformations. In some cases such personalities were placed upon pedestals, though they had played no important role in the transformations or had even taken up positions contrary to the struggle in progress.

What was meant were the critical-historical viewpoints that appeared during Khrushchev's time, especially those related to collectivization and the war years. Trapeznikov also attacked a "few historians" who had underestimated the role of the Party in the struggle for the development of socialism, or even examined it in a biased fashion, as well as a few "pseudo-theoreticians," who had suggested removing Party history from the curriculum and replacing it with courses focused on "the last decade."

Even clearer was Trapeznikov's statement against all those historians and authors who had strongly stressed the difficulties, tragedy, and injustices of the Stalin era: "Therefore it is neither theoretically nor factually correct for some of our scientific and cultural publications to describe life only from the point of view of the personality cult and thereby to overlook the heroic struggle of Soviet people in building socialism." [8]

It was also no accident that the proposal published in January, 1965, concerning the introduction of political science as a separate discipline was rejected at this point.[9] Instead a new textbook on "scientific communism" was to be produced in the shortest possible time.[10] A tougher line was also announced subsequently in regard to Party control over literature.[11] All this suggested a burgeoning tougher line against re-

[7] *Istoricheskii opyt KPSS v osushchestvlenii leninskogo kooperativnovo plana* (Moscow: "Mysl'," 1965).

[8] *Pravda*, October 8, 1965.

[9] See *Voprosy filosofii*, No. 10 (1965), pp. 164-66.

[10] *Voprosy filosofii*, No. 12 (1965), pp. 15-25.

[11] See the article in observance of the 50th anniversary of Lenin's essay on Party organization and Party literature, in *Kommunist*, No. 16 (November 1965).

form-oriented intellectuals. In the first half of October, 1965, Soviet writers Andrei Siniavsky and Iuli Daniel were arrested. Shortly thereafter, Alexander Solzhenitsyn's house was searched. Arrests were made somewhat later of three young writers, Iulia Vishnevska, Vladimir Bykovsky and Leonid Gubanov, who belonged to the underground group of writers known as SMOG (made up of the initials of *Smelost*— Courage, *Mysl'*—Thought, *Obraz*—Form, and *Glubina*—Depth).

A general tide continued in the form of a "further reassessment of Stalin." Brezhnev, in a speech in Kiev, repeatedly referred to "Stalingrad," [12] while Shelest, the Ukrainian Party chief, was equally demonstrative in speaking of "Volgograd." Thus even the tangential, ludicrous question of whether the city should be referred to as "Stalingrad" or "Volgograd" became symbolic of a political dichotomy.

Preparations for the Rehabilitation of Stalin?

The armaments budget was increased from 12.8 to 13.4 billion rubles in December, 1965.[13] The ideological rationale was that the West was preparing for nuclear war and that the Soviet Union had accordingly been forced "to take measures to strengthen its defenses." [14] The great celebrations surrounding the forty-eighth anniversary of the Soviet state security service (December 20) were a further step in the new attitude to the Stalinist past. Film festivals offering movies extolling the state security service as well as "friendship meetings" between KGB officers and the populace were organized; no mention whatsoever was made of Stalin's crimes. At the end of January, 1966, a policy-making *Pravda* article claimed that generalizations regarding the "personality cult" had gone too far. This article maintained that

> In the process of overcoming these serious shortcomings [this apparently refers to the personality cult—W. L.] a new set of mistakes was made, of essentially a subjectivistic character. In various works on historical themes the role of this or that person in history was exaggerated. The false un-Marxian concept of the "era of the personality cult" was disseminated. The use of this concept . . . led to a diminishing of the Party's and the people's efforts in the struggle for socialism.[15]

With this, for the first time since the fall of Khrushchev, a *de facto* halt to the destalinization process was publicly demanded. In early February, 1966, the trial of Siniavsky and Daniel followed. Siniavsky was sentenced to seven and Daniel to five years' imprisonment. At the

[12] *Pravda*, October 24, 1965.
[13] *Pravda*, December 8, 1965.
[14] *Krasnaia zvezda*, December 17, 1965.
[15] *Pravda*, January 30, 1966.

same time, a veritable witch hunt was launched against reform-oriented writers.

In February, 1966, the tenth anniversary of the XX Party Congress of 1956 was passed over in silence even though such events are usually written up in long commemorative articles. Instead, on February 26, 1966, there appeared an extensive article on the seventieth birthday of Andrei Zhdanov, Stalin's cultural dictator, implying that the previous reversal of the Zhdanov decisions had been countermanded. In this article Zhdanov was described as a "great political fighter," who strongly believed in the people, and as an outstanding fighter for the Communist Party and the Soviet state. Interestingly enough, his speech at the founding of the Cominform in September, 1947, was alluded to positively. Zhdanov's life was described as an "example of selfless service to the Communist Party and to the Soviet people."

This demonstrative praise of Zhdanov was especially interesting because in this fashion Khrushchev's destalinization was again being criticized, indirectly but unmistakably. During the Khrushchev era, a resolution of the Central Committee on May 28, 1958, had officially rescinded a Zhdanov-inspired decree of February 10, 1948, against a group of leading composers and artists. Thus the commemoration of Zhdanov's birthday in February, 1966, could be construed only as a warning to artists and writers.

The attempt to curb criticism of the Stalin era reached its peak with the speech by Deva Sturua, the Second Party Secretary of Georgia, at the Congress of the Georgian Communist Party in early March, 1966. Sturua openly demanded a renunciation of destalinization. He argued that the very notion of an "era of the personality cult" tended to downgrade the importance of the entire development of the Soviet Union under Stalin. Under the pretext of fighting against the Stalin cult, he continued, Trotskyism, rightist deviations, bourgeois nationalism, and other "anti-Leninist movements" had been rehabilitated. Sturua also accused Khrushchev of having wished to introduce something like a two-party system. Furthermore, destalinization was responsible for various unhealthy trends:

> The costs of the criticism of the personality cult and also the results of "voluntarism" and "subjectivism" found their expression in a return to "nihilism," "cosmopolitanism," "nationalism," and an apolitical position in assorted works of historians, writers, and artists.[16]

[16] Boris Meissner, "Die KPdSU zwischen Reaktion und Fortschritt," *Osteuropa,* No. 7-8 (1966), pp. 417-18. Meissner gives as his source *Zaria Vostoka,* March 10, 1966.

All this seemed to indicate that someone was making preparations for a partial rehabilitation of Stalin and a condemnation of destalinization at the forthcoming XXIII Party Congress. This, however, was opposed by powerful forces both within the Soviet Union (for instance, by a petition of 27 well-known scientists, writers and artists) [17] as well as outside the Soviet Union (the Communist Party of Italy and probably also the Parties of Czechoslovakia and Hungary). Sturua's speech was not published in the central Soviet (Moscow) press.[18] This could mean that the planned rehabilitation of Stalin was abandoned. One may surmise that at the suddenly convened plenary session of the Central Committee, only a few days before the Party Congress,[19] the reaffirmation of the Stalin tradition, perhaps planned as the sensational high point of the Congress, was dropped from Brezhnev's draft report.

The XXIII Party Congress: Cultural Policy

Even though there was no open rehabilitation of Stalin, the tougher line and the deceleration of destalinization could not be overlooked. The review of the world situation which Brezhnev gave in his report alone was more reminiscent of Stalin's reviews of the international situation at the XVI and XVII Party Congresses (1930 and 1934) than of the report of Khrushchev at the XX Party Congress in February, 1956. Just as Stalin had done over three decades earlier, Brezhnev now spoke of the "general crisis of capitalism," of a new period of contradictions and rivalries in the capitalist world, of an increasing exploitation and intensification of the class struggle. In contrast, such problems as automation, cybernetics, the second industrial revolution, and the social transformations in the Western industrialized nations were not mentioned.[20]

The greatest hardening could be seen in cultural policy. Brezhnev declared that Soviet literature and art must be imbued "with the noble spirit of Party-mindedness." To this end, "the problems of Communist construction in our land must become the chief content" of literature, cinema, theater, painting, and music. While the Party would be against

[17] *The New York Times,* March 21, 1966.
[18] See report on the Party Congress of the Communist Party of Georgia, in *Pravda,* March 9, 1966.
[19] *Pravda,* March 27, 1966.
[20] It is interesting to compare the description of the international situation in Stalin's report on the XVI Party Congress in: Stalin's *Sochineniia,* XII (Moscow: Politizdat, 1949), 235-54; and his remarks on the international situation on the XVII Party Congress: *Sochineniia,* XIII (Moscow: Politizdat, 1951), 282-99, with Brezhnev's remarks on the international situation at the XXIII Party Congress in *Pravda,* March 30, 1966.

"administrative interference and arbitrary decisions" in literature and art, in the future it would continue to indicate "the direction" and would support only "an art and literature that strengthen the belief in our ideals and wage an uncompromising struggle against all manifestations of ideologies alien to us." In an allusion to Siniavsky and Daniel, Brezhnev spoke of the "shameful activity of such people," whom the Party would deal with "as they deserve." Still sharper criticism was expressed by Vasili Mzhavanadze (Georgia) who scored ex-Ambassador Ivan Maisky's memoirs; writer Mikhail Sholokhov, who described Siniavsky and Daniel as "amoral" and declared that he was ashamed for all those "who have attempted and are still attempting to protect these people"; V. S. Markov, who called Siniavsky and Daniel "slanderers" and ideological contrabandists; and Moscow Oblast Party Secretary Vasili Konotop, who attacked the liberal journals *Novyi mir* and *Yunost*. Others who were particularly biting in their remarks were Komsomol chief Sergei Pavlov, Moscow City Party Secretary Nikolai Yegorychev, and Belorussian Party Secretary Piotr Masherov, who reproached both Soviet magazine editors and publishing house directors for having forgotten their responsibility before the Party. Moldavian Party Secretary Ivan Bodiul attacked Solzhenitsyn's *A Day in the Life of Ivan Denisovich,* emphasizing the classical Stalinist formulation that the writers have the freedom to write what they wish, but the Party authorities have the freedom to decide whether it should be printed. Other regime functionaries either did not take part in this "discussion" or were (as in the case of Culture Minister Furtseva) relatively restrained.

The XXIII Party Congress: Party Questions

A similar trend in Party questions was unmistakable. The focal point was the strengthening of Party discipline. Now the Central Committee for Party Control and the regional Party control commissions were to "play a larger part." Admission to the Party was made more difficult, *inter alia,* by the fact that the recommendations of three Party members who have been members of the Party for at least five years (previously three years) are required. An amendment to the Party by-laws stipulated that persons can be expelled from the Party for acting against the program or the by-laws of the Party or for compromising the Party by their behavior. The previous demotion system of "reduction to candidate status" was repealed with the indication that in such cases it was better to expel the Party member altogether. Despite the elastic compromise statement of Brezhnev, the abolition of the personnel rotation principle, introduced by Khrushchev in October, 1961, in fact serves to stabilize the dominant role of the 50- to 60-year-olds in the Party apparatus and makes advancement for the post-Stalin generation in the Party apparatus more difficult. The change of name from Party "Presidium" to "Politburo" was justified on the basis that this designation "more completely expressed the character of the activity" of this organ, despite the fact that almost the same formulation was employed at the XIX Party Congress in 1952 when the Politburo was renamed the Party Presidium. Despite references to the Politburo "as it had been established by Lenin" there can be no doubt that the Politburo concept is chiefly related to the Stalin era, and thus another step was made in the direction of "building a bridge back to the Stalin era." The same holds true for the change in the title of the First Secretary to General Secretary. Yegorychev's claim that the title of General Secretary had been introduced by Lenin at the XI Party Congress was not very convincing. Since Stalin was the only leader to possess this title, the renewal of the Stalin tradition was even more apparent in this case.

The XXIII Party Congress: Changes in Ideology

The deceleration of destalinization was most apparent in the field of ideology. Unlike the Khrushchev period, the significance of ideology as an independent factor was once more strongly emphasized. Typical of this was Brezhnev's demand that an "end be made" to the notion that ideology is only "of propagandistic significance" and should "only clarify and comment on practice." But even more important was the playing down of a number of ideological destalinization theses. No mention was made of the "state of all the people," nor of the "Party of all the people"—concepts introduced five years earlier. But since both theses (whether or not they were ideologically sound) served as an ideological foundation for destalinization reforms, this was of special political significance. The failure to mention the possibility of a peaceful road to socialism, which Khrushchev had always strongly emphasized, must also be seen in the same light. Brezhnev stated merely that there were "different traditions, different economic conditions, and different experiences of struggle" in the Communist Parties of different lands. The concept of "national democracy," introduced by Khrushchev as an intermediate stage along the "non-capitalist road" of the developing nations, was not mentioned.

Finally, it was also striking that disarmament, which since the spring of 1960 had been elevated to the position of a standard part of the ideology ("disarmament is an ideal of socialism") was hardly mentioned, just as was the Khrushchevian thesis, dating from the XXI Party Congress, on the possibility—even if capitalism continues to exist in part of the world—of eliminating world war from the life of society. The doctrine of peaceful coexistence, which under Khrushchev was defined as the general foreign policy line of the socialist nations, was now demoted to a by-product of foreign policy objectives.

All the ideological theses that were no longer mentioned at the Congress (state and party of all the people, the peaceful road to socialism, national democracy, the possibility of preventing world war while capitalism continues to exist, and coexistence as a general foreign policy line) had been fought against for years by the Chinese Communists and by Soviet neo-Stalinists. The failure to mention these theses marked an important step toward the renewal of the Stalin tradition.

Developments Following the XXIII Party Congress

This trend continued after the XXIII Party Congress, when a tougher cultural political line was again closely linked to the defense of the Soviet past (i. e., the Stalin tradition). At the center of the attack was the story of Vasili Bykov, "The Dead Hurt No More," a realistic account of Soviet army life during the Second World War, published in early 1966,[21] and the 1966 essay of V. Kardin, "Legends and Facts." [22] Kardin asserted that there had been no "salvoes from the [cruiser] Aurora" in November, 1917, but rather a single blank round and that there had been no victory of the Red Guard on February 23, 1918, over the Germans—an event that was subsequently celebrated as the Founding Day of the Red Army.

The campaign against Bykov and Kardin was begun under the theme that legends must not be dragged into the dirt. In a letter of protest (signed among others by Marshal Rokossovsky and Old Bolshevik Petrov), Bykov and Kardin were accused of slandering "our heroic history." In April, 1966, in addition to the journal *Novyi mir* (which had published Bykov and Kardin), the "Nauka" Publishing House was also attacked for printing the "subjective memoirs" of former Ambassador Maisky and of Rakitin, as well as books in which the history of the Soviet Union was treated from "un-Marxian positions." [23] A few days later, a dogmatic Party official in cultural affairs, M. Alekseev, warned against simply writing off the books of the Stalin era disparagingly as "cult literature," defended the literature produced under Stalin, and declared that it must not be forgotten that Stalin had been the commander-in-chief during the Second World War.[24]

[21] This story had first appeared in the Belorussian journal, *Maladost,* and in *Novyi mir,* Nos. 1 and 2 (1966).
[22] Also published in *Novyi mir,* No. 2 (1966).
[23] *Sovetskaia kultura,* April 23, 1966.
[24] *Literaturnaia Rossiia,* April 22, 1966.

On the ideological front, subsequent to the XXIII Party Congress, efforts centered on the celebration of the 50th anniversary of the October Revolution, with a good deal of stress on the heroic war period, rather than the horrors of the Stalin era. In this process, "military-patriotic indoctrination" was emphasized more than at any previous time since Stalin's death. This campaign began in May, 1966, at a conference (organized by the Defense Ministry and the Main Political Administration of the Armed Forces) devoted to the "military-patriotic indoctrination of our youth and soldiers." At this conference, Major-General Yepishev and those taking part in the discussions once again attacked the journal *Novyi mir* for publishing such materials as the stories of Bykov, and rejected any unfavorable treatment of the Soviet Army.[25] In late summer, the military-patriotic campaign was continued under the slogan "the youth continue the tradition of their parents," with the aim of exploiting the heroic deeds of Soviet officers and partisans in the Second World War for purposes of indoctrination. The campaign reached its high point in a nation-wide "meeting of young patriots" in Moscow. The meeting ended with a mass assembly in Red Square where the youths in attendance took a pompous military-patriotic oath.[26] Military-patriotic propaganda had, of course, also existed under Khrushchev; the campaign of the summer of 1966, however, significantly surpassed similar events under Khrushchev in scope and intensity.

This line was even more pronounced in the Party's directives of January 4, 1967, concerning preparations for the fiftieth anniversary of the October Revolution. Despite the great amount of detail, the resolution did not contain even the slightest criticism of Stalin or the Stalin era. Certainly anniversary festivities are not particularly well suited for sharp criticism. Nevertheless, it must be pointed out that on another occasion—the September, 1957, theses on the fortieth anniversary of the October Revolution—the Central Committee had not foregone its criticism of Stalin:

> The Communist Party of the Soviet Union did not hesitate to struggle against the personality cult of J. V. Stalin, who had caused great harm to the activity of the Party and to the cause of building communism. The mistakes made in the final period of his rule were condemned so as to make the repetition of such mistakes impossible. . . .

In January, 1967, virtually nothing was said about the Stalin era.[27]

[25] *Krasnaia zvezda*, May 25, 1966.
[26] *Pravda*, September 12, 1966.
[27] Resolution of the Central Committee of the CPSU, January 4, 1967, published in *Pravda*, January 8, 1967.

Similarly, Stalin was scarcely mentioned in the flood of oratory during the anniversary celebrations themselves in October-November, 1967.

All this is evidence of the striving of the leadership to keep political reforms down to the smallest scale possible. In contrast, the problems connected with economic reform are handled in a different way. Though not without opposition, reforms in this sector are continuing. The unwritten motto of the post-Khrushchev leadership might be formulated as follows: "As much economic reform as is absolutely necessary, and as tough a course in the intellectual sphere as possible." The leadership continues a grotesque attempt to forward the transition of the Soviet Union to a modern industrial society while hindering the social, political, and intellectual effects of such a transition.

Although this seems to be the dominant trend in political and ideological development since Khrushchev's fall, it is not the only change. There is a second trend which involves the renunciation of Khrushchev's overly optimistic hopes for the future and a shift to a more realistic outlook.

From Overoptimism to Realism

In the very first days following Khrushchev's fall, in a series of dramatic declarations, his successors announced an important change in Soviet policy.[28] Now all problems of governing would be treated in a more sober, practical, and realistic fashion. The watchwords in the new grammar were: "to analyze the shortcomings soberly" and "to concentrate on the tasks to be solved in the near future." The decisions of the Party and the government had to "correspond to objective laws, to real requirements." In the economic domain, the task was to "analyze soberly" the situation and to "provide rounded analyses of the economic processes" as well as "to make scientifically founded decisions."

This line was underscored by the indirect reproaches leveled against Khrushchev (in which, to be sure, the name of the toppled Party leader was never mentioned). He was charged with "fantasy," "premature conclusions, hasty decisions, and actions divorced from reality," "boasts and empty words," "a penchant for administering," "empty dreams," "making unfounded and dreamed-up decisions." Criticism of these manifestations and the emphasis on a more sober outlook were thus elevated to the level of the general line of Party policy, more or

---

[28] See *Pravda*, October 17 and November 1, 1964; *Partiinaia zhizn*, Nos. 20 and 21 (1964); *Kommunist*, No. 15 (1964).

less strictly adhered to in practice. Already the first plenary sessions of the Central Committee in November, 1964 (annulment of the 1962 Party reorganization) and March, 1965 (agricultural questions) gave evidence of this new practical, sober style. The agricultural plenum in March was further distinguished by more realistic goals; Khrushchev's declaration that the Soviet Union would overtake the United States in the production of milk and meat within a few years was now described by Ukrainian Party Secretary Shelest as "adventurous."

Although the general political line on destalinization began to change drastically in the spring of 1965, the shift to a realistic, practical, sober approach has remained unchanged. All the overly optimistic plans and measures of Khrushchev were either extensively watered down or completely abandoned, including his Party reorganization of 1962, his school reform of 1958 (with the purpose of bringing studies "closer to life"), and his *sovnarkhoz* reform of spring, 1957 (with which Khrushchev believed he could solve the most important economic problems). Nor was any further mention made of his corn and virgin lands campaigns. Even the 1961 Party Program (including the ten- and 20-year plans) was mentioned less and less often. It has been repeatedly emphasized that at sessions of the Central Committee and at other conferences the entire working style has become more businesslike. This (while not completely true historically) was praised as the "Leninist style."

The Renunciation of Khrushchevian Hopes for the Future

The style of the XXIII Party Congress was distinguished by sobriety and realism as well as boredom and the lack of drama. Just as at plenary meetings of the Central Committee, at the XXIII Party Congress the absence of the agile, temperamental, ebullient figure of Khrushchev made itself felt; sober, boring, and bureaucratic apparatchiks dominated the scene.

The new style was particularly evident in the handling of economic policy at the congress. Kosygin openly admitted that the previous plan figures had "not always been in harmony with the real possibilities." Brezhnev spoke of "shortcomings in planning and management." Other speakers criticized the "uncertainty and nervousness" in the economy[29] and the too frequent experiments and reorganization.[30] In contrast, many speakers described the post-Khrushchev economic policy as "well thought out," "realistic," "truly scientific," "precise and theoretically founded," and "practical." No more mention was made of

[29] *Pravda,* March 31, 1966.
[30] *Pravda,* April 3, 1966.

the "main economic task" of overtaking and surpassing the United States.

In social policy, the XXIII Party Congress did announce several new benefits, including the lowering of the income tax, an increase in old-age pensions, and the gradual introduction of the five-day week (with an unchanged work week); but these measures dated back to the Party Program of 1961. Nothing more was to be heard of the promise of the same Party Program to abolish rent by 1980 at the latest and to guarantee the free use of the communal means of transportation and utilities (water, gas, and heating).

In the ideological sphere, the XXIII Party Congress marked the final renunciation of the Khrushchevian vision of the future society, including, most prominently, the hope for a relatively fast achievement of a full-fledged Communist society. The implicit abandonment of the Party Program was clear to everyone. To be sure—and this, too, was typical—the Party leadership neither directly criticized the Party Program nor officially declared it void. Rather, it simply shifted it into the background in the hope that it would slowly sink into oblivion. But the emphasis was shifted from the realization of the future Communist society to the present problems of developing a "socialist" society.

The same trend was reflected in the 1966 May Day slogans of the Central Committee, published in mid-April, 1966. For the first time the Party Program was not mentioned at all. Even the main slogan of the Party Program, according to which the realization of communism would bring "peace, work, liberty, equality, fraternity, and happiness" to all peoples, was no longer to be seen on the banners in the Soviet May Day demonstrations. Instead several times (albeit elsewhere) mention was made of the "socialist stage," a new indication that the Khrushchev thesis of the "all-out building of Communist society" was now a thing of the past. As early as 1965, portrayals of the future Communist society, customary under Khrushchev, were almost completely eliminated. Just before the XXIII Party Congress, Party ideologist P. N. Fedoseev openly criticized attempts to concentrate on the end goal of the Communist society:

> In various works one can note an excessive haste in the treatment of the question of the transition to communism, one hurries ahead of development, skips over the whole stage of socialism in the development of the pure communist social structure.[31]

At the end of December, 1966, fault was found with the new official

[31] *Pravda,* March 16, 1966.

Party handbook, *Fundamentals of Communism.* What this handbook had done wrong was that it "already at this time gave complete answers to certain questions on the future of communist society." [32]

The New Theory of the "Developed Socialist Society"

In this way, the Party leadership made clear which theses were "false." But what then was "true"? How did things stand with respect to the "transition to communism"? At what stage of development did the Soviet Union find itself?

Answers to these questions for which many ideologically interested functionaries in the Soviet Union were waiting, were not forthcoming until the second half of December, 1966—more than eight months after the end of the XXIII Party Congress. According to a policy-making *Pravda* article,[33] the socialist society had *not* triumphed in the Soviet Union in the mid-30's but only the "foundations of socialism" had been laid (which corresponded exactly to what Molotov had declared in February, 1955, and for which he had to indulge in public self-criticism in October, 1955). After the erection of the "foundations of socialism" there was a "more or less protracted period of all-round development of socialist society." How long it was before the stage of "developed socialist society" was finally reached was not stated.

This stage of "developed socialist society" was distinguished by four tendencies (presented here in the briefest form):

1. *Economic*—a new economic system in accordance with the demands the scientific-technical revolution, the harmonious development of the national economy, and an increase in the standard of living;
2. *Social*—the leading role of the working class, unity of the people, the continuation of the collective spirit, camaraderie and the socialist epoch;
3. *Political*—the scientific leadership of society through the Party, the development of the state system and socialist democracy;
4. *Ideological*—the continuation of Marxism-Leninism, and the raising of the general educational level and professional knowledge.

According to this definition, the Soviet Union and the "other socialist countries" were at the stage of "developed socialist society," which was an important stage on the road to communism and would facilitate a "gradual transition to communism."

With this, the shift to a more realistic outlook became evident in all fields. Khrushchevian wishes for the future were replaced by a

[32] *Pravda,* December 27, 1966.
[33] *Pravda,* December 21, 1966.

sober and more pessimistic approach. The style of leadership had changed from activist over-optimism into sober, bureaucratic realism.

Leadership Factions and Hesitations

From the foregoing, one might gain the impression that the ideological and political developments since Khrushchev's fall follow two clear-cut lines, one amounting to the abatement of the process of destalinization and a tougher course with respect to culture, domestic policies, Party and ideology, and the other, amounting to the transition from overoptimism to realism. This picture is incomplete because it lacks the third important phenomenon of the three years following Khrushchev's ouster: the emergence of different factions and groupings, whose disagreements became increasingly apparent. To be sure, these phenomena had existed under Khrushchev and, in part, even under Stalin. However, the new feature in the post-Khrushchev development is that all (or almost all) decisive political questions have been affected, and differences of opinion have been so strong that the leadership has not been able to make clear-cut decisions. Instead, it has continually delayed decisions or hoped to solve important problems through elastic compromise formulations.

The Unclear Stalin Question

In this connection, primary attention may be focused on the Stalin question and the attitude toward the Stalinist past. Thus far, of all the members of the Politburo, only Brezhnev has repeatedly made positive reference to Stalin. Significantly, the other leaders have remained silent. The Sturua incident and the petition of the Soviet intellectuals immediately preceding the XXIII Party Congress underscored the significance of destalinization and of disagreements over it. To date, the top Soviet leadership has failed to reach agreement on the Stalin question. Criticism of the Stalin era is subdued; positive mention of Stalin is made here and there. However, Stalin has not been rehabilitated or, still less, glorified. This ambiguity leaves a peculiarly unclear official attitude toward a quarter-century of Soviet history.

The Absence of Goals

A clear-cut stand on the Stalin issue is a prerequisite for a clear perspective on current and future policy. It is not surprising, therefore, that the Soviet leadership (to an extent that is unprecedented in Soviet history) has been unable to establish clear-cut goals for the further development of the USSR. The aforementioned declaration, in 1966, to the effect that the Soviet Union was at the stage of a "developed socialist society" and in process of "gradual transition to communism" is exceedingly vague. It fails to state when the "gradual transition to communism" begins (or whether it has already begun), what is to happen in the period of the "gradual transition to communism," and in what respect the newly-proclaimed "gradual transition to communism" differs (1) from the "all-out building of Communist society" that was official doctrine following the XXI Party Congress (February, 1959), and (2) from the "transition to communism" which was official doctrine prior to the XXI Party Congress (from 1939 to 1959). This lack of specificity in political and ideological long-range theses is for a Communist a highly unusual, uncertain, and undesirable condition.

In view of the fact that the basic questions are undecided, it is not astonishing that a host of important practical questions in the most diverse areas also remain unsolved. In the jargon of the Communist functionary, these are dubbed "open questions," of which there have never been so many as in the period after 1964.

What are the most important of these "open questions"? Let us refer only to some of the controversies for which there is definite evidence.

The Controversy Over Party and State

Very shortly after Khrushchev's fall, a pronounced controversy broke out over the relations between the Party and the government, that is, over the question to what extent (and within what limits) the "leading role of the Party" was to be realized and what role the government organs were to play, and how the activities of these two power structures were to be separated from one another.

The controversy began with Brezhnev's policy speech of November 6, 1964. The ever-increasing tasks of government, Brezhnev maintained, would increase the role and significance of the Party as the leading and directing force of Soviet society. But in addition, Brezhnev declared that the Soviet Party members had "all rights" for "the effective control of state, economic, and social organizations." Shortly thereafter, Kiselev, Chairman of the Belorussian Council of Ministers, spoke out against this. In "recent years," he complained, the role of the government organs had been "suppressed." An end had to be put to the "petty tutelage over economic organs and to the incompetent interference in their activities." [34] After Kosygin, too, in his speech to the Supreme Soviet spoke out twice against the "petty tutelage" (everyone understood that this meant the Party apparatus), *Pravda*

---

[34] *Izvestiia*, November 27, 1964.

on December 6, 1964, took an official stand on the role of the Party, which came very close to the Kiselev-Kosygin stand. *Pravda* admitted that the role of government organs "in recent years has from time to time been reduced" and declared that it was time that the government authorities "be given more powers." The "leading role of the Party" did not refer to "administrative direction but rather to direction of the highest political type." Nonetheless, the controversy did not end with this. Under the new emphasis on the Party being "responsible for everything" (or, "the Communists being responsible for everything"), the representatives of the Party apparatus continued to fight against encroachments on the power and authority of the Party organs.[35] At the XXIII Party Congress, there were again different views of the relations between Party and state. Brezhnev confined himself to the declaration that the Party "directs and organizes the life of socialist society" and is the "teacher, organizer and political leader of the Soviet people." He did not, however, answer the most important question, which was how this was to come about under the existing conditions. Podgorny, on the other hand, complained that "numerous Party committees . . . take over many of the duties that are incumbent on the soviets." [36] Party Secretary Zolotukhin demanded "that the functions of the Party, state, and economic organs be more precisely demarcated, that the economic functionaries be given more rights, and that excessive regimentation be done away with." The Party committees were not to concern themselves with "the tasks of the economic functionaries." [37]

There has been no clear-cut decision on this question. There is only the famous orchestra analogy which is supposed to "clarify" the matter: just as the conductor must achieve harmony in the orchestra but must not try to play the instruments of the individual musicians, so the Party must lead society without directly assuming the functions of the individual authorities and institutions. The weakness of this picturesque analogy is that it clarifies neither what happens when one of the musicians gets out of line nor how the orchestra should function when, in addition to the principal conductor, there are two co-conductors, Kosygin and Podgorny, who from time to time wave their batons differently.

The Controversy Over Party-and-Leadership Questions

A compromise formulation exists with regard to personnel policy in the Party apparatus and the leadership. At the XXIII Party Con-

[35] *Pravda*, December 13 and 16, 1964.
[36] *Pravda*, April 1, 1966.
[37] *Pravda*, April 7, 1966.

gress, in annulling the rotation principle introduced by Khrushchev, Brezhnev made a "policy" declaration on this subject. Brezhnev proclaimed the "principle of systematic renewal and continuity." According to him, the abolition of the rotation principle was to prevent "good collaborators" from giving up their work in the Party apparatus too soon (in this connection, Khrushchev's ouster was not mentioned) and would supposedly not work to the disadvantage of young officials. Just as in the past, "new, young cadres are to be appointed to leading positions in the Party and the government." In a word, the old remain and the young are appointed.

There are obvious disagreements over the position and functions of the General Secretary of the Party. They became apparent at the XXIII Party Congress, ranging from one extreme represented by Podgorny (who mentioned Brezhnev less often than other speakers) to a raion Secretary, Filinova, who spoke of the "Politburo with the General Secretary at its head" [38] as well as Kirgiz Party Secretary Usubaliev, who referred to the General Secretary as "the political leader of the Party." [39]

In a policy article published on July 6, 1966, *Pravda* declared that the "unity of decisions" was a must and that collective leadership must be "the basis for Party activity in the future as well." [40] Interestingly enough, the same article contains a clear reminder of the precedence of political work over organizational work, which apparently was intended to underscore the leading role of the Politburo (in which diverse currents were represented) as compared to the Secretariat of the Central Committee, which was largely under Brezhnev's influence.

A *Pravda* article published two weeks later went much further. Ostensibly dealing with local Party organizations, it made open allusions to the leadership: collective leadership was "the basic principle of all activity of the CPSU," a principle which must be consolidated and developed further. Whoever "pursues a course of undermining the collectivity of the leadership will be called to account by the Party." A Party secretary was "no boss and had no right to command." He was merely the "elder" in the collective, and in making decisions he had only "the same rights as the other members." [41]

There are considerable differences of opinion and uncertainties in the attitude toward the creative intelligentsia. This is attested to by the Rumiantsev affair in autumn, 1965, discussed earlier, as well as

[38] *Pravda*, April 3, 1966.
[39] *Pravda*, April 4, 1966.
[40] *Pravda*, July 6, 1966.
[41] *Pravda*, July 20, 1966.

by the various attacks on reformist writers at the XXIII Party Congress. While some speakers attempted to outdo Brezhnev in their attacks on writers and artists, other Party officials took no part in the affair whatsoever. Since the XXIII Party Congress, some elements in the armed forces and in the Party apparatus have continued to wage a private war against the intellectuals, while certain important officials and Party leaders have refrained. The divided stand of the leadership, as well as the courage of the writers and artists, was reflected in the fact that the long-awaited Writers' Congress was postponed time and time again. It was first scheduled for spring, 1966; it was postponed to June, 1966, then to January 23, 1967, and finally took place in May, 1967. There is nothing wrong with postponing a congress, but four times is too often.

The Controversy Over Economic Reform

The disputes and the elastic compromise formulations resulting from them over the all-important question of economic reform were especially pronounced; only a few of its political aspects will be mentioned here. The resolution of the Plenum of September, 1965, on economic reform—to give the enterprises a greater degree of autonomy but at the same time to strengthen the control from above through the formation of new central ministries—points to such a compromise. According to Brezhnev, the economic reform was a matter of "strengthening the centralized planned direction of the national economy," which "dovetails with a further development of the initiative and autonomy of the enterprises"—a diplomatic compromise formulation that is easier to proclaim than to carry out.

Even at the September Plenum, there were contradictions between the reports of Kosygin and Brezhnev, both over the question of who was to conduct the economic reform, what incentives (moral or material) were to be emphasized, and what role the Party would have in implementing it. Kosygin declared that the economic reform stemmed from discussions "in the Party-economic *activ*" with the participation of Party officials as well as economists and scholars. Brezhnev, however, stressed the opinion (three times) that it was a matter of suggestions made by the Party Presidium. Kosygin emphasized material incentives, while Brezhnev stressed moral incentives. Kosygin used purely economic arguments in favor of the reform, while Brezhnev placed ideological considerations in the forefront. The economic reform was said to be of a "fundamental nature," a "major political question," and "an effective contribution to the further development of Marxist-Leninist economic theory."

Kosygin had mentioned the Party but a single time at the very end of his speech and had given it the not very respectable and responsible tasks of combating local patriotism and bureaucracy and of stimulating the initiative of the workers. Brezhnev, on the contrary, declared that "highly qualified" and "experienced Party secretaries" must be assigned to the leadership of the Party organizations in the new economic ministries, which were to be established and that these secretaries should periodically report to the Central Committee on the activities of the ministries. The economic reform could be implemented only with the "power of the entire Party"; otherwise it would be impossible to count on "the necessary success." These political differences in the speeches of Brezhnev and Kosygin far exceeded those which their different functions (Party Secretary and Chairman of the Council of Ministers) would warrant.

The vague compromise formulations of the September Plenum and the differing accents in the speeches of Brezhnev and Kosygin gave the critics of economic reform the possibility of expressing their views in word and deed more strongly than would have been possible in the presence of a clear line. The resistance of the dogmatic-conservative circles to economic reform was so strong that the Soviet press publicly complained about it several times. Here are two typical examples: "Some Communists extend a mere temporary *pro forma* recognition to the usefulness of the far-reaching reforms and in reality have strong misgivings about the possibility of implementing the new reforms." [42] And "a certain, even though insignificant, part of the managerial cadres are afraid of the changes; they are afraid of a broad expansion of the economic methods of management." [43] The fact that the press repeatedly spoke of "a few Communists" and the "insignificant part" of management makes it clear that relatively strong forces, primarily in the Party apparatus but also in the economic apparatus, must have been involved.

The Controversy Over "Incentives" and the Armaments Budget

The disagreement over the relation between moral and material incentives was an important feature; as a rule, Party officials favor "moral incentives," while economic personnel prefer material incentives. Here too, the conservative wing of the Party apparatus argued that the reform would engender a "ruble mentality" and thus have a "demoralizing effect" on the Soviet citizen. In reality, these forces feared that with the broader introduction of material incentives the so-called "instructional activity" of the Party apparatus in the enterprises (competition, innovator movements, and "Communist bri-

[42] *Stroitelnaia gazeta,* November 21, 1965.
[43] *Ekonomicheskaia gazeta,* No. 47 (November, 1965).

gades") would decline in importance, and hence the function and scope of activity of the Party apparatus would be diminished. Once more an elastic compromise solution was reached: Stepakov, the new Agitprop secretary, likened the relation between material and moral incentives to a ruble note. Just as one side shows the denomination while the other depicts the emblem of the Soviet Union, so must material and moral incentives inseparably go together.[44]

Similar differences of opinion concerned the increasing defense budget. As previously stated, it was curtailed on the heels of Khrushchev's fall, in December, 1964. With the escalation of the Vietnam war, a campaign was begun to increase the Soviet armament budget (May-July, 1965). The different emphases showed that Brezhnev, Suslov, and Shelepin were in favor of the larger budget, but that Kosygin and Podgorny accepted it unwillingly. At the XXIII Party Congress Kosygin also admitted that armaments had to be strengthened but declared that the defensive might depended on the "economy of the nation." From this he drew the conclusion: "By strengthening our economy, we are strengthening our defensive capability"—a clear declaration not to increase the procurement of weapons at the expense of branches of the economy and to have the interests of the entire economy in mind.

Obscurity in Agricultural Policy

The differences of opinion on agricultural policy were so strong that the post-Khrushchev leadership suppressed almost all its political aspects; this made it possible to discuss these problems publicly and with relative freedom. The focal point of discussion was the new *kolkhoz* statute, which was to have been adopted at the repeatedly postponed Third Kolkhoz Congress. The reformers used part of the preparation time as well as the crop failure of 1965 (the Soviet Union once more had to import 8.5 million tons of grain from abroad) to make far-reaching proposals. One such proposal was known as the "tract reform": the essence of it was that *kolkhoz* land would be divided up into small tracts and a work group of between nine and 12 persons would be responsible for each tract. After many reports (and practical experience as well), it was publicly urged that this reform be introduced throughout the Soviet Union, the plot being permanently placed at the disposal of a given group of persons and that this be legally established.[45] Apparently this proposal won acclaim.[46]

Another suggestion was presented by Tatar Oblast Party Secretary

[44] *Ibid.*
[45] *Komsomolskaia pravda,* August 7, 1965.
[46] E.g., *Komsomolskaia pravda,* September 29, 1965.

F. Tabeev (an economics professor at Kazan University), who as "a reformer in the Party apparatus" had repeatedly introduced interesting proposals. Proceeding from a sharp but well-founded criticism of *sovkhozy* in the Soviet Union, he proposed that *sovkhozy* be made independent of detailed government supervision and control and that the authority of *sovkhoz* directors be expanded,[47] a proposal that also met with acclaim.[48] Finally, the demand was made that the *kolkhozy* be released from the Ministry of Agriculture and that they set up their own "*kolkhoz* associations," which would not only regulate all their own problems but also look after the interests of the *kolkhozy* in their dealings with other institutions.[49]

The Party leadership took no stand on any of these proposals even after a commission of 149 members was formed in January, 1966, for the purpose of drafting the new *kolkhoz* statute.[50] Although Brezhnev, Suslov, and Shelepin were members of this commission, at the XXIII Party Congress the political aspects of agricultural reform were not mentioned. Brezhnev did support—albeit briefly and half-heartedly—the formation of inter-*kolkhoz* associations, and this proposal was taken up by Shelest, speaking in regard to the Ukraine. Almost all the other speakers were silent—apparently from the fear that the *kolkhoz* associations might become independent entities. It was finally decided that this question be "given further study."

Since nothing was heard from the Brezhnev *kolkhoz* statute commission, the reformers made further proposals, including the legal allocation of private farmland, assigning the purchase plan directly to the *kolkhozy* instead of the procurement organs (as in the past), and permitting the *kolkhoz* members to choose their own *kolkhoz* chairman freely on the basis of a secret ballot—rather than having him appointed from without.[51] An especially far-reaching proposal came from V. G. Venzher (who had been severely attacked under Stalin, in 1952). He proposed almost complete autonomy for the *kolkhozy*. At the end of May, 1966, when the Plenum of the Central Committee met to discuss the problems of agriculture, all these problems were once more left out. Following discussion of the report given by USSR Minister of Reclamation and Irrigation E. E. Alekseevsky, Brezhnev gave a speech and the Central Committee confined itself to a decision on a major irrigation program,[52] on the probably

[47] *Selskaia zhizn,* September 12, 1965.
[48] *Ibid.,* September 23, 1965.
[49] *Ibid.,* September 18, 1965.
[50] *Pravda,* January 26, 1966.
[51] See Keith Bush, "Suggestions for the Kolkhoz Congress," Radio Liberty Research Paper No. 9, 1966; and *Sovetskoe gosudarstvo i pravo,* No. 2 (1966).
[52] *Pravda,* May 28, 1966.

correct assumption that this was one question in Soviet agriculture over which no political disputes could be expected.

Only in the late summer of 1966—after an extraordinarily good harvest which, politically speaking, gave the leadership a greater feeling of authority and self-assurance—did the conservative dogmatists feel strong enough to come out openly against the reformers. In August, they proclaimed the "strengthening of state control over the *kolkhozy*" [53]—a line which was to set the tone thereafter.[54] In early September, there was another sharp attack on Venzher's earlier reform proposals.[55] But the most important political problems in Soviet agriculture remained unresolved.

The Postponed Constitution

Just as in the case of the new *kolkhoz* statute and the *kolkhoz* congress which have been postponed from year to year, Soviet citizens and Party members have been waiting (in vain) for the new Constitution. As early as 1962, the drafting of a new Constitution and the formation of a Constitutional Commission were announced.[56] After Khrushchev's fall, at the session of the Supreme Soviet on December 11, 1964, Brezhnev (in place of Khrushchev) was elected Chairman of the Constitutional Commission.[57] But subsequently nothing was seen or heard of it. After all, in the new Constitution such issues must be spelled out as the present stage of development of the USSR and prospects for further development, the role and function of the Party, the relations between Party, state, and economic organs, the function and sphere of activity of the Supreme Soviet and its Presidium and their relation to the government (Council of Ministers), the election system—in short, all the questions which in the post-Khrushchev period have *not* been clarified and upon which decisions are being postponed. Not until December 5, 1966, did a *Pravda* lead article finally indicate that the long-awaited Soviet Constitution was to be completed by the fiftieth anniversary of the October Revolution. Yet when the anniversary came, no Constitution was unveiled.

The Wait-and-See Attitude of the Leadership

These examples alone provide evidence of a new and important phenomenon in Soviet politics. While in the earlier periods, the public disclosure of differences of opinion was the exception, in the three

[53] *Ekonomicheskaia gazeta*, No. 36 (August, 1966).
[54] See *Sovetskoe gosudarstvo i pravo*, No. 7 (1966).
[55] *Selskaia zhizn*, September 2, 1966.
[56] *Pravda*, April 26, 1962.
[57] *Pravada*, December 12, 1964.

years after Khrushchev's downfall, it has become the rule. On almost all crucial questions of policy, a multiplicity of different, in part even conflicting views come into full public view; in several cases even the top leaders have taken an active part in these disputes.

Under these conditions, the Soviet leadership has increasingly been obliged to avoid making decisions. It accomplishes this in three ways: first, by postponing decisions that are urgently needed (for example, on the *kolkhoz* congress, the *kolkhoz* statute, the writers' congress, and the new Constitution); second, by covering up the contradictions by elastic compromise formulations (for example, the centralization of national economy with the simultaneous increase in the autonomy of the enterprises, "renewal and continuity" in the Party apparatus, Brezhnev's declaration at the XXIII Party Congress concerning the strengthening of both the legality and the activity of the state security organs simultaneously). The "picturesque analogies" (of the sort that use the two sides of a ruble note as an "explanation" of material and moral incentives or the example of the orchestra to "clarify" the relations between the Party and state organs) serve as special variants of these compromise formulations. Finally, the third method consists of simply keeping quiet about delicate political problems that are obviously tied up in disputes, in the hope that no one would notice them (for example: the Party Program is no longer mentioned, with no indication whether it is completely void or has been partially "overhauled"; the role of the Party organizations in the economy; the question of whether *sovkhozy* or *kolkhozy* should be given preference in agriculture). What these different methods have in common is the tendency to dodge burning political issues, to avoid decisions, to "wait and see."

Discussions in the "Party-Free Sphere"

The longer the leadership and the Party apparatus delay taking a stand or attempt to cover up by means of elastic formulations, the greater will be the possibility for forces *outside* the top leadership and, in increasing measure, *outside the Party apparatus* to express their own opinions on the many "open problems."

In addition to the often far-reaching reform proposals on important political questions, there have been interesting discussions on other topics in the expanded "Party-free sphere," including even such problems as telepathy, immortality, and the autonomy of academic life.[58]

[58] See, e.g., *Literaturnaia Rossiia,* August 12 and September 23, 1966; *Izvestiia,* May 12 and August 14, 1966; *Literaturnaia gazeta,* May 5, August 13, and November 12, 1966, and January 11, 1967.

The "Party-free sphere" has increasingly taken the form of public discussions on topics which the Party leadership and the Party apparatus are no longer in a position to control to the extent they did previously. Meanwhile the compromise formulations and the dodging and postponing of decisions have intensified the open expression of differences of opinion. Thus the "Party-free sphere" increases. Forces outside the Party apparatus have gained, in turn, the possibility of broaching astounding topics and of putting forth interesting proposals for discussion.

Conclusions

The political and ideological changes since Khrushchev's fall can thus be summarized under three main points:

(1) After a brief continuation of destalinization immediately following Khrushchev's fall, there was a change of line. Beginning in the spring of 1965, it became clear that the aim was to limit the political modernization and, at the same time, to pursue a tougher course in certain important fields—cultural policy, ideology, Party affairs, domestic policy.

(2) After Khrushchev's fall, a more sober, practical, and realistic attitude was adopted toward economic, political, and ideological problems confronting the USSR. This is reflected also in the style of governing.

(3) More than ever before—at least since the end of the twenties—there were, following Khrushchev's ouster, far-reaching and often violent disagreements over major political questions, so that the leadership postponed or even completely dodged necessary and urgent decisions. This served to encourage the open airing of disagreements and to enlarge the opportunity for forces outside the Party apparatus to present reform proposals and new ideas for discussion.

But there has also been a far-reaching change in the role and activity of the Party apparatus. The Khrushchev period was distinguished by the fact that the top leadership and the Party apparatus would drive Party members and the population at large from one "campaign," reform, or reorganization to another. Even if the campaigns, reforms, or reorganizations were ill-founded and had to be abandoned before completion, they served as a mobilizing and policy-making force. The situation has changed greatly since Khrushchev's fall. Increasingly, the top leadership and the Party apparatus have forfeited their function as a policy-making, driving force; more and more, they are limiting themselves to reacting after the fact (sometimes with great delay, sometimes with compromise formulations, and sometimes not at all) to an altered situation or to new problems. In so doing, the leadership and the Party apparatus have changed from a driving to a driven force; they no longer lead but limp along after the event.

The reason for this lies in the deep contradiction in the general line that has been in force since the spring of 1965, between the attempt to continue the adaptation to new problems of an industrial society in the economic-technical area and the effort to hinder or at least to decelerate the requisite changes in the political-intellectual-ideological area. This grotesquely contradictory approach can be explained by the fact that in the leading apparatuses as well as in the top leadership, two groupings with completely different political orientations have formed. This was discernible even before the fall of Khrushchev.

Indeed, there is evidence that Khrushchev was toppled by a "united front" of two very different groupings. They shared a dissatisfaction with Khrushchev's methods of ruling and united in their goal of ousting Khrushchev and of clearing the way for a new approach. One group was chiefly opposed to the governing style and techniques of Khrushchev but was thoroughly in agreement with the fundamental concepts of the ousted Party leader (coexistence, criticism of Stalin, and reforms aimed at modernizing Soviet domestic, economic, and cultural life). The unwritten motto of this group, who could perhaps be described as "moderate modernizers," could have been "Khrushchevism without Khrushchev" or more aptly "Khrushchevism but better than under Khrushchev." Their political aim was to continue the modernization process but in a more sensible way, without the rash reorganization and improvisation so typical of Khrushchev. They wanted to continue those reforms which would not endanger the basic power relations and their own positions of power. In this "camp" there were reformers such as Liberman and V. A. Trapeznikov, who sought major economic changes, and liberals among the artistic intelligentsia, such as the group around *Novyi mir*. Neither was well represented in the decisive organs.

While the "moderate modernizers" were chiefly represented in the economic and government apparatus, they had a small foothold in the more modern and accessible part of the Party apparatus. One might include Mikoyan (until his retirement in December, 1965), Kosygin, and Podgorny (and perhaps Shelest) among them.

The second group, while also opposing Khrushchev's ruling methods, was chiefly opposed to some basic tenets of Khrushchevian destalinization. In the fall of Khrushchev, this group—which could best be designated as "conservative"—principally saw an opportunity for changing the general line of the Party, of stopping the destalinization process, and of turning to a tougher line in domestic, foreign and cultural policies, as well as of keeping the reforms in economic policy within minimal limits. Their unwritten mottos could have been: "no experiments," "order," "authority," and, above all, "an end to the unjust criticism of our past and to superfluous discussions." Their aim was to stop all reforms which "went too far," to revive the Stalin tradition, and to reassess (but not glorify) Stalin. (In this respect, the conservatives differed from the "ultra-dogmatists" or neo-Stalinists, who sought the open rehabilitation of Stalin and thereby the *de facto* re-establishment of Stalinism in modernized form, although without mass terror which might threaten their own power and security.)

The conservatives have been relatively strong in army circles, the state security service, the Party apparatus, and, to a lesser degree, in the government and economic apparatus. In the top leadership (with very considerable differences from one individual to another) the conceptions of the conservatives have been represented by Brezhnev and Suslov and probably to the greatest extent by Shelepin. The interest of both groupings in toppling Khrushchev explains why Khrushchev's ouster came about so rapidly and with so little friction. However, just as clearly revealed were the divergent political conceptions of the "moderate modernizers," on the one hand, and those of the conservatives, on the other.

With the escalation of the Vietnam war (most importantly, the bombing of North Vietnam by the United States) and the accompanying sharpening of international tensions, the conservatives saw a chance to make a breakthrough. Their efforts led to a change in the internal balance of the Soviet regime. In this, the "moderate modernizers" served as a brake that prevented the pendulum from swinging even further. Sometimes they openly opposed the new course; sometimes they expressed their displeasure by a meaningful silence. Beyond this, the "moderate modernizers" have been striving, not without success, to promote the reforms in "their" various areas as well as to strengthen their own apparatus. The result has been the contradictory general line described above.

Such a highly unusual situation can hardly endure indefinitely. There are two basic possibilities for breaking out of it. The first would be a return to Stalinism in a modernized and "enlightened" form, i.e., a return to more authoritarian ruling methods, but without mass terror. Such a possibility is not as improbable as it would have seemed a few years ago.

The other possibility is to tone down the tougher course and return to the reforms of the Khrushchev era in a more sober and realistic form. In this way, the contradiction between economic reform, on the one hand, and the hard course in culture and domestic policy, on the other, would be overcome, by making the "superstructure" fit the "base." Such a change in policy would depend in some measure on a change in the international situation (reduction in tensions between East and West).

Modernization and destalinization are in the interests not only of the "moderate modernizers" and the liberals but also—and this is new—of the Soviet Party apparatus. Some elements of this apparatus are becoming aware of the fact that such a policy presents the only way to overcome the present "blockage" and to transform a power which reacts after the fact into a leading and mobilizing force.

The contradictory political and ideological line of the last three years may continue for sometime. But it can hardly serve as the long-range political plumb line for the USSR.

4 Economic Policy and Economic Trends*

ALEC NOVE

This essay is an attempt at an interpretation of very recent history, and an even more hazardous attempt at predicting the direction being taken by current developments. It cannot, however, begin in October, 1964. Much of what has been happening under Brezhnev and Kosygin can be understood only against the background of Khrushchev's own acts and omissions, as well as in the context of long-standing problems and issues which both Khrushchev and his successors have inherited from past history.

ECONOMIC CAUSES OF KHRUSHCHEV'S FALL

No serious observer can doubt that Khrushchev's economic policies and methods were among the main causes for his removal, and so a very significant portion of subsequent actions were designed to correct his errors. This is not to say, of course, that economic causes were the sole reason for his downfall, or to deny that his "style," plus an increasing tendency to arbitrariness in all spheres, contributed greatly to his colleagues' desire to depose him.

ALEC NOVE is Professor of Economics at the Department of International Economic Studies of Glasgow University. He is also editor-in-chief of the quarterly journal, *Soviet Studies*. Born in Russia, educated in England, he has served the British government, has been a participant in Soviet-British trade negotiations, and has lectured over the BBC. He was previously with the University of London and was visiting professor at the University of Kansas (1963) and at the University of Pennsylvania (1968). He is the author of numerous studies, including the standard work, *The Soviet Economy*.

* The author gratefully acknowledges the assistance of Mr. Roger Clarke in preparing this chapter.

Agriculture

Khrushchev was held responsible for disorganization in that he wrecked the Ministry of Agriculture, dismissed Minister V. V. Matskevich, and confined the ministry's function to research and advice. The State Committee for Procurement and the All-Union Farm Machinery Agency (*Soiuzselkhoztekhnika*) were not responsible for anything outside their respective spheres. Furthermore, the Party was shaken by the remarkable decision to divide it into industrial and agricultural components. The net effect was to create confusion, irresponsibility, uncertainty.

Another charge against Khrushchev involved his penchant for "campaigning." His campaigns forced local Party officials to issue orders about what to sow (corn, sugar beet for fodder, legumes—not grass, no fallow), often in disregard of the nature of the soil, the availability of labor and machines, the advice of local agronomists, the desires of the chairman and directors of farms. The Party officials were then abused by Khrushchev himself (as at the February, 1964, Plenum) for overruling the farm management. Severe losses in agricultural production occurred, and morale suffered. The formerly virgin lands were condemned to monoculture, and the almost complete ban on fallowing resulted in weed infestation, wind erosion, and falling yields. Because Khrushchev's campaigning emphasized other areas, the non-black-earth lands (i.e., the entire center, west, and north) were starved of capital and fertilizer. The livestock campaign led to overcommitment of scarce fodder supplies and to a running-down of reserves, which made the harvest failure of 1963 particularly disastrous in its impact. Khrushchev toured the country, haranguing audiences, blustering, and dismissing officials. Campaigns succeeded each other quite unpredictably. Crop rotations and long-term plans were repeatedly disrupted. Procurement campaigns, which encouraged Party secretaries to vie with each other in making promises, led to ruthless collection of produce, including seed grain (contributing to a sharp decline in quality of grain),[1] arbitrary imposition of delivery obligations, and a fall in payments-in-kind to the peasants.

Peasant welfare was adversely affected in several other ways. There were bitterly resented restrictions on private livestock, taking the form of unpublished instructions to reduce issues of hay and pasture rights, and to revise the rules governing the kinds of livestock which could be kept in which places. The number of private animals

[1] See Iu. Chernichenko, "Russkaia pshenitsa," *Novyi mir*, No. 11 (1965), pp. 180-200.

fell, and thus also peasant consumption of meat and milk. Market turnover fell, adversely affecting cash incomes. Moreover, the terms of the sales of tractors and combines to *kolkhozy* and the price reforms of 1958 had the effect of reducing the *net* revenues of collective farms, so that in many areas peasant incomes from collective work also declined.[2] Of course this had unfortunate effects on incentives and on morale and therefore on production. Peasants who were prevented from obtaining fodder for their *kolkhoz* were apt to spend more time and effort in obtaining it by "hook or by crook," so that they worked even less for the collective. Repeated promises to call a *kolkhoz* congress or to consider a new pay structure remained on paper.

Machinery maintenance suffered severely in the aftermath of the abolition of the MTS. As Matskevich pointed out,[3] repair workshops were often transferred to other activities, mechanics left agriculture (being little attracted to work as *kolkhoz* hands), and many farms were incapable of looking after the machinery they had, in effect, been compelled to buy.

Lower investment as well as lower personal incomes was a consequence of the 1958 reform. Farms had less to invest, after paying the high price for machines, replacements, spare parts, and fuel. The state's program of farm machinery production was scaled down after 1958, apparently (according to Matskevich) in the belief that the *kolkhozy* would be much more economical in their use than were the MTS, or possibly because *kolkhozy* automatically rated lower priority in official minds. Similarly, supplies of building materials, trucks, tires, and spare parts remained very tight or actually worsened. The net effect was a serious lack of necessary investments on the farms, especially in the livestock sector (mechanization was still very deficient, labor costs very high). Khrushchev supposedly annoyed his colleagues by overstressing the priority of agriculture. This view is not supported by actual events since 1958 (unless he did not determine the course of these events). In 1954-58, 11.3 per cent of all investments were devoted to agriculture. After this date the figure fell to 7 per cent.[4]

Price policy was muddled and unfavorable to the farms. The livestock campaign had been launched under conditions in which the prices (as fixed in 1958) were very unprofitable in the entire livestock sector. A promise in 1958 that grain procurement prices would be revised downward in good years, upwards in bad, led to a downward revision in 1958, and there they stayed.[5]

[2] V. Matskevich, in *Voprosy ekonomiki*, No. 6 (1965), p. 4.
[3] *Ibid.*, p. 5.
[4] *Ibid.*, p. 6.
[5] *Ibid.*, p. 5.

Industry

Ample evidence indicates that Khrushchev disagreed seriously with the planners over the chemicals program. Some Western commentators contrasted his view of the priority of chemicals with that of the so-called "metal-eaters," and Khrushchev himself felt that chemicals fell victim to the planners' conservatism. However, his program, especially as enunciated at the Party Plenum in December, 1963,[6] was simply impossible to carry out, since so vast an increase in investments could not be absorbed and specialists could not be made available in time. The attempt to enforce impossible tempos imposed intolerable losses on other sectors of the economy, including metal-production. Planners may be "conservatives," but they also have a duty to strive for input-output balance, and they did not necessarily have to be "metal-eaters" to see that there would not be enough metal to meet requirements. This was not, in all probability, connected with conflicts over military priorities, but rather with Khrushchev's characteristic impatience with any needs other than his own pet project.

Another, less familiar example of this kind of planning was the creation of a coal shortage,[7] apparently through too enthusiastic an insistence on a swift shift away from solid fuels. As in the case of chemicals, the trend was sound, but the tempos and methods were not. In September, 1964, on the very eve of his downfall, Khrushchev is known to have rejected a version of the five-year plan, probably because it contained too few chemicals and in other respects did not accord with his overly sanguine prognostications for 1970.

As to management organization and disorganization, a growing confusion followed the *sovnarkhoz* reform of 1957. The reform itself was a futile, and predictably futile,[8] attempt to cope with a very real problem. Khrushchev saw the ministries not only as politically undesirable power-centers, but also as autonomous empires which disrupted national planning, while almost making regional planning impossible. The ministries, be it noted, were also to be downgraded in the December, 1956, reform proposals, which all agree to have been the work of Khrushchev's opponents; the latter would have placed the ministries under the control of a super-ministry (*Gosekonomkommissiia*), which Pervukhin was to head. However, this solution, whatever its other deficiencies, had the marked advantage of being based on centralization.

[6] *Pravda,* December 10, 1963.
[7] A. N. Kosygin, in *Pravda,* December 10, 1964.
[8] I predicted it, for one; see *Problems of Communism,* VI, No. 4 (November-December, 1957).

It is a characteristic of the Soviet planning model, as both Khrushchev *and* the "anti-Party group" understood it, that the criterion of operation of all subordinate authorities should be the plan, i.e., orders from above. But the logic of such a "command economy" system is a centralizing logic, since the task of collecting, evaluating, and acting upon information can be undertaken only by organs of country-wide responsibility, at least for all but purely local industrial activities. All large-scale industrial enterprises necessarily transcend regional boundaries, both as producers and as "consumers" of inputs. The common problems of given industries (output mix, input needs, technical policy, training of labor, investment choice) are more pressing and urgent than the problems of a given region, the more so when the number of regions was fixed at over a hundred, for political reasons in all probability.

Starting on the wrong foot, Khrushchev moved further and further away from good sense under pressure of events. Sensing the need for recentralization but unwilling to concede the error of the original decision, he improvised. State committees were set up for the various industries, but with no operational powers. Gosplan was split, first on one conceptual principle (long-term: short-term), then along another (plan: implementation). Republican powers were considerable on paper, unclear and confused in practice.[9] The *sovnarkhozy* lost many of their powers, but retained nominal control over most enterprises. The latter found themselves at the receiving end of commands of numerous supply and sales organs at all levels, none of which had any knowledge of or interest in the enterprises' over-all plans or capacities. By 1962-63 Khrushchev was clearly becoming aware that something was amiss, but either he had no clear notion what to do, or he was unable to enforce any viable solution, because of opposition on the part of his colleagues. The situation was thus made even more confused, with plain and unnecessary overlap between the USSR *Sovnarkhoz* (under V. E. Dymshits), which was given power to issue commands over a wide range of subjects in 1962, and the VSNKh (Supreme Council of National Economy, under D. F. Ustinov), which, early in 1963, was given power to issue commands over much the same fields and to which the USSR *Sovnarkhoz* was nominally subordinated.

All this must have seemed quite intolerable to someone, like Kosygin, devoted to orderly, systematic administration. The 1962-63 reforms did reduce the number of regional *sovnarkhozy* but had the effect of bringing regional and Party boundaries out of line with one

[9] See V. Vasiliev, in *Planovoe khoziaistvo*, No. 1 (1965), pp. 60-67.

another, and causing yet another change in organization without correcting any of the previously existing deficiencies. On the whole, the centralization of construction activities was probably wise, but it was undertaken during a period of investment cuts and doubtless caused much annoyance.

As to economic reform, it went at a snail's pace. Khrushchev understood that the planning model needed radical alteration and authorized widespread discussion about its defects and about possible lines of change. Cautious experiments were attempted in individual plants and the results praised. However, Khrushchev seemed unwilling to move far or fast. This is hardly surprising, if we keep in mind his entire life's experience and his predilection for Party-directed intervention to deal with bottlenecks.

Economic Policy, the Party, and Ideology

In 1962 Khrushchev brought about a separation of industrial and agricultural organs at many levels in the Party, and this was the first major Khrushchev measure to be overturned after the new leaders took control in 1964. What possessed Khrushchev to divide the Party in two? It was surely clear that many functions of the Party could not be split into agricultural and industrial sectors. One function was precisely linking together industrial and agricultural activities and reconciling their interests. His reason—that otherwise the Party secretary would pay too much attention to one sector, particularly agriculture—seemed all the more absurd when one recalls that in March, 1962, he specifically instructed the First Secretaries of republics and oblasts to take personal charge of the new agricultural committees. True, this particular reform went awry, but the division of the Party was no way to correct this. In any event, it was politically unwise in the extreme: at a blow every *obkom* First Secretary in every "divided" oblast was demoted, losing either the industrial or the agricultural portion of his bailiwick. This was indeed no way to win friends and influence people in the Party.

Khrushchev spoke much of Party control and guidance. His tendency to weaken or divide state organs could be interpreted as an indirect way to strengthen Party organs. Yet, in fact, he confused and weakened Party organs too. For example, an *obkom* secretary's area no longer corresponded, save in a few instances, with that of a *sovnarkhoz*. Yet the division of the Party was supposedly effected, in part, to strengthen the control of oblast Party organs over industrial planning! It was as if Khrushchev did desire stricter Party control but so feared "localist" deviations (*mestnichestvo*) that he also weakened it, except at the center. He struck further at the principle on which republic Party organs operated by setting up a Central Asian Bureau, to which four of the republic Party bodies were subordinated. All this was bound to create nervousness and a general feeling of insecurity, which could not but affect efficient working of the apparatus, in economic and other questions.

Khrushchev had little patience with ideology as such. Yet he found it necessary to announce not only grandiose plans such as those to "overtake America" in the near future, but also to promote specific installments of communism by 1980: free rents, free urban transportation, free canteen meals. This seemed to many to be not only unrealistic but out of tune with the needs of the time, since the logic of a more prosperous society involves wider choice, of a kind requiring the use of money (e.g., steak rather than what the canteen cook decides is good for you).

SOVIET ECONOMIC DIFFICULTIES

Rate of Growth

In recent years the USSR has experienced a persistent lag in its rate of economic growth. No doubt Khrushchev's policy contributed to this decline, but evidently there were some long-term factors at work. Two of these are discussed in the next section, but others should be mentioned here.

The economic statistics indicating a slowdown in output were affected by the use of weights of recent years in calculating indices of industrial growth. The high figures of the years prior to 1950 tended to exaggerate growth rates by continuing to use as weights the prices of the middle twenties, which were very high precisely for the items which grew fastest. This source of "inflation" has disappeared, and so, while for other reasons the official figures can still be questioned, the difference between them and the "real" rate of growth is now much smaller than in the past. This should be borne in mind before arriving at conclusions regarding the *scale* of the slowdown. It is also noteworthy that changes in quality are seldom adequately reflected in growth statistics. When, as in the early thirties, quality declined, the aggregate figures overstated growth. Conversely, when quality has improved, as in recent years, this too is underrated. Similarly, closer attention to demand can conflict with the aim of maximizing the volume of output.

Therefore *some* of the decline in growth rates may be illusory or a consequence of purely statistical changes. Nonetheless, Soviet economists and their critics agree that a decline has occurred. Some of the

Soviet critics blame errors in investment choices. These doubtless occur, but there is no reason to suppose that they occur more frequently than under Stalin, unless, of course, the greater maturity of the economy makes errors of this kind more costly.

A real decline in growth did occur, however. Thus, the Soviet Union suffered from exhaustion of easily-accessible or already-existing resources of minerals, timber, and transport. Further growth requires bringing into operation new territories, which have ample reserves of minerals and power (e.g., East Siberia), but which need very substantial investments in infrastructure, including new railways and roads, housing, amenities. Development of these resources had the effect of increasing the capital-output ratio, even if it is assumed that investment decisions were correct.

The switch of resources into housing, services, consumers' goods, and the like, also slows down growth, if, as seems reasonable, investments in machine-tools and steel are more "growth-inducing" than investments in the clothing industry or dry-cleaning establishments. This would be so (in the author's view) even if services were included in national income statistics.

Structural Deficiencies in Industry

In regard to industry it is necessary to allude to a whole series of structural deficiencies. It is now generally recognized that the "Stalinist" model of centralized planning was inadequate for a modern industrial state. Complexity grew as the economy expanded in size. It is easier to plan centrally a small rather than a large economy. Aims and objectives became less clear-cut as the Stalinist priorities were diluted. This, and the death of the autocrat whose decisions on priorities were accepted without question, complicated still further a system based on the pursuit of a few chosen objectives at the expense of all others.

The traditional "Stalin" system was too inflexible; there was no direct link between demand and the production program. The system responded clumsily to changing requirements not only in the field of consumers' goods but also in meeting the increasingly sophisticated needs of industrial enterprises.

While in theory the plan covered all eventualities, in practice there was an inevitable degree of aggregation. Plans were (sometimes) fulfilled in global units, such as rubles'-worth of clothes, tons of metal, meters of cloth. But the produce mix was distorted to "fit" into these aggregate measurements, with familiar consequences (metal goods too heavy, and so on). Less obvious but equally important was another source of waste: the rewarding of enterprises providing intermediate goods and services for the quantity of their output, a fact which often conflicted with the need to economize in the volume of intermediate goods required to produce a given amount of final output. An example among many cited by O. K. Antonov:[10] goods transport enterprises do their utmost to fulfill and overfulfill a plan expressed in ton-kilometers and so undertake useless journeys to no purpose. Of course, an ideal centralized plan would include every journey made by every truck, but no such plan could possibly exist.

Whereas the need for rational investment choices was appreciated, there was at first strong resistance to the use of investment criteria of the rate-of-return type. When this resistance was overcome, calculations were none the less rendered difficult and sometimes meaningless by a distorted price system. This also distorted planners' choices in allocating resources of all kinds. If to use X is cheaper than to use Y, this could constitute a reason for increasing the output of or investment in X. This "cheapness" may be quite illusory, because prices had generally been fixed many years earlier and were out of line with costs, and in any event the relative scarcity or abundance of X and Y were not reflected in their relative prices, since even in theory they were not affected by supply and demand. Faulty prices strengthened the tendency to proceed by "material balances," or input-output tables. Present or future shortages of some given item could be deduced from these, but they give no indication of how to choose between alternative means to a given end. One result was a built-in conservatism; past technological relationships were projected into the future (input-output tables are backward-looking, based as they are on a previous year). When the resultant distortions were observed, the reaction was over-precipitate and gave rise to further losses, as in the compensation for past neglect of non-solid fuels and of synthetics.

Initiative and innovation were discouraged at enterprise level. Management bid low, concealed its potential, and hoarded, so as to avoid being saddled with a plan which could not be fulfilled, and to anticipate difficulties in supplies of materials and components.

Some of the items mentioned above represent defects inherent in centralized planning as such, others explain why the system became increasingly difficult to operate at a particular historical period. Defects which existed under Stalin were increasingly felt to be intolerable, partly because of the new freedom of discussion of defects, partly because of consciousness of scarcity of resources in relation to numerous competing ends, which stimulated the search for efficiency. It is also relevant to note that the Stalin system was evolved

---

[10] In a booklet, *Dlia vsekh i dlia sebia* (Moscow: "Ekonomika," 1965), which is almost an encyclopedia of wasteful planning.

at a time of acute shortage of reliable, educated men. It had outgrown itself. These difficulties and defects were connected with Khrushchev's errors, but were in no sense due entirely to Khrushchev's actions. On the contrary, many of the latter were attempts (often ill-judged) to overcome these difficulties and defects. To an extent which no one can measure, all this must have contributed to the slowdown in growth rates.

Structural Deficiencies—Agriculture

Not all of the recent troubles of Soviet farming were due to Khrushchev's unwise policies, for here again there were long-term causes at work.

The *kolkhoz* system led to negative attitudes on the part of peasants toward their work and toward authority in general. This was partly due to poor and uncertain pay, but many other factors were involved. *Kolkhozy* and especially *sovkhozy* were too large for efficient management. The belief in the advantages of large size was widespread among Party officials.

The habit of replacing local knowledge and initiative by centrally devised plans, detailed Party supervision over *kolkhoz* chairmen, political campaigning, and other deficiencies had existed long before Khrushchev. The habit had its origins in the absence of any material interest, for peasants or for farm chairmen, in fulfilling the output and delivery plans or indeed in carrying out farm work generally. When prices and incomes were improved after Stalin's death, the habit of issuing detailed orders persisted, not only on what to sow but also when and how to sow, cultivate, and harvest. This may be attributed to the vested interest of local officials, but also to the fact that price relationships were irrational, in the sense that they conflicted with the desired pattern of production. If, for example, potatoes could be sold for food at a higher price than could be obtained if they were used to feed pigs, it was necessary to order that they be fed to pigs.

The private plot was an essential part of peasant life and welfare. An attack upon it was deeply resented and had adverse effects on agriculture, as both Stalin and Khrushchev learned. Yet it did (and does) compete with the time available for collective work. It is not just a question of prices. The fact is that a peasant's own family eats much of the produce, which the present still primitive food distribution network in the villages cannot supply (it is not a choice between a peasant's "own" milk and purchased milk; there is usually no milk to purchase). As for sales on the market, it is not enough to demonstrate that—as is the case for many products—the present price at which *kolkhozy* sell to the state is close to the free market price (from which must be deducted the peasants' marketing and transport expenses). The point is that the peasant pockets the whole of his receipts, whereas if a *kolkhoz* sells at 100 rubles, its members are unlikely to share more than 30 to 40 rubles, the rest covering running expenses, capital investments, administrative, and other overheads. So there is competition for labor time at busy periods of the year. One Soviet writer has advocated the sale of labor-saving devices to peasant households, such as mechanical cultivators, to free them for collective work. Such an approach would require a great change in attitudes on the part of the authorities. Long before Khrushchev, they regarded the private plot as a tolerated evil and provided no facilities for its operation; on the contrary, they obstructed, taxed, deprived. (One is reminded of English economic history: landlords around 1820 were aware of the bad effect on their laborers of having too large a plot of land.) So long as the peasants feel this conflict of "allegiance" to private and "collective" interest, they may regard collective work as a necessary minimum duty to perform (the old word *barshchina* is sometimes used, to indicate the parallel with labor service to the lord of the manor). This cannot be conducive to efficiency.

Though not strictly "structural," there are the familiar deficiencies in capital assets, due in large part to a generation of neglect. Lack of machinery has been mentioned already. Perhaps more important is the lack of roads, which paralyzes all movement in spring and autumn. Marketings, supplies of fuel and components, retail distribution, movement of men and equipment within farms are brought to a painful halt. Yet farms still carry the main responsibility for rural "roads" (dust-tracks and muddy channels) and bridges. It is not coincidental that Estonia, which has considerable successes to its credit, inherited a good road system from its "bourgeois" past.

Finally, two other long-term obstacles to agricultural efficiency must be mentioned. The low level of the rural labor force must be regarded as a negative factor, in Russia as in many other developing countries. Of course, the *kolkhoz* system has done much to discourage the use of the peasants' knowledge and experience, but, as elsewhere, the effect of industrialization has been to drain away the young, the enterprising, the energetic. One cannot assume that the bulk of the *muzhiks* would behave like American farmers if only the Soviet system were to disappear (though some of them would).

The other matter of great importance concerns soil and climate. No matter who rules Russia, the fact remains that the fertile areas are short of rain, the areas with reliable precipitation are infertile, and most of the Asian lands are either permafrost or desert. This calls for heavy expenditures in irrigation, drainage, liming, and fertilizing. No change of political system would create in the USSR the combination of sunshine, rainfall, and soil of the American Middle West. Under these relatively unfavorable natural conditions, the neglect of the authorities and the deficiencies of the *kolkhoz* system ensured very low yields.

THE POLICIES OF BREZHNEV AND KOSYGIN

In the pages that follow an attempt is made to outline the principal policies and organizational measures taken since the downfall of Khrushchev to correct errors committed by Khrushchev or to grapple with the long-term problems which face the Soviet economy.

Agriculture

Khrushchev's attempt to divide the Party into rural and industrial organizations was promptly abandoned. The same decree (published on November 17, 1964) abolished the clumsy designation of "Party committee of the *kolkhoz-sovkhoz* production administrations" and restored the *raikom*. Presumably the Territorial Production Administrations for agriculture were abolished at the same time. There are now agricultural production administrations, at the raion level. These changes have re-established symmetry and order in the rural bureaucracy.

The decree of March 1, 1965, "on the increased role of the Ministry of Agriculture of the USSR in controlling *kolkhoz* and *sovkhoz* production" once again placed the Ministry of Agriculture, with V. V. Matskevich reappointed as Minister, in a central position in the planning of agricultural production and all other relevant matters.

The March, 1965, Plenum of the Central Committee was addressed by Brezhnev, who promised that farm managers would be given much greater scope and would not be hampered by central instructions about exactly what to grow and how to grow it. No more was heard of the corn campaign or of any ban on grasses and fallowing. Indeed, Brezhnev found it necessary to warn the comrades against "going to the opposite extreme," i.e., excessively cutting down the corn acreage. He emphasized that corn is a valuable crop in the right place and at the right time.

It was realized that one cause of excessive pressure on farms has resided in the high procurement targets insisted upon by the center. Therefore at the March, 1965, Plenum it was decided that delivery targets were to be planned ahead for long periods, were not to be altered arbitrarily, and were to be fixed at a level below the known needs of the state and the people. The additional produce that would be required would be bought by voluntary contract. Matskevich deplored the past tendency to divide all procurements of all products among all the farms in a given region, since this was destructive of rational specialization. However, he evidently feared that too rapid a move in the direction of specialization would or could threaten supplies of particular products, and so he urged caution. A minority school of thought has emerged, which has been advocating the abolition of all compulsory procurement targets, leaving farm management free to sell or not to sell.

PEASANT WELFARE. Brezhnev criticized the restrictions on the ownership of private livestock imposed by his predecessor and the new taxes and difficulties in fodder supply for which he was responsible. These measures were promptly repealed. An immediate effect of this was the reversal of the downward trend in the private ownership of livestock. Despite the further fodder shortages due to the bad 1965 harvest, the increases were as follows:

Livestock ownership
(number, in millions)

| | Jan. 1965 | | Jan. 1966 | | Jan. 1967 | | Increase in Private Animals | |
	Total	Pri-vate	Total	Pri-vate	Total	Pri-vate	Num-ber	Per Cent
Cows	38.8	16.2	40.1	16.6	41.2	17.1	0.9	5.6
Pigs	52.2	14.5	59.5	18.2	58.0	16.5	2.0	13.7
Sheep and goats	130.7	30.5	135.3	32.3	141.0	33.3	2.8	4.2

Source: *Pravda*, February 3, 1966, and January 29, 1967.

Peasant incomes from collective work benefited, and were intended to benefit, from the changes in prices. As a result, the incomes of peasants rose much more rapidly than those of state farm workers. Money pay of collective farmers rose by about ten per cent in 1965,[11] and in 1966 their incomes in money and kind from the farms rose by a further sixteen per cent.[12] The disposable income of farms was also increased by a change in the tax laws. Previously payments made to

[11] *Pravda*, February 3, 1966.
[12] *Pravda*, January 29, 1967.

peasants in cash and in kind were subject to taxation as part of the farm revenues, but under the new rules payment to labor was recognized as a cost. Such payments were not included in the net taxable income of farms (unless they exceeded a monthly average of 60 rubles per worker). This meant a considerable reduction in the tax burden on farms generally, and the poorer farms benefited most. The farms and farm-members also benefited from the writing-off of about 2 billion rubles of long- and short-term debt, this being roughly half of the total indebtedness of farms. It was also decided, at last, to abolish the so-called "rural addition," i.e., the differential between rural and urban prices of consumers' goods. This was done in two stages—in May, 1965, and in January, 1966.

Last and far from least, there was an important new decision on pay of collective farmers which came into operation in July, 1966. This introduced guaranteed pay in money and produce for all collective farm labor, based on the rate of pay for similar work on state farms. Collective farm members must be paid at least monthly, and such payment becomes the first charge on *kolkhoz* revenue, before allocations to the "indivisible fund." Credits will now be granted to farms to enable them to pay their members at state farm rates, whereas previously the very inadequate agricultural credits could not be utilized to pay peasants. These five-year credits are to be on favorable terms, with repayment to start in three years' time. Additional payments to members, linked to the quantity and quality of production, can be made out of the net income of the farms if this income is sufficient to pay more than these basic guaranteed rates. The abolition of the notorious *trudoden* (workday unit) system of paying collective farmers must be expected to provide more effective incentive for better work on farms, as the tenants will now know how much they are earning when they do any particular job.

Having deplored the fall in investments in agriculture and agricultural machinery under Khrushchev, his successors took prompt measures to increase greatly these investments. (By contrast, the fertilizer program was somewhat slowed down.) The 1966 annual plan provided for a rise of 15.6 per cent over 1965 in state investment in agriculture, compared with an increase of 6.3 per cent in total state investment; state agricultural investment in 1966-70 is to be 17.4 per cent of all state investment, compared with 11.3 per cent in 1959-65;[13] output of tractors in 1970 is to be 69.0-76.1 per cent, and of other agricultural machinery, 72.9 per cent greater than in 1965. Fertilizer production is now planned to reach 62 to 65 million tons in 1970,

[13] *Finansy SSSR*, No. 5 (1966), p. 27.

less than Khrushchev's 1970 target of 77 million tons announced in 1961, but still double the 1965 production level of 31.3 million tons.

The new five-year plan contains an extensive program of land improvement: 6-6.5 million hectares are to be drained; not less than 28 million hectares of acid soil are to be treated with lime, and a further 9 million hectares are to be improved; irrigation of another 2.5-3 million hectares is to be undertaken. *Soiuzselkhoztekhnika* is now to provide the necessary maintenance service for collective farm machinery, and a wider range of specialized equipment is to be provided on hire as required.

A rise in milk prices was already included in the 1965 plan and budget presented in December, 1964. Other increases in procurement prices were announced at the March, 1965, Plenum of the Central Committee. The exact extent of the rise is difficult to measure. First, there is now a very much greater regional price differential, the biggest gains being registered by the relatively high cost areas—in the case of grain the center, west, and north. Second, for a number of commodities the multiple price system has been restored. This means that sales to the state over the fixed quota qualify for a higher price, the bonus in the case of most grains being 50 per cent. There will thus be particularly large benefits for those farms that have big surpluses over and above the quota, and for the country as a whole it also means that the average price payable will be higher in a good harvest year. To illustrate this one may take the figures for 1966, a year of excellent harvest. Under the decisions taken in 1965, a compulsory procurement target for grain was to be fixed at 55.7 million tons (3.4 billion poods) for every year until 1970. Procurements in 1966 have been officially given as 74.9 million tons,[14] so a large proportion must have benefited from the bonus price. As with grain, the 1965 procurement targets for meat and poultry were cut (from 9 million tons to 8.5 million tons), and the milk, egg and wool targets were also reduced. However, unlike grain, procurement plans for subsequent years were not left stable but were increased for each year up to 1970. No doubt because the prices are so high as to necessitate a large subsidy, no bonus price was provided for. The following table gives some idea of the scale of price increases decided in 1965.

At the same time prices charged to farms were significantly reduced. Thus the price differential between electricity supplied to industrial and agricultural consumers was abolished, and there were reductions in prices of spare parts, farm machinery, tractors, motor vehicles and tires.[15]

[14] *Pravda*, January 29, 1967.
[15] *Finansy SSSR*, No. 1 (1966), pp. 11, 12.

Agricultural Procurement Prices

	Old prices		New prices	
	(Rubles per ton)			
Milk (changed with effect	100-125	*(sovkhozy)*		
from 1/1/65)	106-165	*(kolkhozy)*	130-230	
Wheat (March 1965)	33-69	*(sovkhozy)*	45-130	*(sovkhozy)*
	67-85	*(kolkhozy)*	76-130	*(kolkhozy)*
Rye	28-65	*(sovkhozy)*	45-130	*(sovkhozy)*
	64-85	*(kolkhozy)*	76-130	*(kolkhozy)*
Buckwheat	200		300	
Rice	220		300	
Millet	80		110	
Barley	55	*(sovkhozy)*	90	
	70-75	*(kolkhozy)*		
Oats	34-35	*(sovkhozy)*	75	
	64-65	*(kolkhozy)*		
Cattle	850-970		+20-55%	
Pigs (meat)	1,000-1,150		+30-70%	
Sheep	510-680		+10-100%	

Source: *Pravda*, March 27, 1965; and J. F. Karcz, "The New Soviet Agricultural Programme," *Soviet Studies*, XVII, No. 2 (October, 1965).

Industry

The new leadership modified its industrial priorities. Thus it took immediate steps to bring the chemicals program into line with reality. Despite all Khrushchev's goading and oratory, the chemicals program for 1965 was in any case going to be very much behind schedule. There is no doubt that Brezhnev and Kosygin appreciated the importance of more chemical fertilizer, plastics, etc., but plans were drastically modified. For example, the 1965 investment plan adopted under Khrushchev's guidance envisaged an increase over 1964 of investments in the chemical industry by 32 per cent. Actual investments in 1965 declined by two per cent. As the table below demonstrates, many of the 1970 targets adopted by Khrushchev were substantially scaled down in the draft of the new five-year plan, but the reduction in the case of chemicals was particularly severe.

It was stated that shortages had arisen in metal and in coal, and therefore the investment programs for these products were stepped up. As already suggested earlier, these measures would seem to be a reasonable response to identified instances of imbalance and shortage. This change of priorities is explained in some quarters by military expenditure, and some analysts point to the considerable rise in 1965 in the budgetary residual within "allocations to the national economy," which they believe can be explained by a larger volume of hid-

Comparison of Plan Targets for 1970

	1966-70 Plan	*Khrushchev 1961*	*Percentage reduction in new plan*
Steel (million tons)	124-129	145	12.8
Coal (million tons)	665-675	683	3.3
Oil (million tons)	345-355	390	10.3
Gas (billion cubic meters)	225-240	317	26.7
Electricity (billion kilowatt hours)	840-850	950	11.1
Plastics and synthetic resins (million tons)	2,100-2,300	5,300	58.5
Chemical fibers (million tons)	780-830	1,350	40.4
Mineral fertilizers (million tons)	62-65	77	17.5
Cement (million tons)	102-105	122	16.0
Fabrics (million square meters)	9.5-9.8	13.6	29.0
Leather footwear (million pairs)	610-630	825	24.8

den military expenditure. However, this increase is at least equally likely to consist of payments made necessary by the substantial increase in agricultural procurement prices. Of course there has been an increase in overt and possibly concealed military expenditure, and some of this may have given rise to higher demand for metal. However, it is interesting to note the striking increase in the output of a number of consumer durables, in particular motor vehicles, of which more anon. The new policies are distinguished by relatively unspectacular soundness, and the stress is on businesslike choices rather than on campaigning. One hears no more of overtaking America at an early date.

The speedy reunification of the Party has already been mentioned. It took nearly a year to decide how Khrushchev's planning system was to be changed, though there must have been unanimity about its inadequacy. Wide-ranging reforms were announced by Kosygin in September 1965.* Gosplan was again made responsible both for current and long-term planning, though there was created a state committee for material supplies to take charge of the regional supply depots, the sole remnant of the former regional structure. V. E. Dymshits, the former head of the USSR *Sovnarkhoz*, has been put in charge of this body, which is responsible for implementing supply plans by Gosplan and the industrial ministries. The new industrial ministries are once more fully responsible for subordinate enterprises, thus eliminating the intolerable degree of what some critics called "multi-stage re-

* See also above, Chapter 2.

sponsibility." As Chairman Kosygin put it, "Ministries will plan and control production, decide questions of technical policy, material supplies, financing, labor, and wages." [16] The effective powers of the ministries, Gosplan, and especially the new supply body will all be affected by the implementation of reforms announced at the same time.

As to reforms, the key element in the new system announced by Kosygin is the reduction in the number and modification of the type of plan indicators which are sent down to enterprises by superior organs. They are to be reduced to five: volume of sales, basic assortment of output, total wages fund, amount of profit and profit rate on capital, and payments to and allocations from the state budget. In addition, major investment in additional capacity or major technical modernization will still be centrally determined or approved. The operational plans of enterprises will of course contain other indicators, including costs and gross value of output, but these will be set by the enterprises themselves on the basis of the five key indicators received from above.

The role of profits is to increase very substantially, as profits are at least partly to determine the magnitude of the increased incentive fund and are to constitute the principal source of managers' and workers' bonuses. Minor investments will henceforth be financed out of a fund formed partly from profits and partly from a portion of the depreciation (amortization) allowances. Enterprises will be free to spend this money without reference to higher organs. There is to be less detailed financial supervision. Managers will be able to use that part of the depreciation allowance formerly earmarked for capital repairs for other purposes as well. Subject to the total wages fund, they will be freer to determine the composition of the labor force. A capital charge is being introduced, a percentage of fixed and working capital employed which becomes payable to the state budget as a first charge on profits. Repayable bank credits are being substituted gradually for non-returnable budget grants as the normal method of financing investments in existing enterprises.

The enterprise incentive fund will generally depend on two indicators: profits and volume of sales. The emphasis given to these two indicators varies in different industries, according to the urgency of increasing the volume of output or of adapting the pattern of production to demand. The substitution of sales for gross output is also intended to discourage production for stock. While enterprises will still be told the broad pattern of their production, detailed specifica-

[16] *Pravda*, September 28, 1965.

tions and details of the product mix are to be agreed upon with other enterprises or the trading organs. As shortages diminish and direct contracts develop, it is intended to reduce detailed control over output and over allocation of material and components.

Profits are henceforth to be expressed as a percentage of capital and not only of the value of turnover. The demand of some reformers, such as Liberman, that profits be adopted as the sole criterion, has been rejected. However, a number of misleading and undesirable plan indicators, such as cost reduction and the notorious NSO,* have been deservedly consigned to the dustbin of history.

The new system is being introduced only gradually and will not be universal until 1968 at the earliest. A group of 43 enterprises was transferred to the new basis at the beginning of 1966, followed by a larger group of 200 at the beginning of the second quarter and 430 more at the beginning of July. These 673 enterprises employed altogether over two million people.[17] At the XXIII Congress, Kosygin announced that by the beginning of 1967 one-third of the industrial labor force would be employed in enterprises under the new system.[18] The first groups of enterprises which were changed over were carefully selected as having a good record of successful operation and only toward the end of 1966 were whole sectors of industry transferred, starting with the tobacco and tea industries and continuing in January, 1967, with parts of the textile and knitwear industries. (It would seem that conversions are taking place rather more slowly than was originally anticipated.) Numerous experiments have been undertaken regarding the enlargement of managerial freedom in retail trade, public catering, and road transport, with encouraging results.

Kosygin's original report announcing the new system left a great many details to be filled in later. It is still far from clear what powers the ministries exercise in practice over the everyday operations of enterprises. How much of the enterprises' production program is in fact going to be determined centrally? How detailed will be the basic assortment which is to be centrally planned? How much choice will be given to enterprises to choose suppliers or customers? We will return to these questions in the last section of this essay.

Meanwhile the financial consequences of the reform are beginning to become clearer. Payment to the state of a capital charge, generally 6 per cent on fixed and working capital, has become the first charge

---

* NSO stands for "normed value of processing"; this was a fashionable but absurdly inadequate means of measuring plan fulfillment, which was used quite extensively from 1960 on.

[17] *Ekonomicheskaia gazeta*, No. 38 (1966), p. 3.

[18] *Pravda*, April 6, 1966.

on profits. (It would have been more logical to make this charge part of costs, but this would have created ideological difficulties, since interest payments must be seen as a part of the surplus product.) In some instances the capital charge is to be lower, in particular where the existing prices provide for a relatively low profit rate. Interest on bank credits is also to be met out of this source if investments are financed by credit. Among enterprises the proportion of gross profits represented by the capital charge varies widely. In one reported instance it was as high as 64 per cent, in another only 3.8 per cent. The average is likely to be around 25 per cent.[19] No capital charge is to be levied for the first two years on any capital assets which have been acquired out of the enterprise's own development fund. There has been some discussion of rental payments, which would also have to be made out of profits, and these would particularly apply to the extractive industries. There has also been talk, but only talk, of differential rent payments for land, which would apply to state and collective farms.

After these capital charges have been met out of profits, there remains a net profit, from which will be formed the material incentive fund, the social, cultural, and housing fund, and the enterprise development fund, the latter being for the purpose of financing minor investment. The total amount paid into these various funds will be determined by a rather complex and varying formula. It will be related to every percentage increase in sales and/or in profits provided for in the annual plan in comparison with the figures for the previous year, and also on an amount related to the profitability rate envisaged in the enterprise's plan. Where profitability and sales exceed the plan, the amount retained is to be lower than for the planned quantities, an idea perhaps "borrowed" from the Liberman proposals, designed to discourage the habit of seeking an easy plan, understating productive potential, and getting an easy bonus for overfulfillment. Allocations to the incentive funds are reduced in proportion to the degree of underfulfillment of plans. The remaining profits, after these incentive funds have been formed, can be used for the following additional purposes: repayment of long-term credits, increases in working capital, financing of additional investments, reserves, and miscellaneous other expenditures. Finally there is left what is termed "the unused remainder." This, contrary to what one might expect from its name, is a planned quantity, which it is an obligation on the part of the enterprise to pay to the state budget.

[19] See *Ekonomicheskaia gazeta,* No. 21 (1966), pp. 19, 20; also No. 38 (1964), p. 4; *Finansy SSSR,* No. 3 (1966), p. 23.

A major price reform has also been launched. Under Khrushchev there was much talk of the need to revise prices, most of which were originally fixed as long ago as July, 1955. However, the date of the new price changes has been repeatedly postponed. The reform of industrial wholesale prices has been completed on July 1, 1967. One complication has been the policy decision according to which the general level of retail prices, agricultural procurement prices, and the prices of industrial goods sold to farms must remain virtually unaltered. This limited the planners' room for maneuver. However, subject to these restrictions, they were told to attempt to arrive at a new price structure which would reflect as far as possible real social cost, quality differentials, and the substitutability of different products. The average profit margin is to be substantially increased to make room for the new payments on the value of capital. The result is to be a general rise in the level of wholesale prices. The turnover tax will diminish, while budgetary income out of profits will increase. Since coal has for some years been produced at a substantial loss, it is not surprising to find that the largest wholesale price increase is to be a 70 to 75 per cent rise in coal prices, but even this will mean that the coal industry will make, on the average, a profit of 7 per cent, well below the normal level, and it will pay a much lower capital charge than nearly all other industries. Electricity prices are to rise by 25 per cent, machinery and equipment prices will fall by an average of 5 to 6 per cent. A fund is envisaged for the regulation of prices at the disposal of the price-setting organs, so that it will be possible to change prices temporarily in the light of particular shortages or gluts without necessitating a revision of the financial plan.

Despite some talk of freezing prices, the chairman of Gosplan's committee on prices, Sitnin, has emphasized that "the state will continue to fix both the general level of prices and the prices of important products—there can be no return to the first years of NEP and to free price formation." [20] This is a reference to a surprisingly wide-ranging debate, to be discussed below, about the role of the market in planning.

Another matter furiously debated has been the role of mathematical methods and programing in planning. Perhaps the fullest published discussion was in the report of a general meeting of the USSR Academy of Sciences held in December, 1965.[21] This also had a very direct bearing on price formation. Thus Academician Fedorenko envisaged an

[20] *Kommunist*, No. 14 (1966).
[21] *Vestnik Akademii Nauk SSSR*, No. 2 (1966).

optimal plan to which all prices would be integrally related. Such ideas are broadly in line with Kantorovich's "objectively determined valuations." By a process of iteration, the optimal production plan and the price level would be influencing each other. Prices would then reflect the degree of scarcity of various items in relation to the optimal plan. Several of the leading Soviet theoreticians considered this whole approach impracticable and demanded to know how one defined and recognized an optimal plan. The price reform of 1967 is not based on the principles of optimality. Nor will relative scarcity and opportunity cost be incorporated in it in any systematic way. This debate too will be considered in the conclusion.

Welfare

No significant change was observable in social insurance regulations and policies or in wage differentials. Though collective peasants' pensions and the long-overdue increase in the pay of teachers, medical staff, and other "service-providers" were introduced in 1965,[22] they had both been announced under Khrushchev. However the effects of these measures, plus the large increase in *kolkhoz* revenues and peasants' pay, were to cause an unusually large rise during 1965 of real incomes: by 7.5 per cent per capita.[23] Since the government set its face against any over-all increase in prices, it followed that an urgent increase was called for in sales of goods and services to the population, if inflation was to be avoided. Since free market prices dropped in both 1965 and 1966, the policies must have had some success. Increased free market turnover contributed only a little to this. Retail sales (state and cooperative) increased impressively, by 10 per cent.

While total purchasing power is most unlikely to rise by as much as this in 1966, the Soviet leadership must be very much concerned with maintaining growth in consumers' goods production, and the good harvest of 1966 provided welcome relief at a time when claims for higher military spending had become too strong to be resisted.

An increase in the minimum wage to 60 rubles was decreed in time for the fiftieth anniversary of the Revolution. This, and other consequential changes in wage scales, will greatly add to purchasing power in and after 1968.

In view of the easing of the labor market, due to the inflow of young people of the larger postwar age-groups, a more generous

---

[22] The pay of those employed in education, medicine, trade, and catering rose on average by 26, 24, and 19 per cent from the 1965 rate.

[23] *Narodnoe khoziaistvo SSSR i 1965 godu* (Moscow: "Statistika," 1966) [hereinafter cited as *Narkhoz,* 1965] p. 593. The average for 1960-64 is stated to have been slightly below 3 per cent.

provision of consumer services of many kinds is accepted as possible. It is certainly very much overdue, as this has been a notoriously weak sector of Soviet life. Many services can be provided without competing for scarce capital assets or with military or space hardware.

Party and Ideology

The "balance of power" between state and Party organs in the economic field seems to rest on the principle that the planners (and Kosygin as prime minister) should carry on their duties unhindered by interference from Party organs in everyday operations. In other words, though the general lines of policy are decided as always by the Party leadership, the government machine executes the policy, Gosplan and the ministries exercise their functions, and *obkom* secretaries (and perhaps also Central Committee departmental officials) know and keep their place.

The situation is rather different in agriculture, where local Party officials remain in a dominant position and, at the center, Brezhnev usually makes the policy statements. But even there the resurrection of the Ministry of Agriculture under Matskevich has strengthened the role of the state organs.

Khrushchev's grandiose "1980 plan" with its perspective of steps toward communism has been forgotten. Instead there is more emphasis than ever on the affluent society. Of course living standards remain low, many goods and services are of poor quality or are lacking altogether. The point is not yet one of achievement, but rather of direction, of goals. Table A below shows the considerable gains already registered in consumer durables. It may be objected that these were planned under Khrushchev; thus the factories which have been making so many more refrigerators would not have been started after October, 1964. This is true, but Khrushchev's mind had not adjusted to the situation which was emerging: the 1980 perspective was attuned to a different epoch. Perhaps Khrushchev felt instinctively that private motoring was a decisive step. He was not prepared to contemplate it: taxis, yes; car-rentals, yes: he would put you in the driver's seat so long as the driver did not own the car. Brezhnev and Kosygin had no such inhibitions—hence the Fiat and Renault deals, parts of the plan to make private motoring a mass phenomenon. Of course, here too there is a very long way indeed to go. Even if 800,000 passenger cars are made in 1970 in the USSR, this, on a per capita basis, would put Russia on a par with Great Britain or France circa 1930. Nonetheless, the change in ideological flavor is unmistakable. It has been duly noted not only by the Chinese but by Castro, too.

Table A

	(a) *Indices*			(b) *Increases, per cent per annum*		
	1960	*1965*	*1966*	*1970 Plan*	*1961-65*	*1966*	*1966-70 Plan*
National income (production)	100	138	(148)	190-195	6.7	} 7.5	} 6.7-7.1
National income (utilization)	100	133	(143)	("National income")	5.9		
Gross industrial production	100	151	164	222-227	8.6	8.6	7.9-8.4
Group "A"	100	158	172	235-240	9.6	9.0	8.2-8.7
Group "B"	100	136	146	194-199	6.4	7.0	7.4-7.8
Electricity	100	147	160	244-247	7.9	9.0	10.7-10.9
Chemicals	100	197	223	394	14.5	13.0	14.9
Machinery & metal working	100	179	201	286-304	12.4	12.0	9.8-11.2
Gross agricultural production	100	112	123	(140)*	2.3	10.0	(4.6)*
Investments (total)	100	136	144	(200)**	6.4	6.0	(7.9)**
Retail trade turnover	100	134	146	—	6.0	8.7	—

* The target stated is that the 1966-70 average exceed the 1961-65 average by 25 per cent.
** The target stated is that the 1966-70 total exceed the 1961-65 total by 47 per cent.

Statistical note: "Inflationary" tendencies in plan fulfillment reports do not affect plan formulation. Therefore a *plan* for an increase of 50 per cent, for instance, may seem "overfulfilled" when an increase of 51 per cent is claimed, but this result may have been influenced by various expedients, such as overvaluation of new products or deliberate choice of a product mix which shows up well in growth statistics. I know of no means to measure or allow for such "inflation," but it needs to be borne in mind. There are also some unexplained upward amendments, notably to the national income figures for 1964, which have been the subject of a published note by the author (*Soviet Studies*, XVIII, No. 1 [July, 1966], 83-85). The original claim to an increase of under 5 per cent became successively 7 per cent and 9.1 per cent. The 1965 handbook increased the figure yet again, to 9.3 per cent.

Sources: Plan fulfillment report for 1965, in *Pravda*, February 3, 1966. Directives of XXIII Party Congress for Development of USSR Economy in 1966-70, *Pravda*, April 10, 1966; English text of these directives as approved at Congress, in *23rd Congress of the CPSU* (Moscow: Novosti Press Agency, 1966), pp. 313-420.

SOVIET ECONOMIC PROSPECTS

Growth and Priorities

By the standards of past years and by those of Khrushchev's original intentions, the tempos of economic growth projected by the current leadership are relatively modest; only in agriculture do they markedly exceed the rates actually achieved in the five years ending in 1965. The industrial growth pattern envisaged by Brezhnev and Kosygin may be seen in the figures in tables A and B.

Is the five-year plan feasible? We have so far only the version of the plan approved by the XXIII Party Congress in April, 1966. The final version, yet to appear, has clearly been the subject of a prolonged dispute. One cause of dispute is probably over military and/or space expenditure and over the sectors to be cut back to make room for such expenditure. It seems reasonable to assume that the Soviet leaders face perplexing choices. American policy in Vietnam, large increases in United States military spending, the possibility of disagreeable incidents on the long border with China, the escalating expense of modern weaponry are among things which compete with more prosaic and insistent calls of agriculture, consumer services, roads, housing, and other "civilian" needs.

The first question to ask in considering future growth rates in relation to the five-year plan is whether this plan has not already been amended significantly. While changes in allocations would probably not significantly affect global output statistics, because an ICBM or a rocket launcher is as much a part of the value of material output as houses, shoes, or vacuum cleaners, they would affect the composition of the national product and the share of personal consumption within it. Surely the 1967-68 increases in military spending were not in the minds of those who drafted the original plan.

If allowance is made for this uncertainty, the *industrial* part of the plan seems basically sound. Care has apparently been taken to preserve balance in the input-output sense. With the moderation of Khrushchev's excessive chemicals targets, there is nothing in the targets for industrial commodities which seems out of reach, given past performance and known resource availabilities. This is not to say that the plan as a whole would necessarily be achievable, even apart from increases of military and space expenditures. Every goal taken in isolation may be attainable and the planned inputs may match the planned outputs; and yet total resources may still be insufficient to fulfill in time the investment program implied by the plan goals, unless resources are used more efficiently. Greater efficiency, in turn, would depend both on wiser decisions by the central planners *and* on the effective working of the new economic model.

The leadership has reasserted the need to reduce the gap in the growth rates of the so-called group A and B industries, i.e., to give more emphasis to consumers' goods. This was a familiar slogan in Khrushchev's time, too. But in practice, the gap widened, particularly in investments, as the following figures demonstrate:

Investments, in million rubles

	1960	*1964*	*Increase/per cent*
Industry group A	10728	14644	36.5
Industry group B	1945	2074	6.6

Source: *Narkhoz*, 1965, p. 531.

Thus a declaration of intention is not evidence. Yet the intention seems serious, and certainly production of consumer durables is advancing impressively. The deals with European car firms are evidence of serious intention. More cars will mean more expenditures on garages, motels, service stations, and the like. There is a vast pent-up demand for such things. In some sectors, however, increases in sales must depend on improvements in quality and design. Thus the unsaleability of the antique sewing machines made by a Podolsk factory has led to a drastic cutback in production. Nor is there any hope of increasing the volume of sales of textiles to the planned extent unless they become more attractive to consumers, who already leave part of the offerings of the textile industry lying on the shelves. It is important to note the significance of consumer demand as a factor limiting production of a number of items. In the USSR this is a relatively new phenomenon; it is, in fact, one of the motives for the reforms in planning.

Table B below, contrasts Soviet past and planned industrial output with that of the United States, for 1965. The growth rate envisaged by the latest Soviet plan—even if one were to accept that by 1965 the USSR had already reached 60 per cent of the United States level (and some would hotly dispute this)—would still leave Soviet production in 1970 some way short of the United States output of 1965. Nonetheless, the achievement of the bulk of the industrial goals for 1970 would represent a big step forward on the part of the Soviet Union.

What of agriculture? The poor performance of this sector in 1960-65 adversely affected general growth in the period and represented a very striking contrast with the grandiose targets of the seven-year plan. What happens under the new management? Was the excellent harvest of 1966 primarily due to an exceptional conjuncture of climatic circumstances? Does it mean that the almost unanimous denial, by Western experts, of the feasibility of the 1970 targets was premature?

On the whole, the 1970 target does seem beyond reach, if we assume (as we must) that it refers to an average year. The targets for total grain harvest and supplies of fodder appear to be unrealistically optimistic. Yet, in asserting this, we are in effect passing judgment on the efficiency of present agricultural policies and implicitly or explicitly "weighting" the impact of various deficiencies on agricultural production. Thus "campaigning," neglect in the non-black-earth regions, inadequate fallowing, insufficient incentives, lopsided mechanization, shortage of fertilizer cause losses. If, year after year, grain and potato yields in (say) the Novgorod, Vologda, Yaroslavl and Kaluga oblasts were abysmally low, to what extent was this due to failure to fertilize and lime the *podzol* soil, a failure which guaranteed poor yields regardless of anything else that was done or not done? Why cannot yields in such areas be raised by 50 per cent? Such questions cannot easily be answered; yet the fate of the agricultural plan depends on the answers to such questions.

We are accustomed to failure on the agricultural front, just as we are accustomed to poor service in shops and breakdowns in food distribution. We attribute these negative phenomena to "the system." Yet they are often due at least as much to purely physical lacks. Agriculture was undersupplied, under-equipped, underpaid. So was retail distribution. If milk is often unobtainable, it is because of the absence of sufficient refrigerated storage, bottling plants, bottles, cartons, transport facilities, roads. We cannot seriously assert that farm laborers or shopkeepers work well only if they own their farms or shops, when many a paid employee of an American farm or supermarket is quite capable of efficient effort. For these reasons, we must beware of assuming that the impressive investments in agriculture *must* yield disappointing results.

However, there is still a good case for skepticism. Brezhnev himself complained of planners "balancing their accounts" at the expense of agriculture, thus keeping it down at the bottom of the priority list, regardless of resolutions by Party planners. *Pravda* (December 28, 1966) reported editorially that many farms are still disregarding the decree which entitles *kolkhoz* peasants to *sovkhoz* rates of remuneration, since it saves financial worries to go on treating peasants as residuary legatees. Promises to allow farm management greater free-

Table B
Industrial Output Statistics

	U.S.S.R.						U.S.A.
	1960	*1965* Plan	*1965*	*1966*	*1967*	*1970* Plan	*1965*
Electricity (bill. kwh)	292	500-520	507	545	589	830-850	1,220
Oil (mill. tons)	208	230-240	243	265	288	345-355	385
Gas (bill. cub. met.)	47.2	150	129.2	145	159	225-240	456
Coal (gross total) (mill. tons)	—	600-612	578	585	595	665-675	—
Coal (hard coal equiv.) (mill. tons)	444	—	505	—	—	—	476
Pig-iron (mill. tons)	46.8	65-73	66.2	70.3	74.8	94-97	80.5
Steel (mill. tons)	65.3	86-97	91.0	96.9	102.2	124-129	121.9
Iron ore (mill. tons)	105.9	150-160	153.4	160	168		91.0
Mineral fertilizer (100 per cent equiv.) (mill. tons)	3.3	—	7.4	8.4	9.4	—	11
Mineral fertilizer (gross weight) (mill. tons)	13.9	35	31.3	35.8	40.1	62-65	50
Sulphuric acid (mill. tons)	5.4	—	8.5	9.4	9.7	—	22.5
Synthetic fibers (thous. tons)	211	666	407	458	511	780-830	1,499
Diesel & electric locomotives (units)	1,699	—	2,126	2,129	—	1,500-1,600*	1,806
Tractors (thousands)	239	—	355	382	405	600-625	672x
Motor vehicles (thousands)	523.6	750-856	616.3	675	728.8	1,360-1,510	11.1 (million)
Passenger	138.8		201.2	230	251.4	700-800	9.3 (million)
Trucks and buses	203.3		379.6	445	477.4	600-650	1.8 (million)
Commercial timber haulage (mill. cub. met.)	262	275-280‡	274‡	258	267	—	273xx
Timber haulage (mill. cub. met.)	370	372-378	378	—	—	350-365	301xx
Cement (mill. tons)	45.5	75-81	72.4	80	84.8	100-105	65
Cotton fabrics (mill. sq. met.)	4,838	5,900-6,100**	5,502	5,701	5,915		9,026
Wool fabrics (mill. sq. met.)	439	640**	466	509	547	9.5-9.8 billion sq. met.	244
Rayon & silk fabrics (mill. sq. met.)	675	1,233**	799	869	938		3,492
Linen fabrics (mill. sq. met.)	516	584**	548	591	642		
Footwear, leather (mill. pairs)	419	515	486	522	561	610-630	630
Clocks & watches (millions)	26.0	—	30.6	32.4	34.4	—	—
Radios (millions)	4.16	—	5.16	5.8	6.4	7.5-8.0	14.1
Paper (mill. tons)	2.4	3.5-4.1	3.23	3.5	3.8	5-5.3	18.9
Television sets (millions)	1.72	—	3.65	4.4	5.0	7.5-7.7	11
Refrigerators (millions)	0.53	—	1.67	2.2	2.7	5.3-5.6	6.1 (incl. electric freezers)
Washing machines (millions)	0.89	—	3.43	3.9	4.3	—	4.5
Sewing machines (millions)	3.10	—	0.80	—	—	—	—

dom of choice of crops have been made before—and ignored before. Talk of rational specialization by farms and regions has gone on for years, but little has yet been done. Fertilizer is indeed available in substantially greater quantities, but its distribution is still seriously deficient, as is the equipment needed to transport and spread it on the farms. There is a grave shortage of skilled young people in rural areas, and they are needed to operate and maintain the modern equipment which is being provided. Amenities are still too often primitive, and the contrast with the advantages of the city too great. Brezhnev is well aware of this, and he and his colleagues have spoken up about the need to narrow the gap between town and country. This is reflected in plans and also in the considerably larger rise in rural rather than urban incomes of the past two years. Yet the great distances and lack of hard-surface roads represent serious handicaps, hard to overcome quickly even with the best will in the world.

The best will in the world cannot, of course, be assumed, and long history must have taught the peasants to be suspicious—and farm managers, too. After all, they have been told before that they would be free from detailed interference from above. Did not Khrushchev say in 1953 that arbitrary upward amendments in delivery plans would cease? But they continued and were denounced yet again by both Brezhnev and Matskevich in 1965. Have times changed? The words of an editorial in *Ekonomicheskaia gazeta* (No. 29, 1966) must have a familiar ring:

> The organization of sales of grain surplus in order to cover the needs of the country fully and to create sufficient reserves is a major state task. To its fulfillment it is necessary to devote the energies of Party, soviet, agricultural, and procurement organs, and all the toilers of the village.

How voluntary will be the voluntary overplan sales? At least in the case of grain they are remunerative. But they will often not be so for

---

^x Includes small garden tractors.
^{xx} 1964.
* Diesel only.
** Fabric goals for 1965 in square meters are based on conversion from goals expressed in linear meters. Ratio between square meters and linear meters was derived from Soviet figures for 1960 production. Conversion factors applied to linear meter figures were 76 per cent for cotton fabrics, 128 per cent for wool, 83 per cent for rayon and silk, and 92 per cent for linen.
‡ Includes *kolkhozy*.
Sources (including U.S. comparisons): *Narkhoz*, 1965, pp. 95, 96, 132-39, 222-23; *Pravda*, January 29, 1967, and January 25, 1968; Directives of XXIII Party Congress for Development of USSR Economy in 1966-70, in *Pravda*, April 10, 1966; English text of these directives as approved at the Congress, in *23rd Congress of the CPSU* (Moscow: Novosti Press Agency, 1966), pp. 335-36.

Table C

Agriculture

	1960	1961	1962	1963	1964	1965	1966	1970 Plan
Gross agricultural production (index)	100	103	104	96	110	112	123	(140)*
Grain harvest (mill. tons)	125.5	130.8	140.2	107.5	152.1	121.1	170.8	169.4**
Potatoes (mill. tons)	84.4	84.3	69.7	71.8	93.6	88.7	87.2	—
Cotton (mill. tons)	4.29	4.52	4.30	5.21	5.28	5.66	6.0	—
Sugar-beet (mill. tons)	57.7	50.9	47.4	44.1	81.2	72.3	73.8	—
Meat (mill. tons)	8.7	8.7	9.5	10.2	8.3	10.0	10.8	—
Milk (mill. tons)	61.7	62.6	63.9	61.2	63.3	72.6	76.1	—
Wool (thousand tons)	357	366	371	373	341	357	372	—
Cattle ⎤	74.2	75.8	82.1	87.0	85.4	87.2	93.4	—
Cows ⎟ (mill.	33.9	34.8	36.3	38.0	38.3	38.8	40.1	—
Pigs ⎟ head)***	53.4	58.7	66.7	70.0	40.9	52.8	59.6	—
Sheep ⎦	136.1	133.0	137.5	139.7	133.9	125.2	129.8	—

* 1966-70 average to exceed 1961-65 average by 25 per cent.
** 1966-70 average, which is to exceed 1961-65 average by 30 per cent.
*** As of January 1.
Sources: *Narkhoz*, 1965, pp. 259, 262, 264, 367; *Narkhoz*, 1962, pp. 234-35; and *Pravda*, January 29, 1967.

livestock products. Price relationships are awry. Yet to put them right by raising livestock prices is impossible unless retail prices are increased; already the procurement price of beef is 165 per cent of the retail price.[24] Arbitrary interference has in the past been the result of irrational price relationships.

Other uncertainties concern the private plot. At present it is growing, and there is talk of direct links between private suburban holdings and state retail stores. Will the authorities accept this development, or will there be yet another wave of restrictions, as in 1938-41, 1947-53, 1958-63?

What will happen to the size of farms? A possible alternative to reducing their size is to split them up into units autonomous for operational purposes, and/or into groups (*zvenia*) for particular crops, so that a small group grows onions or carrots, while large-scale

[24] *Finansy SSSR*, No. 8 (1965), pp. 12-13.

mechanized units deal with wheat. We may also see a narrowing of the differences between *kolkhozy* and *sovkhozy* with the possibility of a merger of the two into a new type of farm, perhaps embodying some features of each.

The services sectors appear destined for serious and continued improvement, and this can make a great difference to the standard of living of the community, especially in view of the past neglect of these sectors. Employment statistics show that a real change is in progress. The labor economist Manevich expects very much more rapid growth in numbers of those engaged in what he prefers to call "non-material production." [25] Voices are now raised to urge the redefinition of the national income to include the rapidly-growing service sectors.[26] Housing, on the other hand, has been lagging behind plans and in 1966 still did so, though the downward trend has been reversed.

The planners' task is both lightened and complicated by the greater abundance of labor, due to the higher birth rate of the postwar years. In 1957-62 there was an abnormally small intake of young workers, because of the small number born in 1942-47, and this contributed to the slowdown of growth in these years. The scale of the change, down and up again, may be gauged by the following figures of age-groups 7-11 (grades I-IV in primary schools), in millions:

1950-51	*1952-53*	*1954-55*	*1955-56*	*1958-59*	*1964-65*
20.1	13.4	12.9	13.8	17.7	20.0

Now there are increasing problems of job placement, particularly for young people, and also serious geographical maldistribution. The administration is not able to cope well with the new situation, which requires adaptation of wage-rates to the needs of different regions, organization of retraining and provision of labor exchanges. But at least the problems are discussed, and we cannot assume that they will not be overcome. With efforts being made to dispose of "the many persons whose presence is quite unnecessary" [27] and who remain employed for lack of alternative occupation, efforts which should be encouraged by the emphasis on profits under the reforms, the difficulties arising from labor shortage should be gradually eased in those sectors or areas in which they hold back production.

[25] Manevich, *op. cit.*, p. 28.
[26] See, for example, A. Kumacheva, in *Ekonomicheskie nauki*, No. 5 (1966), p. 84.
[27] Manevich, *op. cit.*, p. 28.

Economic Reform

It is one thing to announce the intention of changing the structure of the economy and quite another actually to alter it in more than a purely superficial way. How much has actually changed, even in the sectors which have been converted into the new model? It is too soon to say. *Pravda* and various periodicals have printed some complaints about the detailed supervision still exercised by ministries over output plans and other matters supposedly within management's sole jurisdiction.[28] Polish and Czech experience should teach us that the infamous "gross output" indicator can be retained as long as there is a wages fund "ceiling," which can be exceeded only on condition that the enterprise overfulfills the output plan.

These could be the inevitable muddles which happen in the process of a big change. But what is the objective of the reform? Is there clarity in the minds of Kosygin and his colleagues about the kind of economic model they are aiming to create?

A number of schools of thought have emerged. The "radicals," typified by Lisichkin,[29] have found a historical precedent and legitimation in a reinterpretation of Lenin's views in the period between the introduction of NEP and his final illness. Lisichkin suggests that Lenin's support for market relations among state enterprises (and the convertibility of the ruble, and even the free circulation of gold) represented a long-term view of how the business of a socialist economy should be run and was not a forced compromise. The market, in Lisichkin's view, is the means by which the validity of planners' decisions is tested. Without it, they themselves cannot know that what they do is right. The market and the plan must be integrally linked and not counterposed.

Many, probably most, Soviet economists would not go as far as this. They accept a bigger role for "commodity-money relations," the need for utilizing profits, and a more flexible price system. But they accept it as a means of getting done more effectively what the politicians and planners want done. They dislike the word "market" and criticize Lisichkin's version of Lenin's ideas.[30]

The "conservatives" have several strong arguments. The old system at least ensured that priority needs were met. It was based on an assessment of total material requirements by planners, who took into account policy objectives, *zaiavki* (requisitions from below), material

[28] See, for example, *Ekonomicheskaia gazeta*, No. 31 (1966), p. 18.
[29] See his *Plan i rynok* (Moscow: "Ekonomika," 1966), and other works.
[30] See for example, *Ekonomicheskaia gazeta*, No. 44 (1966), pp. 12, 13.

balances, foreign trade, and so forth. By this means they could identify shortages and take appropriate decisions: to reduce utilization, to import, to produce more, to invest in new capacity. Would a market function—for cabbages or footwear maybe, but for sulphuric acid, steel, fuels, cement, capital equipment?

It would be absurd to expect the necessary decisions to be made at the level of an enterprise, which corresponds to a Western plant. What decisions are made by the manager of a plant which is part of Dupont, U.S. Steel, or General Electric? These giants are bigger than many a Soviet ministry and perhaps no less centralized. It is also significant that there are no capitalists and no capital market in the Soviet Union to record and react to new investment opportunities. Finance for major new departures would need to be provided by the state. As for an agricultural market, demanded by some reformers (the abolition of procurement quotas), this is rejected because at present prices farms are coming to see the advantage of being sure of selling a quantity at a guaranteed price, especially as free market prices are sometimes lower or not sufficiently higher to make it worth the trouble to sell other than to the state. Besides, Western experience hardly suggests that an agricultural free market is an unmixed blessing, for in what Western country is there such a market?

It is these questions and the closely related one of prices, which have continued to be the subject of discussions after the introduction of Kosygin's reforms. Writing very soon after the September, 1965, Plenum, Yevsei Liberman[31] evidently envisaged a very considerable degree of enterprise independence. He said that enterprise control figures were to be not so much targets as guaranteed minimum sales levels, and enterprises would make direct contracts for large orders or else deal through wholesale organizations. For the time being, physical production targets would be retained only for items like fuel, energy, and metals, which are of direct interest to the government. He spoke of competition for orders in terms of price, delivery dates, and quality and said that prices would vary around a fixed level. Another economist, Sukharevsky, writing at about the same time, said that profits would not regulate what kind of commodities were produced but were a criterion of the efficiency with which a given category of consumer wants were satisfied.[32] Obviously the significance of this in terms of enterprise independence depends on how wide the "given categories" are. A category could be all clothing, with the decision as to what proportion of coats, suits, or dresses shall

[31] *Pravda,* November 21, 1965.
[32] *Ekonomicheskaia gazeta,* No. 49 (1965).

be produced taken on the basis of profits earnable, or it could be that the planners will specify the quantity or value of men's suits of a given material, with the sphere of enterprise decision confined to the choice between different styles, colors, and sizes.

A much greater degree of independence for enterprises producing consumers' goods was advocated by the well-known aircraft designer, O. K. Antonov.[33] He proposed that for consumers' goods the single test for enterprises should be that they sold what they made; that they should be free to make changes in their production program within quite wide limits. For producers' goods he advocated a system of indicators which would measure the objective utility of the goods produced and suggested that makers of producers' goods could be discouraged from overfulfilling their plan in quantitative terms, but encouraged to overfulfill the amount of total utility they produced (by higher quality, improved design, greater durability, etc.). Far from being opposed to the mathematics-and-computers school of thought, Antonov advocated their use, but insisted that even with their help the amount of central decision-making must be reduced, and enterprises given more autonomy. Mathematical techniques should then be used to improve the quality of the decisions taken centrally.

The other major question on which there has been extensive discussion and disagreement is that of prices, which are central to the whole reform. The essential point is: who fixes what prices? To leave them free would be to lose control. To maintain central price-determination would conflict with the need for flexibility: there are too many prices to set.

Not surprisingly, the leadership is proceeding slowly and carefully. The materials allocation system is being retained, for the time being, and ministerial powers do not seem to be materially diminishing. Yet the need to decentralize is great, too, and some moves toward a market-oriented economy are probable. As problems of glut and salesmanship become more common, the methods of planning even in and by ministries will become more "commercial," and the trading organs will take more seriously their role in studying consumer demand and influencing the production plans of industry.

There may also be some greater toleration of small-scale private enterprise, especially in the personal services sector. Warsaw has had competition between private and municipal taxis without much harm befalling, and Budapest and Warsaw both have private res-

---

[33] *Op. cit.*

taurants. Those who let a room to casual visitors in holiday areas in the USSR are now allowed to provide meals (which they doubtless did all along, though it was technically not legal).

There is another vast question concerning the likely impact of computers and programming on planning. A lively and talented group of mathematical economists has emerged, and has been putting forward far-reaching proposals which would revolutionize planning methods. Most of them advocate a system of "optimal" planning, which reflects consumer demand and which is thus market-oriented, though, like their non-mathematical colleagues, they often disagree among themselves and freely debate the various issues involved. Most Soviet experts would probably agree that no fundamental change will be wrought by these methods until the next decade; methodology, computers, programmers, and information flows are all inadequate. There is also the problem which can be briefly summarized by the question: "optimizing what?" But even in the next few years the tasks of central planning can be lightened and speeded up by computers, giving more time and information for a choice to be made among alternatives. This would be of no mean help.

Economics and Strategy

For reasons which have deep roots, the USSR seeks to become a modern and efficient industrial society. Greater attention to consumer demand and to services, the trend toward reforms, the real effort to provide more comforts of life, the consumer durables expansion, the car deals are all aspects of a change which is hardly surprising, fifty years after the Revolution, however much it may horrify Mao Tse-tung. Of course, all this represents, *inter alia,* an adaptation of the policy of the ruling group, which is seeking to maintain its monopoly grip on power. The leaders are bound to use some of their economic strength to win friends and influence people in other countries. For both "normal" nationalistic and residual-ideological reasons, the Soviet leaders feel they must maintain their country in the front rank of world power. This involves competition with the United States in a wide variety of areas, including that of military power. Much as the Soviet leaders would like to reduce arms spending, they find it impossible to do so at present.

But with the combined pressure for more arms (and outer space) spending and the urgent need for more resources for pressing domestic needs, it may be assumed that other things will suffer, for the next few years at least. There will probably be no large increase in Soviet aid (the offer of wheat to India in a year of bumper harvest in Russia—and famine in India—was virtually forced on them). The emphasis in foreign trade will be on economic advantage, just as the planners will be doing their utmost to achieve efficient disposal of resources to meet as many as possible of the competing needs which press upon a leadership which is more responsive than before to the pent-up demand for better living.

In the long run, the impact of the Soviet system on the outside world—whether by way of example to follow, or aid, or capacity to threaten—depends in some considerable part on economic power. Therefore a judgment of the efficacy of the system and its ability to reform itself to meet new challenges is of evident strategic significance.

Also in the long run, success (or failure) affects the mental attitudes of the upper strata who determine or influence policy and so causes them to see the world in a different light. Needless to say, a good harvest in 1966 does not of itself cause Brezhnev or Gromyko to "soften" their foreign policy attitudes. On the contrary, one could even argue that, by relieving immediate pressure on resources, it enables them to devote more to foreign aid, or to aid for North Vietnam, or to military expenditure. True, their priority concepts being what they are, a large part of the additional resources may be spent on consumers' goods. (Thus the greater the shortage of foreign currency, the more strictly it is devoted to "essentials," i.e., capital goods and raw materials.) The point is that attitudes and objectives can be taken as fixed in the short run. In the longer run, of course, this cannot be assumed, and most would agree that comfortable living and proselytizing ardor do not go well together.

In the short run, resource allocation is always a matter of reconciling numerous objectives, and the task of reconciliation is always made easier if output is higher. The most painful arguments arise over cuts in actual or planned expenditures. The long delay in approving the final version of the five-year plan *must* mean that a tough argument has been in progress. Individual leaders have, of course, been doing the arguing, and so this amounts to an assertion of the existence of political disagreement.

The defense allocation may or may not be at the center of controversy; it could be that they have agreed about defense spending, and the struggle concerns investment priorities within the civilian sector. It would, in the author's view, be dangerously misleading to identify particular leaders with a given view on priorities by making deductions from *obiter dicta* concerning heavy or light industry or metals versus chemicals. To this day it is not clear just where Khrushchev stood on the question of military spending, in relation to those who overthrew him. It is this author's guess that the 1964 conflict was not primarily concerned with arms at all, and this could well be so again in 1967-68.

5   *Soviet Military Policy after Khrushchev*

THOMAS W. WOLFE

In the period since Khrushchev was removed from power in October, 1964, his successors have had to deal with a wide range of problems growing out of developments both within the Soviet Union and upon the international scene. Within the Soviet Union the new collective leadership under Leonid Brezhnev and Alexei Kosygin has found itself deeply engaged in efforts to improve the performance of the Soviet economy, to redefine the Party's proper role in the management of a modern society, to bolster the country's defense posture, and to restore ideological *élan* among youth and the intelligentsia in general. On the international scene, the lengthening crisis in Vietnam has cast its shadow over East-West relations, the Sino-Soviet dispute has grown increasingly bitter and seems to be edging closer toward an open break, and the political dynamics of an evolving Europe have both opened new opportunities for Soviet diplomacy to promote and utilize divisions within NATO and have complicated the Soviet Union's task of maintaining the cohesion of its own Warsaw bloc. Needless to say, such developments have cut across many areas of Soviet policy. The purpose of the present survey is to take stock

THOMAS W. WOLFE is Senior Staff Member of The RAND Corporation and a faculty member of George Washington University. He has combined academic work (having studied at Columbia, the Naval War College, and other service schools, and received his Ph.D. from Georgetown University) with a career in active military service, which saw him posted as Air Attaché to the U.S. Embassy in Moscow. His last assignment, before retiring as Colonel from the U.S. Air Force, was as Director, Sino-Soviet Region, in the Office of the Assistant Secretary of Defense for International Security Affairs. He has written widely on Soviet strategic thought, civil-military relations, and Communist policies, including a book-length study, *Soviet Strategy at the Crossroads*, and articles in *Foreign Affairs, Current History, Slavic Review,* and other journals.

111

of the situation in one of these areas—that of Soviet military policy
—at the fifty-year mark in Soviet history.

Before turning to specific issues of defense policy under the present
regime, one should make the general observation that there has been
no radical change of direction in Soviet defense preparations or in the
strategic philosophy underlying them since Khrushchev left the
scene. It is true that some of Khrushchev's strategic ideas have come
under criticism, and the new leadership evidently has made its own
decisions on certain important questions which Khrushchev had left
unsettled, as we shall see presently. However, there has been no outright repudiation of the military policy course he sought to chart for
the Soviet Union, the essence of which was to place primary emphasis
on the deterrent effect of Soviet nuclear and missile power.

In regard to the Soviet military establishment itself, Khrushchev's
successors in the main have not tampered basically with the organizational structure nor the professional command of the armed forces he
passed on to them, which in itself is a tacit endorsement of his stew-
ardship over Soviet military affairs. The post-Khrushchev period thus
far has been marked by no major organizational and theoretical reforms in the military domain comparable to those which followed the
death of Stalin. This is not to say, however, that the Brezhnev-Kosygin
leadership has been without substantial problems in the realm of
defense policy. Among the major issues with which it has had to
grapple is that of military claims upon Soviet resources—a perennial
problem sharpened by the new regime's commitment to an ambitious
program of domestic economic reform and improvement.

The Resource Allocation Issue

During the first year of the new regime, signs appeared that the
issue of resource allocation was (as it had been before) the source of
some disagreement within the Soviet leadership. In the summer of
1965, for example, the Soviet military press began to advance a series
of theoretical arguments implying that one-sided emphasis on war
deterrence, as practiced under Khrushchev, could lead to neglect of
all-around strengthening of the armed forces and to questioning of
"the need to spend large resources on them." [1] These arguments
sought to make a case for large, well-balanced forces, and especially
for having adequate forces-in-being prior to the outbreak of any

[1] See, for example, Major General K. Bochkarev and Colonel I. Sidelnikov in
Krasnaia zvezda, January 21, 1965; and also Colonel I. Sidelnikov, *ibid.,* September
22, 1965.

war which might occur. It was also asserted, contrary to the view which had gained some currency in Khrushchev's time, that technology had not reduced massive manpower requirements for a modern military establishment.[2]

At the same time that military spokesmen were suggesting that there were no ruble-saving short cuts to Soviet security, indications of divergent views on the question of resource priorities for defense showed up within the political leadership itself. One côterie of leaders tended to place priority on resource allocation for internal economic development, while a second group put more emphasis on the need for further strengthening of Soviet defenses to meet the external threat posed by a deteriorating international situation.[3] The extended crisis growing out of the war in Southeast Asia tended during 1965 and 1966 to buttress the position of the latter group in the internal policy debate over economic-defense priorities.

As of the winter of 1967-68, arguments for larger defense expenditures, even at the cost of some cutback of investment in other sectors of the economy, seem to have prevailed. There was, for example, a five per cent increase in the military budget for 1966, and the budget for 1967 showed a boost of about eight per cent—14.5 billion rubles compared with 13.4 billion for 1966. A further increase, of 15 per cent, was scheduled for 1968, with military allocations reaching 16.7 billion rubles. These figures, it should be emphasized, are what the Soviet Union has chosen to announce publicly. According to competent Western estimates, actual military expenditures, part of which are buried under other budgetary headings, are generally somewhat higher—at least one-third higher.[4]

The supposition that military requirements are taking an even bigger bite out of Soviet resources than the published figures indicate is strengthened by the delay in ratifying the new Five-year-plan for 1966-70. The guidelines for this plan were issued in early 1966 and discussed at the XXIII Party Congress in April, 1966, where Kosygin

[2] Among typical articles, see: Colonel V. Larionov, in *Krasnaia zvezda*, March 18, 1965; and G. Miftiev, *ibid.*, June 4, 1965.

[3] The first group included N. V. Podgorny, A. P. Kirilenko, and D. S. Poliansky; the latter, M. A. Suslov and A. N. Shelepin. Brezhnev and Kosygin seemed to seek positions roughly midway between the others, alternately stressing the case for domestic economic improvement and strengthened defense. For a fuller account of this intra-leadership dialogue, with documentation, see the present writer's "The Soviet Military Scene: Institutional and Defense Policy Considerations," The RAND Corporation, RM-4913-PR (June, 1966), pp. 64-68.

[4] See, for example, J. G. Godaire, "The Claim of the Soviet Military Establishment," in *Dimensions of Soviet Economic Power*, Joint Economic Committee, U.S. Congress, December, 1962, pp. 35-46.

said the plan should be ratified by the Supreme Soviet within four or five months.[5] However, only the yearly plans have thus far been approved, and publication of the whole plan has been considerably delayed under circumstances suggesting that unresolved difficulties of resource allocation, among defense and other sectors of the economy, are still being threshed out. One of the defense questions which has complicated Soviet planning appears to center around deployment of an ABM (missile defense) system, an undertaking involving very substantial new expenditures at a time when other investment will also have to be stepped up to meet the economic goals of the current plan.

Soviet Appraisal of the Likelihood of General War

It goes without saying that the degree of urgency accorded Soviet military preparations depends in no small way upon what the Soviet leadership thinks about the likelihood of a major war in today's world. Khrushchev's views, beginning with his revision in 1956 of Lenin's "inevitability of war" thesis, had gradually moved to the point where he apparently felt there was little danger of a deliberate Western attack on the Soviet Union.[6]

Under the new Soviet regime, there has been some tendency to revive tendentious charges that the West is preparing for war against the Soviet camp. These accusations began to reappear after the Vietnam crisis deepened in early 1965. The Soviet press took up the theme that the "aggressive character of imperialism" is increasing, making it the "most important duty" of the Soviet Party and other Marxist-Leninist parties "not to permit an under-evaluation of the danger of war."[7] The new leaders themselves also have expressed concern that the danger of war has increased in light of the international situation. The critical question, however, is what distinction should be made between Soviet declaratory utterances on the likeli-

[5] Directives of the XXIII Congress of the CPSU on the Five-Year Plan for Development of the National Economy of the USSR, 1966-1970: *Pravda*, April 6, 1966.
[6] See discussion in the present author's *Soviet Strategy at the Crossroads* (Cambridge, Mass.: Harvard University Press, 1964), pp. 115-17.
[7] For typical examples, see General P. Kurochkin, in *Krasnaia zvezda*, July 9, 1965; Fedor Burlatsky, in *Pravda*, June 24, 1965. See also speeches by Brezhnev, in *Pravda*, September 11, 1965, and *Izvestiia*, October 24, 1965; by Kosygin, in *Krasnaia zvezda*, July 1, 1965; by Suslov, in *Pravda*, October 31, 1965; Kosygin interview with James Reston, in *The New York Times*, December 8, 1965; Garbuzov, in *Pravda*, December 8, 1965; Brezhnev speech at the XXIII Party Congress, in *Pravda*, March 30, 1966.

hood of war—which serve various purposes of internal argument and external propaganda—and the private convictions of the leadership.

Any opinion ventured on this subject is bound to be speculative. The present writer would be inclined to believe that the incumbent Soviet leadership still considers a major war between the rival systems to be unlikely—if not thanks to benign United States intentions, then because of a combination of Soviet deterrent military power and the various political forces described as the "world peace movement." A qualification should be added with regard to Soviet concern that a local war, such as the one in Vietnam, might get out of control, or that the policy of a resurgent Germany might one day draw the United States and the Soviet Union into war. In the latter case, especially, there would appear to be what might be called a fixation in the Soviet "political psyche" which generates fears that go beyond what a rational calculus of the German military threat under present-day conditions would justify.

In any event, assuming that the incumbent Soviet leaders do entertain somewhat more concern about the possibility of war than was the case before the East-West détente began to deteriorate in early 1965, it is not without interest that doctrinal ferment has again arisen in the Soviet Union around the question of whether war in the nuclear age has become obsolete as an instrument of policy.

War as an Instrument of Policy in the Nuclear Age

This issue, one may recall, touches one of the major points of Sino-Soviet difference. The Chinese have argued that nuclear weapons have not made war obsolete, and that wars against imperialism are necessary if the world revolution is to be successful. The Soviet Union, on the other hand, has charged that the Chinese fail to appreciate the destructive consequences of a nuclear war and have in effect courted it by being willing to provoke the United States. Peking in turn has retorted that the Soviet leaders have capitulated to Western nuclear blackmail and are so afraid of nuclear war that they have allowed this fact to paralyze their policy.[8]

Leaving aside a certain amount of polemical exaggeration in this clash of views, there certainly seemed to be an increasing tendency in some Soviet quarters during Khrushchev's tenure to admit that nu-

[8] These points of difference between Moscow and Peking are examined more fully in the present author's "The Soviet Union and the Sino-Soviet Dispute," The RAND Corporation, P-3203 (August, 1965), pp. 16-22.

clear war was likely to be militarily unmanageable and that Lenin's dictum on war as a continuation of politics required revision.

This whole issue, which had subsided in the Soviet Union for some time after Khrushchev's ouster, was reopened with an article in September, 1965, in the semimonthly journal, *Communist of the Armed Forces*, by Lieutenant Colonel E. Rybkin.[9] The article attacked by name such prominent Soviet writers as General Nikolai Talensky for having spread the "fatalistic" doctrine that it is no longer possible "to find acceptable forms of nuclear war." While subscribing to the view that nuclear war would create great havoc and that one should do everything possible to prevent it, Rybkin asserted that one should not succumb to the doctrine that victory in nuclear war is impossible. To do so, he said, "would be not only false on theoretical grounds, but dangerous also from a political point of view."

Rybkin went on to argue that victory was feasible provided a country conducted a nuclear war in such a way as to minimize damage to itself. "We must remember," he wrote, "that victory in war depends not simply on the nature of the weapons but on the power relationship of the belligerent countries." Depending on this relationship, according to Rybkin, two complementary ways may be envisaged to limit the damage of a nuclear war. One lies in achieving "quick" defeat of the enemy, "which will prevent further destruction and disaster." The other lies in "the opportunity to develop and create new means for the conduct of war which can reliably counter the enemy's nuclear blows," an apparent reference to ABM defenses.

At the same time, Rybkin warned that attainment of the requisite military posture would call for great effort, without which it would be a dangerous mistake "to assume that victory was reliably assured" simply because of the "innate superiority" of the Communist system.

Rybkin's views have been echoed, at least in part, by other military writers. At the same time, there has been some pointed criticism of certain aspects of Rybkin's argument. For example, in July, 1966, an article by Colonel I. Grudinin approved of Rybkin's attack on the "no-victory" notion, promulgated in the Khrushchev era by military publicists like General Talensky, but took Rybkin to task for adopting ideas which smacked too much of "bourgeois" theorizing about

---

[9] *Kommunist vooruzhennykh sil,* No. 17 (September, 1965), pp. 50-56. For a detailed examination of the Rybkin article, see Roman Kolkowicz, *"The Red Hawks On the Rationality of Nuclear War,"* The RAND Corporation, RM-4899-PR (March, 1966). Rybkin, although not widely known outside the USSR, is the author of an earlier book in which he argued that modern war, no matter how destructive, is bound to have politically significant consequences. See his *Voina i politika* (Moscow: Voenizdat, 1959), pp. 25-26.

modern war.[10] In particular, Grudinin argued that Rybkin had strayed from Marxist-Leninist analysis by pragmatically stressing the material balance of forces, or what in the Western idiom might be called "hardware factors," while failing to give sufficient weight to the ideological advantages possessed by the Soviet system.

Still another military theorist to be heard from on this subject was Lieutenant Colonel V. Bondarenko, who argued in September, 1966, that the key to victory lies essentially in a massive and imaginative research-and-development effort to assure military-technological superiority.[11] Asserting that a properly-managed research program should avoid the dangerous mistake of concentrating merely on improvement of existing weapons, he advanced the thesis that new breakthroughs in weaponry "can abruptly change the relationship of forces in a short period of time." A further contribution to the discussion stimulated by these various military theorists appeared early in 1967 in an unsigned editorial article in *Krasnaia zvezda*.[12] Noting that writers like Rybkin had taken a "creative, independent approach" to problems of modern war, the article stated that he and Grudinin had unfortunately skirted some of the changes to be taken into account under nuclear-age conditions. Although the article itself reiterated doctrinaire claims of Communist victory if war should come, its main emphasis lay upon the need for "anti-imperialist forces" to oppose nuclear war "as a means for resolving international disputes," thus seeming to imply that theorizing on the prospects of victory should not be carried too far.

The revival in the Soviet Union of theoretical argument about modern war as a policy instrument does not necessarily mean that a hard-line element has begun to urge a current policy shift involving much higher risk of war than hitherto. The central point stressed by the various military theorists cited above seems to be not that the correlation of forces *today* would offer a good prospect of Soviet victory if war should occur, but that a future change in the power rela-

---

[10] *Krasnaia zvezda*, July 21, 1966. This article by Grudinin commented on "the virtues and faults" of a lecture given by Rybkin, rather than upon Rybkin's published article. However, the lecture apparently followed the same line of argument as the article. For an analysis of Soviet theoretical writing on politics and war which places the Rybkin-Grudinin dialogue in a broader framework, see Joseph J. Baritz, "Soviet Military Theory: Politics and War," *Military Review*, September, 1966, pp. 3-10.

[11] *Kommunist vooruzhennykh sil*, No. 17 (September, 1966), pp. 7-14. For a detailed analysis of the Bondarenko article, see Benjamin S. Lambeth, *The Argument For Superiority: A New Voice in the Soviet Strategic Debate* (Washington, D.C.: Institute for Defense Analyses, N-419 R, January, 1967).

[12] *Krasnaia zvezda*, January 24, 1967.

tionship between the Soviet Union and its adversaries might do so. This suggests, in turn, that Soviet military theorists may feel that better prospects are now at hand than previously for attempting to reverse the strategic power balance between the Soviet Union and the United States, making it worthwhile to reopen what had tended to become a closed chapter of discussion at the end of the Khrushchev period. At the same time, as we shall see, the new leadership itself—after having taken positive steps to improve the Soviet Union's strategic position—appears to be hesitating whether to proceed with programs which are likely to precipitate a new intensified round in the strategic arms race, or whether to seek ways of redressing the strategic balance by other means, such as arms control agreements with the United States.

THE STRATEGIC BALANCE AND
THE ISSUE OF MILITARY SUPERIORITY

Where Khrushchev's successors stood with regard to the problem of improving Soviet strategic power relative to that of the United States was by no means clear in the first year or so after they took office. They labored under many of the same constraints that forced Khrushchev to come to terms, however reluctantly, with the situation in which he found himself.[13] On the other hand, they seemed increasingly less disposed to nurture the détente in United States-Soviet relations which had served in the 1963-64 period to ease some of the pressures upon Khrushchev. This implied that they might find it necessary not only to cultivate an *image* of impressive Soviet strategic power, but to try, where Khrushchev failed,[14] to alter the *substance* of the strategic balance as well.

The initial approach by the new regime indicated, if nothing else, a determination to improve the technological base upon which any effort to attain strategic superiority would ultimately depend. Appropriations for scientific research were stepped up,[15] and, as made

---

[13] For a discussion of the contradictions which arose in Khrushchev's time between the doctrine of military superiority and the necessity of putting up with a position of strategic inferiority to the Soviet Union's major adversary, see *Soviet Strategy at the Crossroads,* especially pp. 76-90.

[14] A comprehensive examination of Khrushchev's efforts to exploit the *image* of Soviet strategic power for political gains may be found in the study by Arnold L. Horelick and Myron Rush, *Strategic Power and Soviet Foreign Policy* (Chicago: University of Chicago Press, 1966).

[15] Published Soviet allocations for scientific research have risen as follows: 1963—4.7 billion rubles; 1964—5.2; 1965—5.4; 1966—6.5; 1967—7.2; 1968—7.9; *Pravda,*

evident among other things by public display of new families of
weapons, the Soviet military research and development program was
pushed even more vigorously than hitherto.[16]

In the case of decisions affecting the operational strength and deployment of the armed forces (as distinct from efforts to broaden the
Soviet Union's technological base), the new leadership also showed
itself disposed to take several steps which for one reason or another
were left up in the air in Khrushchev's latter days. One of these, attended by comparatively little fanfare, evidently was a decision to
accelerate the deployment of ICBM's. As indicated by informed accounts in the United States press, the number of operational Soviet
ICBM's has grown substantially in the past few years.[17] By the beginning of 1967, the number had reached more than 400, mostly in
hardened sites, as compared with a deployment of less than 200 ICBM
launchers, many of which were early-generation types of "soft-site"
configuration, during the entire Khrushchev period. In other words,
the *rate* of operational deployment of ICBM's not only was stepped up
after Khrushchev's departure, but the qualitative character of the
ICBM force was also improved.

What the ultimate size of the Soviet ICBM program will be remains
uncertain at the moment, but the implication is that the new Soviet
leaders have decided upon a larger strategic force build-up than their
predecessor found himself in a position to undertake. Also, as emphasized in Marshal Malinovsky's report at the XXIII Party Congress,
"special importance" has been attached to developing mobile landbased missiles for the strategic missile forces,[18] a step which would
further diversify the Soviet Union's strategic delivery potential. Meanwhile, as Malinovsky's report pointed out, the Soviet Union continues

---

December 11, 1962; December 17, 1963; December 8, 1965; *Izvestiia,* December 16,
1966; *Pravda,* October 16, 1967. A substantial amount of spending for military
research is evidently included in these figures. See discussion in Nancy Nimitz,
"Soviet Expenditures on Scientific Research," The RAND Corporation, RM-3384-PR
(January, 1963), pp. 12-14.

[16] See Wolfe, *The Soviet Military Scene,* pp. 96-97.

[17] Among such accounts, see "Russian Missiles Estimated at 400," *The New York
Times,* June 9, 1966; Hanson W. Baldwin, "U.S. Lead in ICBM's Is Said to be
Reduced by Buildup in Soviet Union," *ibid.,* July 14, 1966; William Beecher, "Soviet
Increases Buildup of Missiles and Deploys a Defensive System," *ibid.,* November
13, 1966; Beecher, "A New Round on Missiles," *ibid.,* December 18, 1966. See also
Institute for Strategic Studies, *The Military Balance, 1966-1967* (London, September,
1966), p. 2.

[18] *Krasnaia zvezda,* April 2, 1966. For a subsequent claim that Soviet development of a mobile, solid-fuel ICBM is among the factors upon which alleged Soviet
military-technical superiority rests, see the previously-cited article by Colonel V.
Bondarenko in *Kommunist vooruzhennykh sil,* No. 17 (September, 1966), p. 9.

to count upon the additional contribution to its strategic delivery capabilities provided by long-range bombers equipped with air-to-surface missiles for "standoff" attacks against enemy targets and by missile-launching submarines.[19]

Another step intended to bolster the Soviet strategic posture relates to ABM deployment. As was made known late in 1966 by the United States government,[20] after some months of speculation in the press that ABM defenses were being installed around such cities as Leningrad and Moscow, the Soviet Union evidently embarked upon deployment of an ABM system—the ultimate extent and effectiveness of which is still a matter of considerable debate in the West.[21] According to some accounts, it remains unclear whether or not the system is confined to Moscow alone.[22] Speculation about the effectiveness of ABM measures taken thus far by the Soviet Union has been further heightened by public expression of differing opinion on the subject among Soviet military officials.[23]

[19] As is the Soviet custom, Malinovsky gave no figures for the size of the Soviet Union's long-range bomber and missile-launching submarine forces. According to recent Western estimates, the Soviet Union possesses some 200 heavy bombers (M-4 "Bisons" and TU-95 "Bears") and about 35 submarines capable of firing an average of three ballistic missiles each. In addition, about 40 submarines are equipped to fire cruise-type winged missiles, which could be used against land targets but which probably have a primary mission against the adversary's naval forces. See *The Military Balance 1966-1967*, pp. 3, 5.

[20] The first official United States cognizance of "considerable evidence" that the Soviet Union was deploying an anti-ballistic missile defense system was given by Defense Secretary Robert S. McNamara in an interview on November 10, 1966. *The New York Times*, November 11, 1966. Among earlier reports and analysis of Soviet ABM activity, see: *Missiles and Rockets*, April 4, 1966, p. 7; May 2, 1966, p. 12; *Technology Week*, June 20, 1966, p. 16; *The New York Times*, April 23, May 11, June 26, 1966; *The Washington Post*, April 21, 1966; John R. Thomas, "The Role of Missile Defense in Soviet Strategy and Foreign Policy," in *The Military-Technical Revolution: Its Impact on Strategy and Foreign Policy*, ed. John Erickson (New York: Frederick A. Praeger, Inc., 1966), pp. 187-218. According to one estimate attributed to American officials in early 1967, the Soviet Union had spent up to that time from $4 billion to $5 billion on development of its ABM system, compared with something over $2 billion spent by the United States on development of the Nike-X missile defense system. *The New York Times*, January 29, 1967.

[21] See, for example, Hanson W. Baldwin, "A New Round Begins in the Battle of Sword vs. Shield," *The New York Times*, November 27, 1966; Henry Cemmill, "The Missile Race," *Wall Street Journal*, December 14, 1966.

[22] See Hanson W. Baldwin, "Soviet Anti-missile System Spurs New U.S. Weapons," *The New York Times*, February 5, 1967; and *The Washington Post*, February 22, 23, 1967.

[23] For several years, Soviet military leaders have publicly advanced claims for Soviet ABM progress, varying from outright assertions that the Soviet Union had solved the ABM problem to more guarded statements like that of Marshal Malinovsky in April, 1966, that Soviet defenses could cope with some but not all enemy

Why the Soviet regime decided to deploy an ABM system and to claim a significant advantage in this field is not altogether clear. The Soviet leaders were undoubtedly aware that "first deployment" of ABMs has been widely regarded in the West as a step which could "destabilize" the strategic environment and set off a new round of the arms race. In light of the earlier example of the "missile gap" which in the late fifties and early sixties greatly stimulated United States missile programs and had the net result of placing the Soviet Union in a relatively unfavorable position with respect to strategic forces, one might have supposed that the Soviet leaders would think twice about stirring up an "ABM gap" psychology. However, the Soviet predilection for building strategic defenses, possibly combined with overcoming of earlier technical obstacles in ABM development, apparently prevailed over the economic costs and the risks of stimulating the strategic arms race, in the judgment of the present leadership.

Whether this decision will hold up in the face of American efforts to persuade the Soviet government to reconsider its ABM policy, remains to be seen.[24] At this writing, it is not clear what may emerge from the exploratory United States-Soviet talks on this subject.[25] However, by hinting that any negotiations which may develop should also take up the issue of strategic delivery forces, in which the United

---

missiles. (For review of such statements, see the present author's *Soviet Strategy at the Crossroads*, pp. 190-96, and *The Soviet Military Scene*, pp. 99, 169.) In February, 1967, the conflicting pronouncements of several Soviet military men on this subject assumed new interest in light of the opening United States-Soviet dialogue on halting a potential ABM race. Two Soviet officers, Generals P. F. Batitsky and P. A. Kurochkin, took the optimistic position that Soviet ABM defenses could reliably protect the country. Shortly thereafter, two senior military men, Marshals A. A. Grechko and V. I. Chuikov, voiced the more pessimistic view that the Soviet Union did not yet possess defenses capable "in practice" of intercepting all incoming enemy planes and missiles. For press accounts of these statements, see "Russians Say Anti-Missile System Will Protect Them From Attack," *The New York Times*, February 21, 1967; "Russians Concede Missile Net Flaw," *ibid.*, February 23, 1967; "Soviet Cities Vulnerable, Red Defense Chief Says," *The Washington Post*, February 23, 1967.

[24] United States hopes of persuading the Soviet Union to agree to a mutual "freeze" of some sort on ABM deployment were voiced by President Johnson in his State of the Union message on January 10, 1967. Thereafter, diplomatic soundings on the matter in early 1967 proceeded in a climate of alternative doubt and cautious optimism about the prospects of reaching an understanding. The general Soviet tone, set by Kosygin in an interview in London on February 10, was rather cool. See, for example, *The New York Times*, January 15, February 10, 1967; *The Washington Post*, February 18, 22, 1967.

[25] These exploratory talks were carried on in Moscow between United States Ambassador Llewellyn E. Thompson and Soviet Premier Kosygin, beginning on February 18, 1967.

States enjoys a putative 3:1 advantage,[26] the Soviet leaders seem to be giving thought to the possibility of improving the Soviet Union's relative position via the arms control route rather than banking solely on a unilateral build-up of Soviet offensive and defensive strategic forces.

SOVIET THINKING ON PROSPECTS OF CONVENTIONAL WARFARE

Let us briefly consider current Soviet thinking with regard to the possibility of non-nuclear "theater warfare" of significant scale between the major powers. In Khrushchev's time, the central conception common to both Soviet military and political discussions of theater warfare, particularly any war in Europe, was that it would be fought within the framework of general war opening with heavy strategic and tactical nuclear exchanges by both sides.

Some signs that a shift in Soviet thinking might be taking place began to appear before Khrushchev's ouster, in the form of professional statements on the need to improve theater capabilities for either nuclear or conventional operations.[27] Under the new regime, there have been further indications of a doctrinal reappraisal of the possibility of non-nuclear theater warfare, the implication being that the theater forces must be better prepared for situations in which it might not be expedient to bring Soviet nuclear power to bear. Marshals Rotmistrov and Malinovsky, for example, have suggested that hostilities might not automatically involve use of nuclear weapons.[28] Other military spokesmen have commented that Soviet military doctrine does not "exclude" the possibility of non-nuclear warfare or of warfare limited to tactical nuclear weapons "within the framework of so-called 'local' wars," which could "take place even in Europe." [29]

It should be observed, however, that Soviet professional military opinion has by no means swung in unison away from previously-held views on the improbability of purely conventional or limited tactical

[26] See, for example, *The New York Times,* February 22, 1967.

[27] See *Soviet Strategy at the Crossroads,* pp. 119-24; and the present author's "Trends in Soviet Thinking on Theater Warfare, Conventional Operations, and Limited War," The RAND Corporation, RM-4305-PR (December, 1964), pp. 41-48. This paper may also be found as a chapter in *The Military-Technical Revolution, op cit.,* pp. 52-79.

[28] Marshal R. Ia. Malinovsky's, Radio Volga broadcast, September 8, 1965; Marshal P. A. Rotmistrov, in *Krasnaia zvezda,* December 29, 1964.

[29] See Colonel General S. Shtemenko, *Nedelia,* No. 6 (January 31-February 6, 1965); Major General N. Lomov, *Kommunist vooruzhennykh sil,* No. 21 (November, 1965), pp. 16, 18.

nuclear operations in Europe. In August, 1965, for example, a military commentator, General V. Zemskov, dismissed the notion of "waging a local nuclear war" in the European theater with these words: "It is obvious that a war in Europe, which is saturated with nuclear weapons and missiles, would immediately assume the broadest dimensions." [30] An article jointly authored in the spring of 1966 by Marshal Sokolovsky and a colleague also illustrated that the doctrinal reappraisal sought by such "traditionalist" leaders as Marshal Rotmistrov was not going undisputed.[31] The article made only passing mention of the possibility of non-nuclear warfare and stressed that the responsibility of Soviet strategy is to plan properly for the use "above all of missile-nuclear weapons as the main means of warfare."

Again, however, one must bear in mind that Soviet declaratory positions do not necessarily tell the whole story. Expressions concerning the dubious prospects for limitation of a European war, intended partly for deterrent effect, may be subject to change under various contingent conditions. Should the private views of the Soviet leadership come to admit a higher expectation that war on a European scale might be conducted on a non-nuclear basis—and in this connection the example of an intensified conflict in Vietnam without nuclear escalation may influence Soviet thinking—then a number of basic considerations affecting Soviet policy would doubtless arise.

The prospect of reduced risk of a nuclear confrontation in Europe, for example, might well dispel some of the caution which has strongly colored the Soviet outlook upon military conflict there. This, in turn, could call for reassessment by the Soviet leadership of its political stance, leading perhaps to the belief that stepped-up pressure for solution of outstanding problems could be more safely applied than hitherto. On the other hand, if Soviet leaders have learned anything from past experience, they may be wary of exerting new pressures upon Western Europe, which could have the effect of stimulating the NATO alliance to close ranks again, as happened on several occasions during the postwar period under both Stalin and Khrushchev.

Evolving Character of the Warsaw Pact

The Soviet Union's military relations with the other members of the Warsaw Pact have changed considerably since the Warsaw Treaty Organization was formally created in 1955, largely as a diplomatic

[30] *Krasnaia zvezda*, August 3, 1965.
[31] Marshal V. Sokolovsky and General M. Cherednichenko, in *Kommunist vooruzhennykh sil*, No. 7 (April, 1966), pp. 59-66.

and propaganda counter to West Germany's entry into NATO. Originally the Pact played little part in Soviet military planning, which was predicated on the assumption that Soviet theater forces would bear the burden of any military undertakings in Europe in which the Soviet Union might become involved. Around 1960-61, however, Khrushchev instituted a new policy of closer military cooperation with the East European members of the Pact, aimed both at improving the collective military efficiency of the alliance and at tightening its political cohesion in the face of "polycentric" tendencies in East Europe.[32]

This policy has been continued under the Brezhnev-Kosygin regime. In particular, the process of joint training and modernization of the East European forces, commensurate with their enlarged responsibilities, has gone forward. Today these forces total over 900,000 men, organized in some 60 divisions, of which about half are at combat strength and readiness, according to Western estimates.[33] Taken together with the Soviet forces deployed in East Europe—which consist of 20 divisions in East Germany, four in Hungary and two in Poland, plus sizeable tactical air elements and tactical missile units— the aggregate Warsaw Pact forces in Europe today represent a rather impressive military potential.

From the Soviet viewpoint, however, the fruits of the new course toward the Warsaw Pact have not been entirely sweet. While the capability for joint action of the East European components undoubtedly has improved, the political aim of tightening bloc unity and cohesion through military integration seems to have gone awry. Instead of being bound closer to Soviet policy interests, the East European regimes have tended to press for a more influential voice in Pact matters affecting their own interests, such as the sharing of economic and military burdens and the formulation of alliance strategy. Rumania, first to jump the traces in the economic field, also has taken the lead in challenging Soviet control of military affairs.[34] Partly perhaps as a response to Rumanian recalcitrance, but probably more because the focus of Soviet political and strategic interest is directed toward Germany, a rather marked regional differentiation has emerged within the Warsaw alliance between countries of the "northern" and "southern tiers." [35]

---

[32] For discussion of these trends, see the present author's "The Warsaw Pact in Evolution," *The World Today*, May, 1966, pp. 191-98.

[33] *The Military Balance, 1965-1966*, pp. 6-8.

[34] See the present author's *Soviet Military Power and European Security*, The RAND Corporation; P-3429 (August, 1966), pp. 38-41.

[35] The "northern tier" countries—East Germany, Poland, Czechoslovakia, and the

In sum, there is growing evidence that the Warsaw Pact is evolving into an alliance beset with the familiar interplay of coalition politics, rather than representing a fully compliant instrument of Soviet policy. It would probably be wrong to jump from this to the conclusion that the Soviet Union has ceased to exercise a predominant role in the affairs of the Warsaw Pact. The residual animosities of the Cold War, skillful Soviet play upon East European fears of a resurgent Germany, and, above all, the Soviet military presence in East Europe continue to place limits on the ability of the Warsaw Pact countries to shape their own policies independent of Soviet interests.

THE VIETNAM CRISIS AND SOVIET MILITARY POLICY

Finally let us consider the bearing of the Vietnam conflict upon Soviet military policy under the new regime, a question upon which the strained state of Sino-Soviet relations also impinges. Although the present Soviet leadership has increased its support of Hanoi's military effort during the past several years, especially by furnishing SA-2 missiles and other air defense matériel, it has not sanctioned the formal commitment of Soviet military forces to the war in Southeast Asia.[36] Presumably, in the interest of avoiding a direct confrontation with the United States, the Soviet leaders would prefer to keep their military involvement limited to furnishing equipment, technical advice, and training to Hanoi's soldiery, although they have spoken of permitting "volunteers" to participate, which would still be something less than formal intervention. Beyond experimenting with volunteers, however, the Soviet leadership's room for maneuver would seem to be constricted not only by the risk of major escalation, but also by the fact that geography makes direct Soviet intervention difficult. Charges of Chinese refusal to cooperate in the overland shipment of Soviet aid to North Vietnam have pointed up this difficulty.[37]

With regard to China, the Soviet Union evidently has had to consider military problems potentially a good deal more serious than interference with shipments to Vietnam. In the spring of 1966, for example, the Soviet leadership reportedly felt obliged to castigate

Soviet Union—have frequently been alluded to by Communist sources as the "first strategic echelon" of the Warsaw Pact. These, of course, are the countries most immediately involved with the question of West German aspirations in Central Europe.

[36] For a discussion of the Soviet Union's gradually increasing military aid to Hanoi, see the present author's *The Soviet Military Scene,* pp. 109-124.

[37] *Ibid.,* pp. 112, 173.

Peking for telling the Chinese people that "it is necessary to prepare themselves for a military struggle with the USSR." [38] Since that time, Sino-Soviet relations have grown still more inflamed in the climate of Mao's "cultural revolution," and reports of frontier clashes and mutual military precautions in the border territories of the two countries have increased.[39] Although an outright military collision between the two Communist powers is still perhaps only a remote possibility, the new Soviet regime has doubtless been obliged to reassess its military preparations with such a contingency in mind. In this connection, according to Peking's allegations, there has evidently been some internal redeployment of Soviet forces in the Asian regions bordering on China.[40]

Neither the Vietnam conflict nor friction with China, however, seems to have counseled any significant redisposition of Soviet military power deployed against NATO Europe. Occasional rumors to the effect that Soviet divisions were being withdrawn from East Germany to bolster the Soviet Union's posture in the Far East have been discounted by Western observers in Europe.[41] For the Soviet leaders to consider troop withdrawals in Europe while the war in Vietnam continues would, of course, leave them vulnerable to Chinese allegations of "collusion" with the United States to ease the European situation and permit the transfer of American troops to Vietnam.[42]

Sensitivity to Chinese criticism, however, probably has no more than an incidental bearing on Soviet military deployments in Europe. The main factor seems to be that, despite the demands of the war in Vietnam and the Soviet Union's increasing stake in Asian affairs generally, priority still applies to maintaining the Soviet Union's European power position and its ability to deal with the political and military problems of Europe, not the least of which, in Soviet eyes, is that of keeping a resurgent Germany in check.

Indeed, the present Soviet leaders have kept their sights fixed in this direction. As Politburo member Alexander Shelepin took pains to point out during a visit to Hanoi in January, 1966, by way of suggesting to the North Vietnamese that they should rely mainly on

[38] *Ibid.*, pp. 137, 174. See also *The New York Times*, March 24, 1966.

[39] See Victor Zorza, "Soviet Press Clamors Over Chinese Military Threat," *The Washington Post*, November 10, 1966; "Chinese Report Soviet Border Clash," *ibid.*, February 14, 1967; Charles Mohr, "Observers Speculate That Tensions Along the Soviet-Chinese Border May Be Rising," *The New York Times*, February 21, 1967.

[40] See remarks to a group of Scandinavian journalists by Chinese Deputy Premier Chen Yi, *The New York Times*, July 21, 1966.

[41] See *The New York Times*, October 24, November 6, 1966.

[42] For a sample of such Chinese allegations, see *Peking Review*, IX, No. 8 (February 18, 1966), 10.

their own resources to oppose the United States, the Soviet Union must continue to bear in mind its own "heavy commitments" in Europe.[43] Subsequently, Andrei Gromyko and other Soviet spokesmen have re-emphasized that the main focus of Soviet interest continues to lie in Europe,[44] where, as the Kremlin sees it, the emergence from the disarray within NATO of a closer Washington-Bonn axis would allegedly constitute the greatest threat to Soviet security.

[43] *Pravda*, January 10, 1966.
[44] See Gromyko's remarks before the United Nations General Assembly in New York on September 23, 1966. *The New York Times*, September 24, 1966. Whether the Soviet Union would find it expedient to play down the idea of a German-American axis in light of signs of emerging strains in their relations had not, at the time of writing, yet become apparent.

6 Foreign Policy Perspectives in the Sixties

VERNON V. ASPATURIAN

INTRODUCTION

The most conspicuous over-all characteristics of Soviet foreign policy since Khrushchev are: the progressive disengagement of foreign policy goals from ideological norms; the diffusion of policy-making; the globalization of Soviet power and influence; the personalization of Soviet diplomacy; and finally, the vigorous pursuit of both confrontation and collaboration with the United States.

All of these trends were set into motion under Khrushchev. Brezhnev and Kosygin have attempted to arrest or attenuate most or all of these trends but without much success. Ideology as a motivational force in Soviet foreign policy continues to wane. Moscow has retrenched somewhat from the global overcommitment of its power and resources made under Khrushchev, but it cannot abjure its global role without serious injury to Soviet prestige and influence. While Soviet foreign policy is no longer symbolized by a single personality, it has not been completely depersonalized either; Kosygin, Brezhnev, and Podgorny now appear on the world stage almost as equals, whereas before there was only one. The division of diplomatic labor symbolizes the collectivity of the current Soviet leadership, but it also reflects the fragmentation of power and authority.

VERNON V. ASPATURIAN (Ph.D., U.C.L.A. 1951) is Research Professor of Political Science at Pennsylvania State University where he has taught since 1952. He has been a visiting professor at the Graduate Institute of International Studies (Geneva, Switzerland), Johns Hopkins University, U.C.L.A., and Columbia University. He is the author of several books on Soviet foreign policy and has contributed numerous articles to the *Journal of International Affairs, Journal of Politics, Yale Review, American Political Science Review,* and *Survey,* among other journals.

The ouster of Khrushchev may have been prompted at least in part by the conviction that he had become too closely identified with the policy of alienating Peking in order to woo Washington, which was viewed with concern by some of the other leaders, who may have favored a different equilibrium between Soviet commitments to China and Soviet cooperation with the United States. As matters turned out, both Peking and Washington have been further alienated.

The de-ideologizing of Soviet foreign policy, set into motion at the XX Party Congress, and the repudiation of some sacrosanct ideological principles within which it operated, served to free it from Stalinist fetters, but it also shattered the myths of Soviet ideological infallibility and political omniscience. This, in turn, released disintegrative forces. Factional politics became the rule throughout the Communist world and have become increasingly institutionalized, making it virtually impossible to coordinate policy or resolve conflicts among Communist regimes and Parties.

De-ideologizing Soviet Foreign Policy

Viewed in historical perspective, ideology has not been a constant in shaping Soviet behavior but a relative factor whose relationship to others relevant to Soviet behavior has fluctuated widely. This protean and variable characteristic has been a prime source of controversy in assessing the significance of ideology for Soviet policy.

Soviet foreign policy has always been the product of ideology in combination with other variables: capabilities, perceived opportunities, personalities, internal group and factional interests, and extra-volitional institutional and functional restraints. The long Stalinist era served to distort and dull the perception and analysis of Soviet behavior from abroad. Soviet policy was judged to be the product of two variables: ideological goals, as interpreted by Stalin, and Soviet capabilities. Ideology determined long-range goals, while short-range goals were limited by Soviet capabilities. An extremely complicated process of interaction and metamorphic development was thus reduced to an oversimplified two-factor analysis and prediction of Soviet policy. Stalinist behavior was mistakenly assumed to be the immutable behavior of the Soviet state. The leader's personality and the internal political order were accepted as constants, while ideology was viewed as an instrumental extension of Stalin's personality. Stalin's long-range ideological goals were no secret; it was his short-run intentions which were inscrutable. On the assumption that Stalin would take what he could get, the most common method for predicting short-run Soviet behavior was the measurement of Soviet capabilities. While such an approach had its utility during the Stalin era, it unfortunately spilled over into the post-Stalin period when it served to obscure the influence of other important variables which had been largely muted or latent until then.

Since the ideological goals of the Bolshevik movement were enunciated long before there was even a problem of Soviet security or interests to defend, ideology in its pristine form cannot be defined as an expedient defensive response to the behavior of a hostile environment. After the Revolution and the Soviet state merged, this dual entity made itself the self-appointed custodian of the interests of the world proletariat. A national revolutionary movement was metamorphosed into a world revolutionary movement; and the interests of the Soviet state were merged with those of the movement.

The relative influence of ideology as a motivating force in Soviet foreign policy cannot be properly separated from the utility of the world Communist movement as an instrument of Soviet policy: the disutility of the latter was bound to subvert the animating force of the former. "In the change from Lenin to Stalin," observes George F. Kennan, "the foreign policy of a movement became the foreign policy of a single man," [1] and one might add that in the changeover from Stalin to his successors, the foreign policy of an autocrat became the foreign policy of an oligarchy.

Under Stalin, the interests of the world movement fused with that of the Soviet state, and the interests of the state were largely merged with the personal and political interests of Stalin. World revolution, i.e., the extension of Communist power, became indistinguishable from Soviet expansion, and while this was largely a hypothetical relationship until 1939, after the outbreak of World War II it became a practical matter which ultimately resulted not only in the territorial expansion of the USSR but in the establishment of a system of vassal states, which was first successfully challenged by Yugoslavia in 1948 and has been in a state of progressive dissolution since 1956.

While Stalin's death set the stage for the disintegration of the world Communist movement into its constituent states and national Parties, the underlying cause for the divorce of Soviet interests from those of other Communist Parties was the rapid growth in Soviet capabilities. As Soviet power grew, so did the risks and costs of implementing a forward policy. The general tendency was for Soviet ideological goals to recede or to erode into ritualistic rhetoric, while the growth in Soviet power created greater opportunities for the pursuit of traditional great-power goals.

---

[1] George F. Kennan, *Russia and the West Under Lenin and Stalin* (Boston: Little, Brown and Company, 1961), p. 223.

In the years since Stalin's death, the Soviet Union has been forced to adjust to changing configurations of interests and power at home, in the Communist inter-state community, in the world Communist movement, and in the international community at large—changes which have resulted in a fundamental restructuring of priorities among the various interests and purposes which motivate Soviet foreign policy.

The progressive de-ideologization of Soviet foreign policy goals under Khrushchev took place more by inadvertence, as a consequence of his opportunism, than by design. Once domestic pressures—for instance, in favor of raising the standard of living—were given equal legitimacy with ideological pressures, it was axiomatic that they would become a factor in internal politics and in turn impel Khrushchev to cater to them, while spurning the simultaneous demands of foreign Communist states and Parties. To assign higher priority to China and the world Communist movement might have been necessary to preserve Soviet pre-eminence in the world of communism. But it was bound to be of little value in preserving Khrushchev's authority at home, which increasingly depended upon his ability to meet the demands of powerful domestic constituencies.

Thus the traditional operational norms and assumptions of inter-state behavior—national interest, security, survival, economic and material well-being, national pride and prestige—have been increasingly supplanting the abstract goals of "world revolution" and "world communism" in Soviet foreign-policy behavior. In the words of Peking:

> The Soviet leaders seek only to preserve themselves and would let other people sink or swim. They have repeatedly said that so long as they themselves survive and develop, the people of the world will be saved. The fact is they are selling out the fundamental interests of the people of the world in order to seek their own momentary ease.[2]

While the Soviet Union appears to have exhausted ideology as a motivating force in its foreign policy because it has become increasingly dysfunctional, ideology has not exhausted its utility in other dimensions. It continues to serve the Brezhnev-Kosygin regime as a valuable instrument of epistemological, political, and social analysis, i.e., as a theory of reality; as a repository of moral truths and standards of ethical conduct; as a medium of communication; as an effective and necessary vehicle for the rationalization and explanation of

[2] "Statement by the Spokesman of the Chinese Government . . . August 15, 1963," *Peking Review,* VI, No. 33 (August 16, 1963), p. 7.

the Soviet social order; and as the indispensable foundation of legitimacy upon which the entire Soviet structure reposes. While ideology wanes as a motivating force, it may simultaneously wax in its other functions, much as religions have undergone similar functional metamorphoses.

In the process of gradually disentangling ideological norms from policy goals, however, Soviet ideology has assumed a new function, whose effects are not altogether an unmixed blessing. It now functions to legitimize Moscow's behavior as a *global power,* i.e., a power which asserts a right to intervene in any dispute or conflict in any part of the globe. While the Soviet leaders have abjured ideology as a norm-defining mechanism, they have by no means abdicated their self-appointed role as the guardian and spokesman of the oppressed masses of the world against international imperialism. Otherwise Soviet global interventionism could be justified only in terms of raw power and naked self-interest, an impression which Moscow avidly desires to avoid.

The Fragmentation of the Decision-Making Apparatus

Under Stalin, policy-formulation and decision-making were tightly centralized in his own person. However, the struggle for power among his successors resulted in the fragmentation of the decision-making structure, distributing power among various individuals and factions, each in command of a separate institutional power structure. Ideology was increasingly divorced from policy formulation, which in turn was frequently out of phase with the administration and execution of policy, as rival factions increasingly assumed control over policy-making and policy-executing bodies. The fragmentation of the decision-making structure was artlessly concealed behind the fig-leaf of "collective leadership." Personalities, factions, and eventually sociofunctional and socio-institutional groupings assumed a more variable role in the shaping of Soviet behavior, and a new, fluid relationship was established among Soviet capabilities, ideology, personalities, and institutions in the decision-making process. While this made it even more difficult to judge Soviet intentions and predict Soviet behavior, it was compensated for by the corresponding inability of the Soviet Union to pursue the single-minded and precisely controlled type of foreign policy which had been characteristic of the Stalin era.

Factional conflict in the Soviet hierarchy has thus introduced a new and fortuitous element in Soviet behavior, since it is by no means predictable whether a given Soviet personality or faction will continue, repudiate, or modify the policies of its predecessors or rivals. Even more significantly, Soviet policy may fluctuate not only in accordance with institutional and personality changes, but also with the changing equilibrium of factions within the hierarchy. As Soviet capabilities expand, these factional conflicts register conflicting perceptions of risks involved in relation to possible returns; they represent shifting configurations of interests and priorities.

Whereas the United States has been accustomed to self-restraint in the exercise of power, the self-restraint introduced into Soviet behavior, partly as a consequence of factional politics, confronts Soviet leaders with a new and bewildering experience, to which they have not completely adjusted. Accustomed to being guided in their behavior by the principle of "pushing to the limit," they have in the past assumed that the American "ruling class" was guided by the identical principle. Since about 1956, it has no longer been valid to assume that the Soviet Union will consistently use its capabilities to its utmost. Although the USSR has tried to stretch its capabilities in some instances by bluffing, Soviet behavior in fact has fallen short not only of its stated intentions, but also of its capabilities. This has been notably true of its conduct toward the Communist states of Eastern Europe, but it has been true elsewhere as well. This self-restraint is not necessarily deliberate or calculated in all instances; it has probably resulted also from institutionalized factors such as internal rivalries, conflicts of judgment, perception and interests, and sheer bureaucratic inertia, i.e., the fragmentation of the decision-making process.

The Globalization of Soviet Foreign Policy

If it was Stalin who transformed the Soviet Union into a great power, it was under Khrushchev that Soviet Russia was transformed into a global power, challenging the United States for paramountcy and asserting the right to influence developments in any part of the world. Khrushchev broke out of the doctrinal shell confining Soviet diplomacy and embarked upon a bold global strategy of reaching out in search not only of possible recruits to the Communist bloc but of diplomatic client states.

Khrushchev's global strategy, pursued against the background of Soviet space spectaculars which he tried to metamorphose into military power, was designed to breach the non-Communist world at its most vulnerable points—in the Middle East, Southeast Asia, Africa, and even Latin America—irrespective of the strength of local Communist Parties. The maximization of possible diplomatic gains in the non-Communist world invited a minimization and dilution of the ideological content of Soviet foreign policy. This was to prove self-defeating (although advantageous momentarily) since it dictated the abandonment of foreign-policy strategies associated with Moscow for decades. Thus it meant, in some instances, sacrificing the future of local Communist Parties in return for diplomatic gains in the third world; it meant the diversion of scarce resources from internal development and from allied Communist countries to seduce the newly-independent countries of Asia and Africa with economic aid; it meant the assumption of new burdens in areas vulnerable to United States sea and air power, far from the centers of Communist power. For a time Khrushchev capitalized on the alleged "missile gap" to unfurl a protective nuclear-missile umbrella over Asia, Africa, and Latin America in the mistaken conviction that the United States could be thereby deterred from interfering with Soviet policy or from intervening to arrest local revolutions.

While Khrushchev successfully transformed the Soviet Union into a global power, he did so at the expense of weakening Soviet control in its own sphere; alienating Moscow's strongest ally, China; over-committing Soviet power; and maximizing the risks of thermonuclear war by his persistent probing of weak spots in the Western world hoping to force the United States into the settlement of outstanding issues on Soviet terms. These were the orientations and relations which the Soviet leaders inherited when they retired Nikita Khrushchev.

KHRUSHCHEV AND SOVIET DÉTENTE STRATEGY

One serious consequence of these trends in Khrushchev's foreign policy was the abandonment of a structurally-assured leadership of the Communist bloc in return for a tacit bid to be a co-ruler of the world with the United States. This simultaneously alienated the Chinese, who saw in Moscow's desired partner their chief enemy, and created a spiritual and power vacuum in the international Communist movement which Peking tried to fill. The consequence was a fracturing of the Communist bloc and the establishment of a new fluid and uncertain equilibrium in Sino-Soviet-American relations.

Soviet and Chinese Perceptions of the United States

Since the United States has become a major factor in the evolving relationship between the Soviet Union and China, its perceptions and behavior become important variables of the situation. It is difficult to ascertain whether Sino-Soviet differences are a consequence of divergent perception of American intentions and behavior or a root cause of these differences. By the November, 1957, conference of ruling Communist Parties in Moscow, it had become rather clear that the United States, its intentions, and the threat it posed were being perceived differently in Moscow and Peking, and this gap was straining the Sino-Soviet alliance. Khrushchev emphasized more and more the horrors of nuclear war and made its avoidance the first objective of Soviet foreign policy. Since the avoidance of thermonuclear war depended also upon the United States, such a policy presupposed a revised image of the United States, which would allow for an equal commitment on the part of the American "ruling class" to the avoidance of such a holocaust.

Khrushchev's policy was facilitated by the fact that, with the exception of the German question, both the United States and the Soviet Union were prepared to accept the political and territorial status quo in Europe. Neither the Soviet Union nor the United States had any direct demands upon the other which could encumber an accommodation. The principal obstacles originated in ideological differences and the inherent tendency of the two hegemonial powers to view one another with suspicion and fear as natural rivals.

China's relationship with the United States was fundamentally different. From China's standpoint, the United States was not only its major ideological opponent, but its major national enemy as well. Not only had China been involved in a proxy war with the United States in Korea, but the United States persisted in its refusal to recognize the Peking regime, remained the decisive force in keeping Peking out of the United Nations, and sustained a rival regime on Taiwan which it recognized as the legitimate government of all China. The United States policy toward China's two major Far Eastern allies, North Korea and North Vietnam, was substantially identical, and since both bordered on China, this created the appearance of hostile encirclement by the United States, which appeared as the major obstacle to the national unification and juridical recognition of China and its two acolytes and directly or indirectly seemed to threaten the interests and very existence of the Far Eastern Communist regimes. Not only did the United States continue to deprive them of territories which they claim as part of their state, but in all three instances it actively supported rival regimes.

No comparable perceptions of American deprivations existed on the Soviet side. The Soviet elite still views the United States as the leader of a hostile ideological-military coalition and as a global power rival in international affairs; but these are matters subject to compromise and accommodation. These differing perceptions of American intentions and expected behavior have shaped corresponding attitudes across a spectrum of issues which, while couched in ideological terms, are actually distorted by the national interests of each side and organized into different orders of priority.

The areas of tangible agreement between the two have shrunk considerably, since Moscow and Peking have divergent perceptions of the nature of the American threat and divergent assessments of the risks and costs necessary to deal with it. Because of these divergent perceptions, the further expansion of communism is no longer viewed by both Moscow and Peking as automatically beneficial; it all depends on, What kind of communism is being proliferated? Whose power is being expanded? Whose interests are being served?

The Realignment of Forces

In the decade between 1956 and 1967, Soviet and Chinese images of one another and the international scene have undergone fundamental alteration. These perceptions, in turn, are a function of changing Soviet perceptions and unchanging Chinese perceptions of American behavior and reflect the essentially conflicting national and state interests of two states unable to manipulate a common ideology in such a way as not to jeopardize the interests of one while advancing those of the other. What the Chinese leaders perceive as necessary for their own security and well-being, the Soviet leaders perceive as inimical to their requirements. These differences arise partly because of divergent internal demands and pressures as well as different security requirements. The limited test-ban treaty of 1963 constitutes the major watershed in the evolution of Sino-Soviet-American relations, with both Peking and Moscow conceding that an important realignment of world political actors has taken place.

In the eyes of both Peking and Moscow, the Soviet Union and the United States had been transformed from total enemies into limited partners-and-adversaries. Cooperation-and-conflict were to characterize their relations, with the center of gravity shifting from conflict toward cooperation. Even American bombardment of a common ally in Southeast Asia was insufficient to restore Sino-Soviet cooperation and friendship, and while the escalation of the Vietnam war impeded the Soviet-American détente, it failed to provoke a direct confrontation. The Soviet reaction has been one of dismay, disappointment, and embarrassment. There is little question but that Moscow expected the nuclear test-ban treaty to be followed up by a series of further agreements, most notably an East-West non-aggression pact, a nuclear non-proliferation treaty, and possibly a German settlement.

On the other hand, the Soviet Union and China were transformed from full allies into partial adversaries and potential enemies. Conflict-and-cooperation were to characterize their relationship as well, with the center of gravity shifting from cooperation toward conflict. The escalation of the Vietnam war, instead of increasing cooperation between them, actually reduced it even further.

From the Chinese point of view, the test-ban treaty and its implications brought about a virtual reversal of alliances. This observation, a typical Peking exaggeration, appears valid as a statement of Chinese expectations, if not fact:

> The leaders of the CPSU have completely reversed enemies and comrades. . . . The leaders of the CPSU are bent on seeking Soviet-United States cooperation for the domination of the world. They regard United States imperialism, the most ferocious enemy of the people in the world, as their most reliable friend, and they treat the fraternal parties and countries adhering to Marxism-Leninism as their enemy. They collude with United States imperialism, the reactionaries of various countries, the renegade Tito clique and the right-wing Social Democrats in a partnership against the socialist fraternal countries. When they snatch at a straw from Eisenhower or Kennedy or others like them, or think that things are going smoothly for them, the leaders of the CPSU are beside themselves with joy, hit out wildly at the fraternal parties and countries adhering to Marxism-Leninism, and endeavor to sacrifice fraternal parties and countries on the altar of their political dealings with United States imperialism.[3]

Strangely enough, the new Soviet and Chinese images of world realignments held much in common. Essentially extra-Marxist, these revised images of world realignments in effect abandoned the canons of class analysis. Instead of a world divided into peace-loving Communist states and warlike imperialist countries with a broad belt of non-aligned states in between, Moscow now perceived the world as being divided into peace-loving states and social forces, on the one hand, and warlike states and social forces, on the other. Some sectors of the imperialist "ruling classes" were numbered among the peace battalions, while some Communist states and Parties were consigned to the warlike forces. The peace-loving forces were united in singling out the avoidance of thermonuclear war as their overriding objective; they enthusiastically embraced the test-ban treaty and were opposed to the dissemination of nuclear weapons and the proliferation of nuclear powers. Acceptance of the test-ban treaty, in the Soviet view, became the litmus test of peace-loving tendencies.

Peking divided the world into nuclear and non-nuclear powers, ir-

[3] *Hung Chi*, editorial, February 6, 1964; translated in *The New York Times*, February 7, 1964.

respective of ideology or social systems. It saw the struggle as one between those who wanted to preserve their monopoly over nuclear weapons and those who wanted to break it. Whereas Moscow argued that proliferation was against the best interests of the "socialist camp" and would increase the possibility of war, the Chinese retorted that the capitalists already had a clear numerical advantage in nuclear weapons and that non-proliferation would freeze the West's advantage.

Concealed in all the verbiage was the implicit Chinese charge that a freeze of the thermonuclear status quo would give the white and developed countries a monopoly on nuclear weapons, which would continue to insure their domination over the non-white, underdeveloped nations of Asia, Africa, and Latin America, who would be denied nuclear weapons. That the Soviet Union was a Communist country was less significant in this connection than the fact that it was European, "white," and developed. It could not be assumed that Soviet interests and those of the underdeveloped countries, including China, were congruent. The Soviet claim that China and other countries could rely upon Soviet nuclear might in defense and promotion of their interests was viewed by Peking as amounting to an intolerable dependence upon the Soviet Union, which meant that in return for Soviet nuclear protection other countries would have to tailor their interests to coincide with those of the Soviet Union and thus become its dependent appendages.

When one slices through all of the invective, esoteric jargon, and self-serving rhetoric of the Sino-Soviet dispute, what emerges are two variants of the classic image of a world divided into revisionist* and status quo forces, with the Chinese enrolled among the revisionist forces and Moscow associated with those of the status quo. A principal objective of the test-ban treaty for the Soviet Union was to deny the forces of revisionism access to nuclear weapons. From Moscow's perspective, the threat came from those who wanted to alter the international status quo through resort to war, if necessary. These included both revolutionary and reactionary opponents of the status quo. Moscow considered both equally dangerous to Soviet interests. They included West German "revanchists," "madmen" in the United States, the Chinese Communist leadership, and the Parties that followed the Chinese lead.[4]

The Soviet leaders correctly perceived that the Soviet Union was the main target of all these forces, East and West, Communist and

---

* The reference to "revisionism" here and hereinafter does *not* imply use of this label in its specific Marxist-Leninist connotation, i.e., "rightist" deviation.

[4] *Pravda*, August 5, 1963.

non-Communist. And although the Soviet Union had only recently been the most revolutionary center in the world, its leaders were realistic enough to understand that revolutionary revisionism was likely to provoke counterrevolutionary revisionism and that, on balance, this would be detrimental to Soviet interests.

The Cuban missile debacle apparently convinced Khrushchev that Soviet interests could best be served by pursuing an essentially status quo foreign policy with residual traces of political and ideological revisionism. Soviet national and territorial objectives were largely satisfied, and Moscow found the existing distribution of power at least tolerable if not enthusiastically acceptable. This was particularly true with respect to the division of Europe, where the juridical status of East Germany and West Berlin constituted the only areas of concern and anxiety. Moscow's European allies were similarly inclined toward the status quo.

The nuclear test-ban treaty highlighted the transition of the Soviet Union from revolutionary global power to a mature state whose national goals have been largely satisfied and whose ideological goals have been largely eroded. The erosion of the Soviet commitment to violence and world revolution reflects the growing maturity of the Soviet Union and further signifies that the manipulation of a world revolutionary movement is no longer either indispensable or perhaps even desirable as an instrument of Soviet policy or purpose.

Khrushchev's repeated call for an international treaty outlawing the use of force in the settlement of territorial questions was a reflection of Moscow's relative satisfaction with the territorial status quo, while the Soviet signature on the test-ban treaty reflects Moscow's relative satisfaction with its status as the second of two global nuclear powers. Content with her state frontiers, equipped with a powerful arsenal of nuclear weapons, and surrounded with a retinue of client states in Eastern Europe, the Soviet Union remains revisionist only in the ideological sense. Ideology has become increasingly ritualistic as Moscow's passion to preserve national gains exceeds its passion to achieve ideological objectives.

Verbally, of course, the Soviet leaders deny that they have become partisans of the status quo, as Khrushchev did in December, 1963:

> No Marxist-Leninist ever interpreted peaceful coexistence of countries with different social systems as preservation of the *status quo,* as a sort of truce with imperialism, as a "safe conduct" against revolutionary processes of national and social liberation. No one applies this principle to the relations between imperialism and oppressed peoples, since the princi-

ple of coexistence by no means places a "veto" on the struggle of these peoples.[5]

But, contrary to Soviet expressions of intent, Soviet behavior and the objective consequences of Soviet policy unmistakably stamp the status quo character of her foreign policy, as the Chinese have correctly assessed.

What remains of Soviet ideological revisionism continues to be blunted for the following reasons: (1) It tends to stimulate ideological counter-revisionism in the United States, which manifests itself among the "madmen" who demand a foreign policy of "roll-back," "liberation," "export of counterrevolution," and "atomic blackmail." (2) It has a tendency to revive and reinforce all other proponents of violent change, especially in West Germany and Japan. Both countries have national claims against the Soviet Union and its client states. As the country most vulnerable to territorial revisionism, Moscow has a conspicuous interest in stifling territorial revisionism in general. (3) Soviet revisionism sustains and reinforces Chinese national and ideological revisionism, which is aimed in large part against the Soviet Union itself.

The Condominium Approach

Khrushchev's détente strategy assumed the faint but definite contours of a Soviet-American condominium, or dyarchy, in the international community, whereby the two super-powers would demarcate their respective areas of vital interest, define their area of common interest, delineate the status quo to be preserved, and establish the guidelines which would govern their competition in areas peripheral to their vital interests. Khrushchev came to believe that no problem of international relations could resist the imposition of a joint Soviet-American solution. Such a condominium would, in effect, ensure American non-intervention in areas of Soviet vital interests and Soviet non-intervention in areas of American vital interests. Thus Khrushchev had on various occasions stressed that "history has imposed upon our two peoples a great responsibility for the destiny of the world," and that as regards the two countries, "our interests do not clash directly anywhere, either territorially or economically." [6]

This approach was most pungently described by Peking with its customary self-serving rhetoric of exaggeration, but it was also discernible in the speeches of Soviet statesmen and in Soviet writings.

[5] *Pravda*, December 22, 1963.
[6] *Pravda*, December 31, 1961.

It finds reflection in two Soviet books published in 1965, *The Motive Forces of U.S. Foreign Policy* and *The U.S.S.R. and the U.S.A.—Their Political and Economic Relations.* Accordingly, the two books were pounced upon by Chinese critics as ample confirmation that the policy of the Brezhnev-Kosygin regime was indistinguishable from that of its predecessor. According to an official Chinese review, the first book

> . . . proclaims that "Soviet-American relations, the relations between the two greatest powers in the world, constitute the axis of world politics, the main foundation of international peace." Using the words of U.S. Secretary of State Rusk, it preaches that "the two great powers—the USSR and the U.S.A.—bear special responsibility for the destiny of the world and of mankind." It says that the Soviet Union "strives for peace and cooperation with the United States, realizing that Soviet-American relations are the primary thing in contemporary world politics and in the question of war or peace. . . ." The book stresses that an "extremely important feature in Soviet-American relations" is the so-called "community of national interests of the two countries." It says, "Except for the black spot—the U.S. participation in the military intervention against Soviet Russia from 1918 to 1920—Russian-American and Soviet-American relations have not been clouded by any military conflicts or wars." "At the present time, too, no territorial or economic disputes or conflicts exist between the two countries, and their national interests do not clash either on a world scale or on any regional scale." [7]

Hence, *Hung Chi* correctly noted, Moscow and Washington can shift the competitive aspects of their relations to the periphery of their vital interests:

> The book asserts that provided there is "peaceful coexistence" between the Soviet Union and the United States, "the competition between the two socio-economic systems and the ideological struggle between the two main antagonists on the international arena will proceed within the confines of broad economic, diplomatic, scientific, and cultural competition and cooperation, without sanguinary collisions and wars." [8]

Khrushchev's détente strategy was thus based upon two assumptions:

1. The Kennedy Administration represented the "sober" forces in the American "ruling class," who perceived a détente with Moscow to be in their self-interest and thus could be "trusted."

---

[7] "Confessions Concerning the Line of Soviet-U.S. Collaboration Pursued by the New Leaders of hte CPSU [*Hung Chi*, editorial, February 11, 1966]" (Peking: Foreign Language Press, 1966), pp. 3-4.

[8] *Ibid.*, p. 3.

2. The United States could speak for the entire West, and thus the détente would assume the configuration of an international condominium between the two major world powers.

As a consequence of the "condominium" Moscow appeared to harbor several expectations:

1. The Soviet Union and the United States together would retain overwhelming nuclear superiority and thus be able jointly to enforce the peace.
2. Japan and Germany would be prohibited from acquiring nuclear weapons and their revisionist ambitions blocked by joint Soviet-American action.
3. The nuclear development of France and China would be considerably inhibited and retarded.
4. China's expansionist aspirations would be contained and blocked by the United States with the tacit support of the Soviet Union.
5. The "madmen" in the United States would be isolated and kept out of power.
6. A general relaxation of international tensions would ensue, which would undercut the attractiveness of the appeals for more aggressive action. Without a Soviet "threat," Khrushchev reasoned, internal social revolution in various parts of the world would no longer be perceived as a threat by the United States.
7. A rapid growth in Soviet economic development would take place with a corresponding rise in the standard of living.

Deficiencies in Khrushchev's Policy

The entire structure of Khrushchev's détente strategy rested upon the assumption that the Kennedy Administration represented the "sober" forces in the United States and that they would continue to determine American policy. This strategy implicitly posed a serious threat to the social position, role, and interests of powerful socio-institutional groups in the Soviet Union, like the Party apparatus, heavy-industrial managers, and the traditional military. Instead of executing his détente policy so that their interests might be painlessly accommodated, Khrushchev brusquely attempted an "end run" by appealing to other constituencies whose interests would be enhanced by his policy. Khrushchev's strategy and behavior also exposed the Soviet Union to new diplomatic and security vulnerabilities. This, too, contributed to a tactical agreement between Khrushchev's associates and his opposition. His opportunistic behavior in going outside the normal arena of Soviet politics, together with his capricious judgments, frightened his own partisans. Khrushchev's policies threatened the interests of his factional opposition; his behavior alienated his own faction. These currents merged to topple him in October, 1964.

It remains a matter of speculation to what extent the background
of his ouster included the concern of the Soviet elite that Khrushchev's détente policy threatened to expose the Soviet Union to new
vulnerabilities. To some of Khrushchev's colleagues it may have appeared that the Soviet Union was being cleverly encircled by shrewd
American diplomacy, aided by an inept and over-zealous Khrushchev,
who had not adequately covered either his eastern or his western
flank. The cutting edge of Peking's revisionist aspirations was now
being turned against the Soviet Union in revenge, without any assurance of a restraining influence by the United States at a time when
West Germany's revisionist edge had not yet been blunted. In August,
1964, for example, Mao Tse-tung virtually invited Japan, East Germany, Poland, Rumania, and Finland to join Peking in dismembering
the Soviet Union:

> There are too many places occupied by the Soviet Union. In correspond-
> ence with the Yalta agreement, the Soviet Union, under the pretext of
> guaranteeing the independence of Mongolia, actually put that country
> under its rule. . . . In 1954, when Khrushchev and Bulganin arrived in
> China, we raised this question, but they refused to talk with us. They
> have appropriated part of Rumania. Detaching part of East Germany,
> they drove out the local inhabitants to the Western area. Detaching
> part of Poland, they included it in Russia and as compensation gave
> Poland part of East Germany. The same thing happened to Finland.
> They detached everything that could be detached. Some people have said
> that Sinkiang Province and the territory to the north of the Amur River
> must be included in the Soviet Union. The USSR is concentrating troops
> on its borders[9]

Khrushchev, in effect, was relying for Soviet security upon the uncertain good will of the Kennedy Administration and upon the even
more dubious trust of his successor, who was an unknown quantity.

Anxieties and Uncertainties

Against this background of Soviet anxiety and uncertainty concerning Khrushchev's possible misperceptions of the Kennedy Administration's intentions and his possible miscalculation of the magnitude of the common interest between Moscow and Washington, the
assassination of President Kennedy could only intensify these apprehensions. Now the Soviet leaders were seriously in danger of being
victimized by their own fantasies about "ultras," "extremists," and
"madmen."

Deciphering Kennedy's motives and intentions was difficult and

[9] *Pravda,* September 2, 1964.

treacherous enough, but their initial doubts about Kennedy had been dispelled in the minds of the Khrushchev faction after 1,000 days of dealing with him. Besides, Khrushchev and Kennedy had experienced a number of harrowing crises together, and a certain mutual respect had developed between the two men, so that an element of "trust" in their relations was conceivable. In short, Kennedy was a known quantity to Khrushchev, whose strategy rested upon the conviction that this known quantity would continue in power through 1972. Actually, Khrushchev's policies were based upon a virtually predetermined assumption that the "sober" group would continue to prevail through any administration.

During the first six months of the Johnson Administration, the Soviet leadership remained non-committal about the character of the Johnson presidency. It was obvious that the Soviet leadership was concerned lest the delicate balance of forces which it detected in the American leadership be upset in favor of the "ultras," whose activities and views were given increasing prominence in the Soviet press.

These doubts and uncertainties continued into the months of the United States election campaign of 1964. If Lyndon B. Johnson was re-elected, Soviet observers seem to have reasoned, the uncertainty would continue; if Barry Goldwater were to become president, all of Khrushchev's assumptions and expectations would be shattered beyond repair.

The tendency of Khrushchev to accept Johnson as a spokesman for the "sober" group in America probably not only alarmed his conservative detractors, who had never accepted his perception of an American "ruling class" divided into "sober" and "mad" groups, and the traditional military (such as Marshal Rodion Malinovsky), who shared an image of the United States with the conservatives, but also frightened his own factional associates as well, who viewed his clumsy and capricious style with apprehension.

Khrushchev's ouster thus came hard on the heels of a number of events which pointed toward crises in Sino-Soviet and Soviet-American relations. What their relevance was can only be surmised. At any rate, the displacement of Khrushchev did not resolve Soviet doubts or end Soviet backstage debate about the entire détente policy.

Soviet Diplomatic Strategy after Khrushchev

Unlike Khrushchev, the new Brezhnev-Kosygin team was probably prepared for any contingency which might develop as a result of the American election, ready to plug the gaps in Khrushchev's détente strategy if the détente policy continued, and also amenable to try a new approach to Peking.

The Soviet Image of the Johnson Administration[10]

For more than three years the Brezhnev-Kosygin team has been taking its measure of the Johnson Administration, and while the latter has not been consigned to the "mad" category (this would have generated irreversible and highly unpalatable implications for Soviet policy and behavior), neither has it been classified as "sober." The doubts and uncertainties about the Johnson Administration persist in Moscow and probably find expression in different ways among various Soviet leaders. Although voices uttering different views are periodically heard in the Soviet press, the dominant view in official Moscow is evidently that the Administration is subject to pressures from both "doves" and "hawks," and this accounts for the vacillation in its policies and behavior. It is noteworthy, however, that Anastas Mikoyan, once the most outspoken advocate of the view that Washington is dominated by "sober" men, was dropped from the new team, perhaps as being too committed to the Khrushchev line.

The image of the Johnson Administration held by the Brezhnev-Kosygin regime is not identical with Khrushchev's image under Kennedy. Whereas Kennedy was perceived as a representative of the "sober" forces in the American "ruling class," Johnson has not been viewed as a member of this group. Voices are still to be heard which seem to assign Johnson to the "sober" camp, while others consign him to a more "bellicose" or "aggressive" wing; still others emphasize that he tries to satisfy both groups and thus vacillates in his own posture.

In May, 1965, after the Administration had involved itself more deeply in the Vietnam war, Brezhnev charged that Johnson had betrayed the American public (and, in effect, double-crossed the Soviet leaders) by contravening his campaign promises. President Johnson, he charged, had campaigned "under the slogan of allegiance to peace and fidelity to the traditions of Franklin Roosevelt," and the American voters,

> aware of the catastrophe a world war would mean for the United States in today's conditions, put their trust in the politician [Johnson] who in campaign speeches had spoken out for peace and a realistic approach to international problems.[11]

[10] See also Chapter 7.
[11] *Pravda,* May 9, 1965.

The following month, Premier Kosygin bluntly charged:

> The government of the United States is in essence pursuing the foreign-policy line proposed by Goldwater at the time of the elections but rejected by the American people. It is carrying out an aggressive policy directed against the countries of socialism, against the states that have liberated themselves from colonial domination, against the revolutionary movement of the peoples.[12]

Moscow's perceptions of the Johnson Administration are also shaped by its view of Chinese intent and behavior, and while it may still have doubts about Johnson, it seems to have none with respect to Mao Tse-tung. Indeed, it has blamed the Chinese leader for discouraging a Vietnamese settlement in the hope that a prolongation of the conflict would inevitably force a confrontation between Moscow and Washington, which the existing regime fervently seeks to avoid. Thus, in a letter circulated among friendly Communist Parties, dated February 23, 1966, the Soviet leaders alleged:

> . . . the Chinese leaders need a lengthy Vietnam war to maintain international tensions, to represent China as a "besieged fortress." There is every reason to assert that it is one of the goals of the policy of the Chinese leadership in the Vietnam question to promote a military conflict between the USSR and the United States. They want a clash of the USSR with the United States so that they may, as they say themselves, "sit on the mountain and watch the fight of the tigers." New facts constantly prove the readiness of the Chinese leaders to sacrifice the interests of the national liberation movement to their chauvinist big-power plans.[13]

For their part, the Chinese retorted that the new leaders were plotting with the United States to encircle China:

> You have worked hand in glove with the United States in a whole series of dirty deals inside and outside the United Nations. In close coordination with the counterrevolutionary "global strategy" of United States imperialism, you are now actively trying to build a ring of encirclement around socialist China. Not only have you excluded yourselves from the international united front of all the peoples against United States imperialism and its lackeys, you have even aligned yourselves with United States imperialism, the main enemy of the peoples of the world, and

[12] *Pravda,* June 19, 1965.
[13] *The New York Times,* March 24, 1966.

established a holy alliance against China, against the movement, and against the Marxist-Leninists.[14]

In spite of all, the dominant view in Moscow has been that the "sober" groups would ultimately prevail, particularly if the Vietnamese war is settled, since this is presumed to be the main inspiration of the more aggressive forces in American society.

The contrast between the cautious, prudent, and restrained style and tempo of the Brezhnev-Kosygin foreign policy and the ebullient, highly idiosyncratic style of the Khrushchev era, with its exercises in adventurism, bluffing, and vulgarity, should not obscure some essential continuities between the two foreign policy lines. The two sets of policies share a common point of departure in pursuit of a common goal but differ in methods and strategies.

One conspicuous departure from the Khrushchev policy was a determined attempt to heal the rift with China, which was made promptly after Khrushchev's ouster and permitted to linger for over a year. Another was to reassert the Soviet presence in Vietnam, and a third but less obvious departure was a new approach to the West designed to provide greater security against Germany. None of these departures signified a shift away from the top priority item in Soviet foreign policy—the avoidance of thermonuclear war with the United States—but rather suggested that the leadership thought the new approaches need not be incompatible with a Soviet-American rapprochement.

The Brezhnev-Kosygin Strategy: Double Encirclement

The retirement of Khrushchev did not solve Moscow's problems of West Germany and China, which the new regime inherited from its predecessor, but it did set the stage for a fresh review and re-examination of policy. The new leaders were certainly aware that West Germany and China were problems which transcended personalities, systems, and ideologies. Moreover, the two countries pose different problems for Moscow. China has already reasserted itself and has successfully rebuffed Soviet hegemonial ambitions in the Far East and established an effective barrier to any further expansion of Russian power southward. Germany, on the other hand, remains divided and thus constitutes as yet only a potential threat to the eroding hegemonial position of Moscow in East Central Europe, either because West Germany might become an instrument of American policy against the Soviet Union or because, under certain circumstances, West

---

[14] Chinese reply to the Soviet invitation to send a delegation to the XXIII Congress of the CPSU, in *The New York Times,* March 24, 1966.

Germany might be able to involve the United States in a war with Moscow in pursuit of her own aspirations.

Moscow perceives of the German threat as real but *potential* or *latent,* and Soviet policy is designed to prevent its development, whereas the Chinese threat is viewed as much more immediate and ominous.

In the Far East, the Soviet Union has envisaged the United States as a partner in the encirclement and containment of China and thus, with some reservations, desires a United States presence in that area. On the other hand, in Europe the United States is viewed as the chief bulwark of West Germany and the main source of her power and influence.

While the détente with the United States established an over-all strategic balance between the Communist and non-Communist worlds and minimized the threat of direct confrontation and possible annihilation, it also diminished the need for bloc unity and afforded individual member-states the luxury of allowing their submerged and latent local and national grievances against one another (inside and outside blocs) to surface. This serves to create instability on the periphery of both power-blocs and disturbs the equilibrium, which was artificially frozen by the bi-polarization of power after World War II.

It is the threat to local balances on the eastern and western marches of the Soviet Union that has agitated the new regime in Moscow. Moscow has sought to maintain the status quo in the West by restructuring a new configuration in the local balance of power, while in the East it has sought to preserve the status quo by maintaining the existing balance of forces.

Isolation and Containment of China

Whereas the United States may have embarrassed, alarmed, and humiliated the Soviet leadership by its conduct in Vietnam, it poses no threat to the Soviet Union; nor does it aim to upset the status quo in the Communist world. The Chinese leaders, on the other hand, seek to overturn the present leadership of the Soviet Union and have hinted that they might even resort to force to redeem China's "lost" lands now "occupied" by the Soviet Union. Thus, on February 23, 1966, the CPSU informed other Communist Parties that Peking was even contemplating war:

> The idea is obstinately being suggested to the Chinese people that it is necessary to prepare for a military conflict with the USSR. The CPSU Central Committee has already informed the fraternal parties that the Chinese side is provoking border conflicts. Such conflicts have again in-

creased in recent months. . . . At the same time, allegations are being spread to the effect that the Soviet Union unlawfully holds Chinese territory in the Far East. The official Chinese representative in the bilateral consultations on border questions threatened directly that the CPR authorities would consider "other ways" of settling the territorial question and stated: "It is not out of the question that we will try to restore historical rights." But the CPR has no "historical rights." The territories of which the CCP leadership now talks have never belonged to China.[15]

The recrudescence of Chinese expansionist ambitions has left the Soviet Union little choice but to pursue a policy of isolating, encircling, and containing China. The efforts, immediately after the ouster of Khrushchev, to heal the rift with Peking were to no avail.

Since the Plenum of October, 1964, the CPSU Central Committee has done everything possible to normalize relations with the CCP and to insure unity of action in the struggle against the common imperialist enemy despite existing differences of view. In this connection we considered the fact that the interests of the Socialist camp and of the entire Communist movement will suffer from the continued differences of view.[16]

Moscow views the United States as its main partner in the encirclement and containment of China, with India and Indonesia playing subsidiary roles.

The United States has always subscribed to an "Open Door" policy in the Orient. The policy implies a door open to all outsiders, not only the United States, since several outside powers are necessary to ensure their presence and are thus mutually reinforcing. The presence of peripheral powers serves to displace a hegemonial equilibrium with a balance of power involving several actors. As a corollary to the "Open Door" policy, the United States, since 1905, has encouraged Russian presence in the area as a counterpoise to Japanese ambitions, and after the Bolshevik Revolution, when a power vacuum developed in the Russian Far East, it was the presence of United States troops and American insistence on the territorial integrity of Russia which deterred the Japanese from detaching the Russian Far East in one form or another, thus allowing the bogus Far Eastern Republic to be reabsorbed into the Soviet state. Moscow is also not unmindful of the fact that Japan's attack upon Manchuria and her further ambitions in the area were instrumental in the recognition of the Soviet Union by the Roosevelt Administration.

Historically, the presence of both the United States and Russia in

[15] *The New York Times,* March 24, 1966.
[16] *Ibid.*

the Far East has been mutually reinforcing. Russian and American interests have come into direct conflict in the Far East only when the indigenous powers have been weakened by internal strife or defeat in war. This was the case after World War II when the defeat of Japan created a power vacuum which could not be filled by a weakened and divided China and thus led to a direct confrontation between Moscow and Washington, and the two indigenous powers of the region, China and Japan, temporarily became instruments of Soviet and American policy respectively.

The reassertion of China's bid for hegemony in the Far East thus once again endangers the interests of both the United States and the Soviet Union, as they interpret them, just as Japan's challenge did in 1931. Since Peking has publicly repudiated Moscow's claim to being an Asian power and has declared the Soviet Union to be a European power "in Asia," the Soviet leaders are under no illusions concerning Peking's conception of the role Moscow is to assume in Asian affairs. Furthermore, the Chinese have claimed virtually the entire Soviet Far East including the Maritime Province (with Vladivostok). Similarly, Peking is determined to drive American power and influence out of the Far East and thus slam the door against both Moscow and Washington, the two remaining foreign "imperialist" powers in East Asia.

Khrushchev's downfall provided an occasion for Moscow to review its relations with China and its Far Eastern policy in general. Essentially, this led to two departures from Khrushchev's policy. The first was a decision to attempt once again to arrest the deterioration in Sino-Soviet relations. The second was to reassert Soviet interest in Southeast Asia and restore Soviet influence and involvement in Vietnam. Khrushchev had virtually dissociated Moscow from Southeast Asia, fatalistically abandoning the area during the Sino-Soviet conflict, assuming that both race and geography favored the Chinese. The escalation of the war and American bombardment of North Vietnam, however, confronted Moscow with serious problems involving the prestige and credibility of the Soviet Union's obligation to defend all socialist states from attack—a commitment which was first made in 1960 (and repeated thereafter):

> Today the whole world has had an opportunity to receive assurance that anyone who dares to encroach upon the inviolability of the Soviet Union's borders, as well as those of other socialist countries, will receive a crushing rebuff. The Warsaw Treaty Organization is based on the principle of "all for one and one for all." The Soviet government has frequently stated that the borders of all its true friends—the socialist countries—will be defended by the Soviet Union exactly as if they were its own borders.

This is how we understand proletarian internationalism and this is how all the peoples of the socialist countries understand it.[17]

Apparently Khrushchev had been unwilling to make even a gesture which would have satisfied the formalities of Moscow's existing obligations toward North Vietnam. The Soviet Union was in danger of becoming an object of ridicule, some Soviet officials held, and the credibility of its commitments was subject to serious erosion.

The reassertion of Soviet influence in Southeast Asia was designed to serve four objectives:

1. To reassert the credibility of the Soviet promise and ability to protect its allies against American power;
2. To find a common ground for a rapprochement with China, whose joint support of North Vietnam would maximize chances for a settlement;
3. To re-establish a measure of control over a situation which might conceivably involve the Soviet Union in another confrontation with the United States, which Moscow avidly sought to avoid; and
4. To be in a position to influence a settlement of the Vietnamese conflict which would not subvert the détente with the United States.

The second and fourth objectives were and are incompatible, but apparently the Brezhnev-Kosygin regime thought that a reconciliation with China and a détente with the United States were possible simultaneously, provided Moscow approached the whole problem in a different way—or at least acted as if no choice between these orientations needed to be made.

An Olive Branch to China Rebuffed

The Soviet approach to Peking was apparently based upon the conviction that the Sino-Soviet dispute had been exacerbated by the personality conflict between Mao and Khrushchev and hence was irreconcilable while both remained in authority. The Brezhnev-Kosygin regime may have felt obliged to explore whether Peking was prepared to find a face-saving formula to heal the split. But, according to Moscow's later review of its efforts to heal the breach, Peking rebuffed every Soviet overture:

We submitted an extensive program for normalizing Chinese-Soviet relations at both the Party and the state level. This program included proposals on implementing bilateral meetings of delegations of the CPSU and the CCP on the highest level, on the mutual discontinuation of polemics, concrete proposals on extending Chinese-Soviet trade and scien-

[17] *Pravda*, May 14, 1960.

tific, technical and cultural cooperation, and on coordinating the foreign policy activities of the CPR and USSR.[18]

The Chinese, for their part, revealed that they had obstinately attempted to impose their views upon the new Soviet leaders and extract a confession of "repentance" which they must have known was unacceptable:

> Since Khrushchev's downfall, we have advised the new leaders of the CPSU on a number of occasions to make a fresh start. We have done everything we could but you have not shown the slightest repentance. Since coming to power, the new leaders of the CPSU have gone farther and farther down the road of revisionism, splittism and great-power chauvinism. The moment you came to power, you declared that you would resolutely carry out the Khrushchev revisionist general line of the XX and XXII Congresses. You told us to our faces that there was not a shade of difference between Khrushchev and yourself on the question of the international Communist movement or of relations with China.[19]

In Search of a Vietnamese Settlement

Khrushchev had disassociated Moscow from the Vietnam war except in the most perfunctory way. In his speech of January 6, 1961, he conspicuously failed to classify the Vietcong uprising as a "just" war, although the Vietminh war against the French was so categorized and described as successful and terminal. Khrushchev's lack of interest in the Vietnam war probably stemmed from a desire to avoid a possible confrontation with the United States in Southeast Asia and perhaps also from a belief that Hanoi would ultimately cast its lot with Peking.

Moscow may have perceived in the American escalation of the war in Vietnam an opportunity to facilitate simultaneously a reconciliation with Peking and also a détente with the United States. But Peking was not interested in settling the war, even on Hanoi's terms, since from the Chinese perspective a Vietnamese settlement would clear the way for a full resumption of the Soviet-American détente. As a consequence North Vietnam was caught in the Sino-Soviet crossfire while being pounded by the United States.

The Vietnam war impaled the Soviet leaders on the horns of a painful dilemma. By restoring the Soviet presence in Hanoi, Khrushchev's successors hoped to regain a measure of control and influence over a matter vitally affecting their interests elsewhere, but they simultaneously incurred the risk that failure to achieve a settlement

[18] *The New York Times,* March 24, 1966.
[19] *Ibid.*

could only worsen relations with Hanoi, Peking, and Washington. Soviet exploration of a reconciliation with China thus did not necessarily signify an intention to repudiate its détente policy, but rather a drive to minimize sources of friction in its foreign relations. Unlike previous Soviet regimes, which frequently perceived opportunities to muddy international waters and were interested in sustaining a degree of tension on the international scene, the Brezhnev-Kosygin team has shown a passion for tension reduction and interest in international stability. The Tashkent settlement between India and Pakistan, engineered by Kosygin, is indicative of this reorientation in Soviet policy.

In retrospect, Khrushchev's judgment that Soviet and Chinese interests and objectives were incompatible appears to have been valid, especially after Mao's startling and gratuitous claim to some 500,000 square miles of Soviet territory in the summer of 1964. While Khrushchev had apparently judged the Chinese situation well if not wisely, the abortive attempt of his successors to heel the rupture was not without its compensations. The basic miscalculation of the Brezhnev-Kosygin team was the obverse of the fundamental correctness of Khrushchev's judgment. As long as avoidance of thermonuclear war remained the top priority item in Soviet foreign policy, Soviet and Chinese interests were bound to collide. China's price for a reconciliation was a complete repudiation and reversal of Soviet policy, including a repudiation of the resolutions of the XX, XXI and XXII Party Congresses. This Moscow was not willing to do. Thus, before the end of 1965, Sino-Soviet polemics were resumed in more aggravated form and were further exacerbated the following year by the sharp factional conflict which broke out in Peking.

What the new team in Moscow managed to convey in the process of dealing with Peking was a novel posture of sensitivity, moderation, and rationality, in contrast to Peking's obstinacy, dogmatism, and rigidity. This served further to isolate China in the Communist world. But Moscow's sobering experience with the Chinese could not but impel it to reintensify the uneasy search for a détente with the United States, made both more urgent and more difficult by the continuing conflict in Vietnam.

Soviet Policy in the West

If it is a major Soviet objective to contain China in the East, a major goal of its diplomacy in the West is to forge a preventive containment of West Germany. But whereas the American presence is necessary in the Far East to encircle China, Moscow views the American presence in Europe as an obstacle to its policy with respect to the German Federal Republic.

Hence, current Soviet policy in the West is designed to eject the United States from Europe, not so much to weaken the United States or to make West Germany more vulnerable (although these are subsidiary objectives) as to remove the protective umbrella of American power under which West Germany might develop into a major military power in her own right. Soviet leaders have viewed with increasing concern the steady rise in West Germany's power and influence. Especially since France's virtual defection, they have claimed to perceive an evolving Washington-Bonn axis within NATO, which might develop a momentum of its own. They see three possible dangers which might develop: (1) the United States might choose to permit the full revival of German military power as a bulwark against the East; (2) West Germany might, in pursuit of her own revisionist ambitions, set into motion a chain of events which would involve the United States and the Soviet Union in war; (3) West German power might evolve to the point where, if it decides to assert an independent policy and chart its own course, its containment by the United States would require measures which Washington might choose not to invoke.

It is the third possibility which has probably disturbed the Soviet leaders most. Just as China managed to develop its power under the umbrella of Soviet protection and then declared its independence of Soviet policy, Moscow sees the real possibility of a similar performance by West Germany. The sudden outburst in West Germany of vehement opposition to a nuclear non-proliferation treaty during Kosygin's visit to Britain in 1967 surprised many in the West and could only reinforce the Soviet conviction that influential forces in West Germany secretly harbor a lust for nuclear weapons.

Moscow seeks to ease the United States out of Europe so as to deprive West Germany of its protective umbrella, which would clear the way for Moscow to devise new arrangements to ensure the maintenance of the status quo in Europe. It would, of course, also create other opportunities for Soviet diplomacy, giving Moscow greater flexibility in pursuing whatever objectives it might choose in Western Europe.

While the Soviet approach to China proved abortive, the new approach to the West has been bearing fruit. Khrushchev may have perceived that the Soviet Union could hardly expect American cooperation in an encirclement and containment of Germany, and during his last few months in power rumors were rampant that he was planning a deal with West Germany at East Germany's expense. If this was so, the new regime reversed this strategy almost immediately, and all talk about a special deal with West Germany in exchange for generous lines of credit and other concessions suddenly ceased. Just as Washington's approach to Eastern Europe aims to isolate East Germany, the Brezhnev-Kosygin approach to Western Europe is designed to isolate and encircle West Germany. Instead of relying on the condominium approach, the new strategy is to deal with Great Britain and France individually, on the assumption that their interests *vis-à-vis* West Germany are different from those of the United States.

Khrushchev's successors perceived that Moscow's willingness to pursue a détente with the United States enabled London and Paris to resume an autonomous foreign policy. Once the Soviet threat was lifted, London and Paris could pursue policies independent of the United States. Since the American presence in Europe not only shielded Western Europe from Soviet power but also implicitly served to protect Britain and France from a possible German revival, a withdrawal of the United States from Europe on the basis of a détente with Moscow would remove the main restraining influence on German power.

With respect to Germany, the Brezhnev-Kosygin regime thus perceives a common interest between Moscow, on the one hand, and London and Paris, on the other, which is not shared by the United States. Moscow's approach signifies a subtle bid to establish an informal containment of Germany as a part of the crypto-entente arrangement with those two countries. Such an encirclement would be reliable because it would rest upon the self-interest of the three countries. It cannot be said that London and Paris were totally unresponsive to these subtle overtures.

The multi-pronged Soviet approach is thus designed not so much to divide Western Europe and open it to Soviet penetration, but rather to protect Moscow's western flank at a time when the main danger appears on the eastern horizon. While it cannot rely upon the self-interest of the United States to contain and limit German power, it can rely upon British and French self-interest to resist the revival of German power.

It should be noted that, while it may not be the intention of the regime in Moscow to weaken the West by this strategy in order to make it vulnerable to Soviet attack or penetration, objectively it does expose the three countries to potential hazards, should the intentions of the regime change, or should a new militant faction come to power in Moscow, or should the present strategic balance change radically in favor of the Soviet Union.

As long as the threat from Moscow was more immediate and real than the threat from Germany, the United States, according to the Soviet view, could impose an ideologically-inspired policy upon the West as a whole, subsume the long-range German threat, and actually sponsor a partial revival of German military power. Once the Soviet threat was lifted, however, the Soviet leaders perceived that West Germany's growing power in NATO and America's increasing reliance upon Bonn as its chief ally in Europe posed a more immediate threat to London and Paris than did Moscow. This view has been outlined by a Polish international affairs expert in a leading Soviet journal:

> Up to the early 1960's, the United States as a rule managed to impose its own political ideas as regards Germany on the West European countries, although these, far from being enthusiastic, even objected to them. It was not until the balance of forces turned against the U.S.A. that the West European countries were able to pursue a more independent policy on the German question among others.[20]

With the United States out of Europe, West Germany's ambitions would be kept in check by the European status quo powers acting in concert. This is the main thrust of the periodic Soviet call for a conference on European security. Thus, in response to a question concerning the possible American participation in such a European security conference, Kosygin replied at his Paris press conference:

> In our opinion the countries of Europe could gather to discuss the situation on the European continent with the aim of easing tension and ensuring security in Europe. As to U.S. participation in this conference, it seems to me that this is a question that should be decided by the European countries themselves. When they do decide the question, you will receive an answer to it.[21]

At the same press conference, Kosygin lucidly described the status quo which Moscow seeks to preserve in Europe:

> I think the major contribution that the Federal Republic of Germany can make to the solution of the problem of European security is that it must have a clear and accurate conception of the situation in Europe, where two German states exist—the GDR [German Democratic Republic] and the FRG—and no forces from outside can change this situation. Any other judgments on this score are unrealistic. This is the first circumstance. The second is that the boundaries in Europe that were formed after World War II are inviolable. Moreover, West Germany must renounce

[20] L. Pastusiak, "Dangerous Bonn-Washington Deal," *International Affairs*, No. 7 (July, 1966), p. 45.
[21] *Pravda*, December 5, 1966.

forever any claims on nuclear weapons. If the FRG recognizes these circumstances, it will make a great contribution to the cause of easing tension in Europe and to the cause of ensuring European security.[22]

Khrushchev's successors do not perceive in de Gaulle's ambitions and anxieties the policies of a front man for nameless French extremists (which apparently was the view of Khrushchev). Rather they view de Gaulle's attitude towards the United States as reflecting a profound conflict over the future of Germany's role in Europe. De Gaulle's emphasis on the "grandeur" of France is perceived as symbolic of his intention to establish and preserve a clear and permanent position of military superiority *vis-à-vis* Germany, which de Gaulle views as France's eternal and natural rival for paramountcy in Western Europe.

> France's withdrawal from the NATO military structure has enabled her to regain freedom of action, which naturally strengthens her positions in the world arena. This step has also removed the danger of France being automatically involved in a world conflict against her free will which, in the nuclear age, would jeopardize the future of the entire country. . . .
> The Soviet Union has always emphasized France's rights as a world power particularly responsible for European security. Naturally, this attitude of the USSR makes it easier for France to defend her rights and interests in the world arena and, in particular, to rebuff the attempts of the United States and West Germany to dictate their will. It is no accident that de Gaulle wrote in his memoirs that the solidarity of the two countries "is in keeping with the natural state of affairs as regards both the German menace and the Anglo-Saxon desire for hegemony."[23]

The Franco-Soviet rapprochement is described in almost rhapsodic terms as not stemming from "temporary expediency," but as "a long-standing tradition to maintain mutual contacts and act jointly in politics," [24] which is frankly put forward as nothing less than a policy of encircling Germany:

> . . . In these circumstances, the interests of the Soviet Union and France dictate the imperative need to join their efforts so as to prevent a dangerous source of tension in the center of Europe.
> Many commentators point out that the interests of the two countries coincide on such important problems of European security as preventing

[22] *Ibid.*
[23] Y. Nikolaev, "Soviet-French Relations—An Important Factor of World Politics," *International Affairs*, No. 12 (December, 1966), p. 12.
[24] N. Yuriev, "Soviet-French Cooperation and European Security," *International Affairs*, No. 6 June, 1966, p. 7.

West Germany from gaining access to nuclear weapons and the inviolability of the existing frontiers.[25]

Britain's interest in isolating and encircling Germany is not viewed in Moscow as being as natural and durable as is the French interest. At times Britain has not been averse to a revival of German military power as a counterpoise to either Russia or France, or both. Furthermore, the Anglo-American relationship is viewed as more intimate and durable than the Franco-American relationship and hence less susceptible to subversion. Whereas French and American national interests may actually come into direct conflict over Germany, it is likely that Anglo-American problems will reflect themselves as differences over policy rather than as a conflict of national interests. Thus, while it is plausible for Moscow to believe that the American presence might be excluded from the continent, it is not likely that it can be expelled from the British Islands.

Nevertheless, the present Soviet leadership views the Wilson Government as at least partly amenable to its encirclement strategy, provided that it is muted and played in low key, recognizing that British policy with respect to Germany is based on fleeting expediency rather than a durable vital national interest as in the case of France.

The present Soviet leaders thus aim for a relationship with Great Britain which falls somewhere in between the crypto-entente with France and the strategic détente with the United States.

Implications of Current Soviet Diplomacy

Khrushchev's détente policy and its implications for the world Communist movement emerge, in retrospect, not as simply reflections of his personal idiosyncrasies but as a realistic course corresponding to the vital interests of the Soviet Union as a global power. This policy could be executed within a different priority of internal interests (heavy industry over light, armaments over butter, etc.), carried out with greater or lesser flexibility, prosecuted with greater or lesser enthusiasm, implemented with more or less finesse, and compressed within the shell of a "harder" or "softer" line, but any Soviet group which placed survival at the top of its priority list would have to seek some form of rapprochement with the United States to maximize its chances for survival. Khrushchev in his own bungling way had intuitively grasped the essentials of a realistic foreign policy. The challenge of Communist China made it impossible for Moscow to con-

---

[25] Nikolaev, *op. cit.,* p. 13.

tinue its half-century of oscillation between being a state and the
center of a world revolutionary movement. Moscow had to choose
between survival and doctrinal virtue. It had chosen the former,
leaving the latter to Peking, which need not yet decide between the
two.

Moscow's decision to seek a rapprochement with the United States
and the American response plunged both alliance systems into disarray. Priorities in the policies of more than a score of states are in
the process of being restructured, and various realignments are likely
to take shape. This process will be accelerated if an over-all strategic
détente between the United States and the Soviet Union becomes
a durable reality, since it will provide a protective umbrella for other
states to resurrect demands upon one another.

Just as the Soviet decision to give higher priority to a détente with
the United States than to China's national hegemonial interests
alienated China from Russia, the United States may have to choose
whether to place a higher priority on a détente with the Soviet Union
than on its support for West Germany's territorial and other national
claims. Moscow's strategy is to isolate West Germany, just as China
has been isolated. One of the nightmares of Western statesmen has
been a replay of the Rapallo scenario, but this is hardly a likely prospect at this time.

Today the Soviet Union is a global power, while Germany is a
dismembered state still slightly tainted by its Nazi past; today, the
Soviet Union holds East Germany in thrall and supports Polish positions on the boundary question and thus holds many prizes which
Bonn would like to retrieve; but what can Bonn give in return? The
relationship is totally asymmetrical. Furthermore, there is reason to
believe that Moscow is implacably committed to a divided Germany,
and there is hardly a conceivable circumstance under which the
Soviet Union might find a reunited Germany in its interest. Even the
hypothetical vision of a united Communist Germany can hardly be a
cause for jubilation in the Kremlin after the Chinese experience. The
Rapallo nightmare of Western statesmen is matched or exceeded
by the Soviet nightmare of being caught between two Communist
great powers with territorial and other national grievances against
Russia.

The erosion of NATO, which has been a consistent goal of Soviet
foreign policy, contributes in turn to the dissolution of the Warsaw
Pact, which Rumania already considers obsolete and superfluous. This,
of course, is an unintended consequence of Soviet policy. The absence
of a Western coalition not only contributes to the erosion of the
Eastern bloc but further encourages the smaller Communist countries

to make their own arrangements with individual countries of Western Europe and thus creates the possibilities of new realignments. The greater the number of ties established with Western countries and the greater the number of Western countries involved, the greater will be the areas of autonomy for the smaller Communist states; and in the absence of a Western threat, these ties cannot be viewed by Moscow as seriously detrimental to its security and vital interests.

Soviet Foreign Policy at the Crossroads

After 50 years of the Soviet state, the successors to Lenin, Stalin, and Khrushchev face painful problems in foreign policy which demand resolution. The Soviet leaders must decide finally whether they are directing a state or a movement; in the face of the Chinese challenge and American pressures, the current transitional attempt to behave like a state while hanging on to the rhetoric of revolution cannot be sustained indefinitely. And if they choose to play out their role as a global power, the Soviet leaders must decide whether to challenge the United States once again for paramountcy or settle for second place, whether to continue to postpone the maximum utilization of scarce resources for internal development in order to maximize foreign-policy options and the achievement of diplomatic goals. Moscow must also decide whether to seek spheres of influence on four continents or retrench to the Eurasian land mass. No matter what the decisions, they will be cause for renewed factional conflict.

There is substantial evidence to suggest that the Soviet leadership is divided over the direction of its next major moves in foreign policy. As a consequence, most decisions have postponed rather than resolved existing differences of opinion. It would be an over-simplification to divide the Soviet ruling group into "hawks" and "doves"; but it is true that the sharpest point of internal factional conflict is over the allocation of resources, which frequently divides the Soviet leadership into two broad groupings: those advocating a greater relaxation of international tensions, a retreat from overcommitments in foreign policy, and a demand that peripheral international disputes be resolved through compromise and mutual concessions; and those advocating a build-up in Soviet strategic capabilities, perhaps even to the point of challenging the United States for strategic pre-eminence, greater assistance to allies under attack to whom the Soviet Union is committed in one form or another, and the deferral of maximizing internal development in the interests of national security.

It would be grossly incorrect to characterize the second group as being made up entirely of expansionist-minded or ideologically-oriented leaders, although both types are undoubtedly included.

Rather, it is, on the whole, a grouping which is skeptical of United States intentions and has little confidence in lasting international stabilization. Instead it envisions a continuous period of challenge and response between the two global powers. It does not rule out the possibility that China may become an object of attention from both sides. Hence, this group may be more amenable to an ultimate reconciliation with China than is the first grouping, even if it retards or reverses the détente with the United States.

The Arab-Israel war, in June, 1967, served to bring these contradictory currents of Soviet attitudes into sharp relief. Soviet policy seemed to veer from one extreme to another during the crisis, as if some leaders were demanding a more vigorous Soviet response while others were counseling prudence. Although there appears to be some evidence to show that at least some sectors of the Soviet leadership encouraged the Arabs in their provocations against Israel, there is also evidence to indicate that part of the Soviet leadership was alarmed at Nasser's excesses as well as those of the Syrians. Once the war broke out, the Soviet government strenuously supported the Arab states diplomatically and politically on every point except the destruction of Israel.

One may surmise that some Soviet leaders called for more vigorous and direct action on the premise that an Israeli victory of the magnitude which it assumed would undercut the credibility of Soviet military and diplomatic support and simultaneously enhance that of the United States as Israel's patron.

The refusal of Moscow to go beyond the strong diplomatic support given to the Arabs suggests that the counsels of moderation won out, and Premier Kosygin's appearance at the United Nations General Assembly was designed as much to emphasize Soviet support for the Arabs as it was to arrange a personal meeting with President Johnson.

Confronted with a wide range of rapidly changing problems, the Soviet leadership will probably continue to "muddle through," allowing itself to be dominated by events rather than domesticating them. Until the Vietnam war is settled, there will always be serious apprehensions and suspicions in the Soviet leadership concerning ultimate American intentions. As a consequence, the Soviet leadership is likely to continue to make compromise decisions, postpone the resolution of problems, and remain vulnerable to the demands of those whose counsels would lead to a new and more dangerous spiral in the arms race. It is a question as to how much longer Moscow can evade some hard decisions on the direction of its foreign affairs.

7 Soviet Perceptions of the United States

WILLIAM ZIMMERMAN

As a result of a major reappraisal during the last years of the Khrushchev era of virtually every facet of Communist doctrine bearing on international relations, the unity of theory and practice, which had always been at the very core of Marxist-Leninist doctrine, was severed and the doctrinal preconditions were created for regarding Leninism as historically transcended and thus irrelevant to the atomic age.[1] The reappraisal touched on the identity of the international actors, the configuration of global power relations, the nature of the political process in the underdeveloped world, the role of international relations in the "world historical process," and the prospects for the creation of an "international relations of a new type" with the global advent of socialism.[2]

The evolution of Soviet perspectives on American foreign policy constituted a particularly important dimension of that reappraisal, for it had a significant bearing on the changing Soviet-American

WILLIAM ZIMMERMAN (Ph.D. Columbia, 1965) is Assistant Professor of Political Science at the University of Michigan. The winner of the Helen Dwight Reid Prize of the American Political Science Association for 1965, he is the author of a forthcoming book on *Soviet Perspectives on International Relations, 1956-67* and has contributed to *Survey* and the *Journal of Conflict Resolution*. His research has been primarily in the field of Soviet policy, Soviet-American relations, and the comparative study of foreign policies.

[1] Particularly vivid illustrations of this theme in Khrushchevian commentary are to be found in Khrushchev's speech at the III Rumanian Party Congress in 1960, where he declared: "One cannot mechanically repeat now . . . what . . . Lenin said many decades ago on imperialism"; and the January 7, 1963, *Pravda* editorial, which cautioned "Communists, and especially Communists who are statesmen and political figures, . . . not [to] rehash old truths from past centuries."

[2] For an analysis, see my "Soviet Perspectives on the International System, 1956-1964," a Columbia University doctoral dissertation.

relationship during the last years of Khrushchev's tenure in office and was central to the charges of "modern revisionism" directed at Khrushchev by the radical wing of the world Communist movement. The present essay summarizes the most important components of the evolution of Soviet perspectives on American foreign policy during the Khrushchev era, compares and contrasts, where possible, Khrushchevian and post-Khrushchevian perspectives on American foreign policy, and attempts to indicate the major divergences in perspective within the present Soviet ruling group and among key Soviet sub-elites evident in the central press and the specialized international relations literature.

It should be emphasized at the outset that, as anyone who has attempted to make inferences about real perspectives from elite articulations realizes, it is not an easy matter to ascertain who speaks for Moscow on which subjects and when the messages transmitted reflect accurately the views of Moscow or even an identifiable segment within the Soviet ruling group. Plural transmitters have existed in Moscow for some time now, which—operating along a narrow frequency band—emit divergent signals on some matters of high policy. The content of the messages transmitted represents an admixture of the perspectives of those who control the means of communication, the continued programming of "old favorites"—routinized symbols bearing little relation to the operative perspectives of those now controlling the communications channels, tactical considerations, and the perceived listening preferences of plural domestic and foreign audiences. With respect to Soviet perspectives on the foreign policy of another state, the task is particularly troublesome. Messages characterizing the motives, capabilities, and even the decision-making processes in another state are used to register approbation or disapprobation of that state's particular moves and short-run policy orientation. Tactical considerations prompt declaratory appraisals which may diverge radically from real perspectives. Soviet spokesmen at times have continued to utilize symbols which did not imply any misgivings about the motives and policies of a state long after Soviet decision-makers had, in fact, determined that the state in question was conducting a policy hostile to Soviet interests. "Hard" declaratory statements, by contrast, on occasion have served as a surrogate for operationally significant behavior or have provided a façade behind which arrangements with another state were made.

THE KHRUSHCHEVIAN REASSESSMENT

It is possible, however, to speak with some assurance about main trends in the evolution of Soviet perspectives during the Khrushchev era on American foreign policy.[3] That evolution embraced a reconsideration of the decision-making process in American foreign policy, a growing specificity and realism in the characterization of American capabilities, and an increasingly benevolent posture toward American motives. Taken together, the result was a Soviet image of United States foreign policy behavior in the atomic age which was considerably at variance with conventional Bolshevik notions about the main enemy.

In the traditional Marxist-Leninist perspective, key political decisions were made by the bourgeoisie. The state was perceived as merely an instrumentality of the ruling class, a front organization for the bourgeoisie. In the sixties, however, a major reappraisal of the relation between the economy and the polity was undertaken by Soviet political economists. In essence, the conclusion of that reappraisal was that a shift in phase in the American system had occurred; the United States had evolved from monopoly capitalism into state-monopoly capitalism. As a result, Soviet writers of the mid-fifties who (following Stalin's formula) had used "subordination" as a term epitomizing the relation of the bourgeois state to the capitalists were attacked [4] and an autonomy was ascribed to the government hitherto undetected in Soviet commentary.

The shift in focus from "Wall Street" to the "White House" was accompanied by a corresponding stress on the "Pentagon" as a force operating relatively independently of both monopoly capital and the White House and exercising pressure on the White House. As a result, the image of American foreign policy in the Khrushchevian perspective bore a marked similarity to C. Wright Mills' "power elite" model, in that the decisions are seen as a product of the intersection of the economic, military, and political orders—with the President playing an especially significant role. The Chinese were on solid ground in 1963 when they asked "the leaders of the CPUSA" whether they "still accept the Marxist-Leninist theory of the state and admit

[3] See also Nathan Leites, "The Kremlin's Horizon," The RAND Corporation, RM-3506-ISA (March, 1963); and Alexander Dallin, "Russia and China View the United States," *The Annals*, Vol. 349 (September, 1963), pp. 154-62.

[4] S. A. Dalin, *Voenno-gosudarstvennyi monopolisticheskii kapitalizm v SShA* (Moscow: "Nauka," 1961), p. 328.

that the U.S. state is the tool of monopoly capital for class rule?"
and if so, how can there be a President independent of monopoly
capital, how can there be a Pentagon independent of the White
House, and how can there be two opposing centers in Washington?" [5]

Moreover, Soviet commentary began to go "beyond the power
elite." During the last years of Khrushchev's tenure in power, Soviet
commentators on the American scene increasingly differentiated
among groups of the bourgeoisie and among policies advocated by
various representatives of monopoly capital. Equally importantly,
the more innovative Soviet analysts—especially in the Institute of
World Economy and International Relations—began during the
last two years of Khrushchev's rule to include elements *outside* the
bourgeoisie in the arena of American foreign policy decision-making.
Lobbying and interest articulation, it was explicitly recognized, were
carried on by groups other than "Big Business." Thus, in one Soviet
enumeration, "trade unions, churches, and other organizations including the AFL-CIO, the National Farmers' Union, the American
Medical Association" were mentioned as organizations having "their
own lobbies." [6]

In short, in the last years of Khrushchev's power, Soviet perspectives
on the American decision-making process evolved in a significant
manner toward a calculus embracing the elements typically considered
by Western commentators on American foreign policy.

Ascertaining Khrushchevian perspectives about American capabilities represents an appreciably more difficult task than that involved
in taking note of the changed Soviet calculus of the American foreign policy process. Generally, Soviet statements about American or
"imperialist" capabilities do not refer to capabilities in the abstract
but rather involve a rough cost calculus—which entails assumptions
about the motives and rationality of American decision-makers. Thus,
the assertion first enunciated by Khrushchev in 1959 that imperialism
was no longer capable of destroying Communist rule in the Soviet
Union by force, constituted a calculus that Western decision-makers
would be unwilling to pay the cost to achieve an intended effect
(in this instance, the re-establishment of non-Communist rule in the
Soviet Union), rather than an assertion that such capability no longer
existed. Similarly, Soviet commentators during the Khrushchev era
in their polemics with the Chinese about the nature of American
imperialism tended to pose a dispute over motives in capability terms.

[5] "A Comment on the Statement of the Communist Party of the U.S.A.," *Peking
Review*, VI, No. 10-11 (March 15, 1963), p. 59.
[6] G. Yevgenev, "Lobbying in the USA," *International Affairs*, No. 6 (June, 1963),
pp. 93-94.

To give credence to the Soviet contention that socialism was "turning into the decisive factor of world development," Soviet spokesmen generally confined themselves to asserting that, while the nature of imperialism had not changed, its capabilities had. This posture was considerably less dangerous tactically than its alternative, which was to state that in the atomic age the priority calculations of United States decision-makers had altered—which virtually denied the imperialist essence of American foreign policy.

Nevertheless, it is possible to describe the broad outlines of the Soviet appraisal of American capabilities during the Khrushchev era. Briefly put, there have been two dominant themes in the Soviet dialogue since 1955. The two seem contradictory at first glance, but are in fact readily reconcilable. The first involves a qualitative decline in the relative power of the United States noted by Soviet observers, which served, *inter alia*, to justify revolutionary optimism.[7] The crucial element, in the Soviet calculus, was the development by the Soviet Union in the late 1950's of an inter-continental ballistic missile. With the ICBM, in the Soviet view, the Soviet Union was able to deprive the United States of the geographically-based impermeability on which the United States' position as the dominant power rested. A second development was the emergence, at the end of the 1950's and in the early 1960's, of the Afro-Asian bloc of independent states. These two developments were seen to have provided an impetus to the third major transformation, namely, the re-emergence of Europe and the resultant weakening of the United States' position within the imperialist camp.

Simultaneously, Khrushchev and other Soviet observers hastened to caution that the United States was nevertheless "still strong"—and thus to urge a minimum risk policy. At no time, not even during the years 1957-61 (a period when Soviet commentary was replete with exuberant assertions concerning the decline in the United States' relative power position) did Khrushchev or Soviet international relations specialists ever deny world power status to the United States. Rather, the thrust of Soviet writings was that the leaders of the United States were faced with the task of adjusting to a world in which they were obliged to treat another power more or less equally,[8]

---

[7] It was as a result of this change in the relative distribution of power that Soviet spokesmen began to speak of the beginning of "a new, third phase of capitalism's general crisis."

[8] For subtle speculation on the *degree* of equality from a psychoanalytical viewpoint, see Leites, *op. cit.* A more detailed account of the perturbations in Soviet characterizations of the global distribution of power is contained in Zimmerman, *op. cit.*

a world in which the United States was merely *one* of "the world's giants." In the years 1957-61, similarly, Soviet claims concerning strategic capabilities were at a maximum,[9] but nowhere in Soviet commentary (in contrast with Chinese writings at this juncture) do we find the suggestion that the United States lacked a capacity to deliver a punishing second strike on the Soviet Union.

During the last years of the Khrushchev era, Soviet statements about American capabilities became appreciably more specific, especially with respect to American strategic capabilities. The most detailed account of American strategic might published was contained in Marshal V. D. Sokolovsky's *Voennaia strategiia*.[10] Drawing, ostensibly, on the figures of the London Institute for Strategic Studies, it presented a detailed enumeration of American strategic capabilities which for those in the Soviet Union cognizant of Soviet missile strength at that time must have been sobering, to say the least.

Moreover, in the last years of the Khrushchev era it became increasingly evident that underlying much of the Soviet analysis of American foreign policy was the implicit assumption that the United States would retain its world power status throughout the remainder of the twentieth century. Soviet commentary seems to have assumed that:

1. Revolution per se in the United States was not on the horizon;
2. The chances of general war were slight;
3. Another great depression or other economic or social catastrophe of such magnitude as to affect appreciably the international position of the United States was improbable; and
4. The growth rate projections for the United States by American economists, while high, were not exorbitant.[11]

Small wonder, therefore, that the Chinese argued that during the Khrushchev era "the only country the leaders of the CPSU [looked] up to was the United States"! [12]

Soviet commentary in the last years of the Khrushchev era also generally manifested a considerably more benign appraisal of the motives of the decision-makers acting in the United States' name

---

[9] See Arnold L. Horelick and Myron Rush, *Strategic Power and Soviet Foreign Policy* (Chicago: University of Chicago Press, 1965).

[10] English translations of the first edition are V. D. Sokolovsky, ed., *Military Strategy* (New York: Frederick A. Praeger, Inc., 1963); and *Soviet Military Strategy* (Englewood Cliffs, N.J.: Prentice-Hall, Inc., 1963).

[11] See especially S. M. Menshikov, *Ekonomicheskaia politika pravitelstva Kennedi* (Moscow: "Mysl," 1964).

[12] "Peaceful Coexistence—Two Diametrically Opposed Policies," *Peking Review,* VI, No. 51 (December 20, 1963), 16.

than that conveyed by traditional Soviet formulations.[13] Traditional Soviet formulations had depicted United States "ruling circles," animated by considerations of power and/or profit, as seeking world domination. The United States was the main enemy, the bulwark of global reaction. From 1959 on, Khrushchev generally adopted the position that "reasonable men" or "realists" were in the majority in the American ruling group. As Khrushchev appears to have become increasingly attracted by the prospect of a genuine Soviet-American détente, moreover, the concept "reasonable men" underwent an evolution. Initially in 1959-60, "reasonableness" or "realism" referred to the propensity, which Khrushchev professed to detect, on the part of the majority within American ruling circles to adjust to the realities of the changed global distribution of power and to acquiesce in the onward progression of the world historical process. Gradually, the notion of realism became transformed: especially after the Cuban missile crisis, it came increasingly to refer simply to those who recognized a common stake in the avoidance of nuclear war and who consequently were disinclined to resort to war as an instrument of policy.[14] Finally, "realism" became so broad that persons like General Maxwell Taylor and members of the Morgan financial dynasty began to be included; i.e., the realists among American decision-makers were those intelligently pursuing American interests under conditions of mutual deterrence.[15]

[13] For a striking example of an article completely at variance with the mode of Soviet commentary in these years, see L. Zubok, "V. I. Lenin ob amerikanskom imperializme i rabochem dvizhenii SShA," *Novaia i noveishaia istoriia*, No. 2 (signed to press March 1, 1963), pp. 50-64. This article is belligerently anti-American in tone and makes no mention of Khrushchev. It may, therefore, be further ammunition for those who argue that Khrushchev suffered an eclipse in the aftermath of the Cuban missile crisis.

[14] During the latter years of the Khrushchev era and in the succeeding years as well, there has been on-going controversy as to whether and to what extent the Clausewitz dictum has become irrelevant to the foreign policy behavior of socialist and capitalist countries. The reluctance of the military to accept the view of Khrushchev and the Institute of World Economy and International Relations that the dictum was irrelevant in the atomic age is noted in Thomas W. Wolfe, *Soviet Strategy at the Crossroads* (Cambridge, Mass.: Harvard University Press, 1964), pp. 70-78.

[15] In one sense, this latter perspective was consonant with the Chinese view, since the Chinese contend that "if the representatives of U.S. monopoly capital are 'sensible' at all, they are 'sensible' only in safeguarding the fundamental interests of their own class, in oppressing the American people at home and plundering other peoples abroad, and in executing their policies of aggression and war." ("Confessions Concerning the Line of Soviet-U.S. Collaboration Pursued by the New Leaders of the C.P.S.U.," *Peking Review*, IX, No. 8 [February 18, 1966], 8.) The difference, of course, was that for Soviet commentators, such "sensibleness" was commendable, whereas it was not for the Chinese.

Implicit in the latter assessment (which was as revealing of the Khrushchevian reappraisal of *Soviet* goals as of Soviet perspectives on American motives) was an assumption that the successful pursuit of American interests was compatible with an improvement in Soviet-American relations. The gains, therefore, of the one country were not necessarily the losses of the other.[16]

Underlying *all* these notions of "reasonableness" was a rather strange image of the main enemy. Indeed, it is seriously open to question whether for Khrushchev in the last years of his rule the United States was the main enemy. Rather than a view of the world in which the United States was located at the enmity pole of an enmity/amity continuum, the Khrushchevian imagery became more akin to the perspective of the minority leader in a two party national system. To Khrushchev—the Everett Dirksen of the world Communist movement —the men of reason in the United States constituted the leading forces in the ruling opposition party, to be sure, and as such were the major adversary. Unlike the radicals of both systems ("It is truly said," Khrushchev declared, "if you go left, you come out right") ,[17] however, the men of reason in the American "party" were people with whom "struggle *and* cooperation" [18] were necessary, desirable, and possible; and—because they used power responsibly—represented a lesser threat to Soviet values than either the Goldwaters or the Maos.

OCTOBER, 1964—SEPTEMBER, 1965: KHRUSHCHEVISM WITHOUT KHRUSHCHEV

The months immediately following October, 1964, witnessed the appearance of a number of specialized works on American foreign policy as well as on international relations generally which demonstrated an almost total continuity with the trends in the evolution of Soviet perspectives in the last years of the Khrushchev era.[19] Of these,

[16] For a Soviet statement explicitly characterizing international politics in the atomic age as a non-zero sum game, see G. Gerasimov, "War Savants Play Games," *International Affairs*, No. 7 (July, 1964), p. 80.

[17] *Pravda*, December 13, 1962.

[18] It was the dialectical unity of struggle and cooperation which represented the "new content" of peaceful coexistence. For an analysis, see Robert C. Tucker, *The Soviet Political Mind* (New York: Frederick A. Praeger, Inc., 1963), pp. 201-22.

[19] Among the more important were AN IMEMO, *Dvizhushchie sily vneshnei politiki SShA* (Moscow: "Nauka," 1965); I. M. Ivanova, *Mirnoe sosushchestvovanie i krizis vneshnepoliticheskoi ideologii imperializma SShA* (Moscow: "Mezhdunarodnye otnosheniia," 1965); AN IMEMO, *Stroitelstvo kommunizma i mirovoi revoliutsionnyi protses* (Moscow: "Nauka," 1966); AN IMEMO, *Mezhdunarodnye*

a collective work by several specialists in the Institute of World Economy and International Relations entitled *The Motive Forces of U.S. Foreign Policy* was the most important in that it, in a relatively systematic fashion, brought together in one place most of the innovative trends in Soviet commentary on American foreign policy. That works such as *Motive Forces* bore a marked similarity to books and other treatments of the United States in the years immediately prior to Khrushchev's ouster was scarcely surprising, since they were conceived and largely written[20] before Khrushchev's removal. What is most significant about these works is that (1) they *were* published, and (2) in certain respects they were even closer to typical Western perspectives on American foreign policy than the modernist trend in Soviet commentary had been during the Khrushchev era.

With respect to American foreign policy decision-making, several themes were noted in Soviet accounts in the months immediately after Khrushchev's removal. Soviet specialists continued to lay great stress on the importance of the state apparatus in United States foreign policy decision-making.[21] The same two explanations were advanced: (1) the increased significance of foreign policy matters "in public affairs," and (2) the change in the relationship between the state and the economy within the United States. On the latter point, for instance, the authors of *Motive Forces* specifically attacked Stalin for having used "subordination" to describe the position of the bourgeois state vis-à-vis the capitalists and informed their readers that "the founders of Marxism-Leninism" had "always emphasized . . . that the government is not only a shop assistant but also a stock holder." "One must not," they cautioned, "underestimate the relative self-sufficiency and the active role of the state [and] its unfailing tendency to transform itself from a servant into a master." In fact, "the bourgeois state," they declared, "sometimes even acts against the will of the majority of the ruling class."[22] Similarly, Soviet writ-

---

otnosheniia posle vtoroi mirovoi voiny, III (1956-1964 gg.) (Moscow: Politizdat, 1965).

[20] V. N. Baryshnikov's competent dissertation, *"Taivanskii vopros" v kitaisko-amerikanskikh otnosheniiakh* (unpublished dissertation, AN SSSR, Institut Ekonomiki Mirovoi Sotsialisticheskoi Sistemy [Otdel Istorii]), was completed during 1964 and then revised to account for Khrushchev's removal by the simple expedient of covering Khrushchev's name with such phrases as "the Soviet government."

[21] See especially *Stroitelstvo,* p. 389, and *Dvizhushchie sily,* p. 21.

[22] *Dvizhushchie sily,* pp. 20-21. In an article which repeats the substance of the introductory chapter of *Dvizhushchie sily,* I. Lemin put it even more strongly by omitting "of the majority," i.e., it "sometimes even acts against the will of the ruling class." (I. Lemin, "Vneshniaia politika SShA: dvizhushchie sily i tendentsii," *Mirovaia ekonomika i mezhdunarodnye otnosheniia,* No. 6 [June 1965], p. 26.)

ings in the months after Khrushchev's removal (both before and after the November, 1964, American election) took pains to emphasize the unique role of the American president "in the carrying out of foreign policy, in particular on questions of war and peace." [23] Soviet commentators in this period, moreover, stressed that the "contradictions and conflicts in the United States ruling circles about disarmament, the Cold War, East-West trade [had] become a permanent factor of the internal political life of the U.S." [24] Finally, Soviet specialists on American foreign policy continued to show attention to forces outside the bourgeoisie which influenced foreign policy, and, for the first time, some specialists began to ascribe major significance to the influence of public opinion on American foreign policy making.[25]

In gross terms, the Soviet appraisal of American capabilities also underwent no appreciable changes in the months immediately following Khrushchev's removal. Books as widely divergent in authorship, character, and/or audience-targeting as *Marxism-Leninism on War and the Army, Motive Forces, The Construction of Communism and the World-Revolutionary Process,* and Volume III of *International Relations Since World War II* analyzed the capabilities of the United States from essentially the same perspective on the nature of power as had been the fashion in the Khrushchev era: namely, that economic (including scientific)[26] and military capacity and potential are the essential components of the United States' power internationally and that in these terms the United States remains far ahead of all countries other than the Soviet Union. Furthermore, there were indications that Soviet specialists on the American economy—"dogmatists" notwithstanding—continued to regard a major depression in the United States as improbable, that they were impressed by the use of Keynesian techniques by the Kennedy and Johnson administrations, and that they considered the minimum growth rate projections to the year 2000, contained in the book *Resources in America's Future* (which was deemed sufficiently significant to warrant translation) not out of line. Again, with regard to strategic capabilities, there was nothing to suggest that Soviet observers in any way either questioned that the United States had the capacity to render a damaging second-strike on the Soviet Union or thought that any other bour-

---

[23] *Ibid.; Stroitelstvo,* p. 389.

[24] *Dvizhushchie sily,* p. 22.

[25] See, especially, the controversial dissertation by E. I. Popova. *SShA: bor'ba po voprosam vneshnei politiki 1919-1922 g.g.* (Moscow: "Mezhdunarodnye Otnosheniia," 1966).

[26] Indeed, there seems to have been a definite upgrading of science as a variable making for political power internationally. See, for instance, *Marksizm-Leninizm, o voine i armii* (Moscow: Voenizdat, 1965), p. 265.

geois state could ever approximate significant strategic capability.[27]

On at least one important matter relating to the Soviet appraisal of American capabilities there was no consensus in Moscow in the first months after the October, 1964, coup. The question at issue was whether under any envisionable circumstances an outcome amounting to a Soviet "victory" might result from a thermonuclear exchange with the United States. The prevalent (but not unanimous) view in the last years of the Khrushchev era had been that prospects were close to nil for ever denying the United States the capacity to cause the Soviet survivors of a thermonuclear exchange to "envy the dead." Khrushchev's removal, coupled with the American bombing of North Vietnam appears to have created conditions in which those at variance with what had been the prevalent view during Khrushchev's tenure in office attempted to reassert their position. From the modest evidence available, it is possible to infer that during the first year after Khrushchev's ouster this effort was not successful. In March, 1965, G. Gerasimov, one of the few Soviet civilian commentators knowledgeable about strategic matters, published an article[28] in which he polemicized against the view that, through the creation of an antiballistic missile system, it might be possible to achieve "victory" in a thermonuclear exchange. It would require "a discovery bordering on a miracle," he argued, to achieve the "means for the 100 per cent interception of nuclear missiles," and nothing less would be adequate. "The means of defense," he declared, "lag behind the means of attack." Further evidence of on-going controversy as to whether victory might result from a thermonuclear exchange appeared in May, 1965, when Nikolai Talensky, a retired general who for more than a decade had been identified with modernist trends in the Soviet Union on questions of war and peace, warned that there could be "no more dangerous illusion" than to believe that thermonuclear war could be an instrument for achieving political goals.[29]

Perhaps the most startling assertions about American foreign policy to appear in the period immediately after Khrushchev's ouster pertained to American motives and behavior. Once again, the Institute of World Economy and International Relations' *Motive Forces* serves as the prime example. The typical Khrushchevian characterization of all three recent American Presidents—Eisenhower, Kennedy, and Johnson—as reasonable and prudent men, disinclined to risk-

[27] *Mezhdunarodnye otnosheniia*, III, 251.

[28] G. Gerasimov, "The First Strike Theory," *International Affairs*, No. 3 (March 1965), pp. 44-45.

[29] N. Talensky, "The Late War: Some Reflections," *International Affairs*, No. 5 (May, 1965), p. 15.

taking and aware of the realities of the nuclear age, was advanced. The United States, the authors of *Motive Forces* argued, was less inclined to use force as an instrument of foreign policy in its relations with the Soviet Union and other socialist countries.[30] For the first time in Soviet commentary, the authors of *Motive Forces* redefined (albeit hesitantly and contradictorily) the alleged American drive for world dominance. Rather than construe "world domination" literally, they hinted, the United States should be seen as seeking merely to retain its position of leadership in the capitalist world. The authors in addition stated explicitly that a "community of national interests"[31] exists between the United States and the Soviet Union, and declared —in a book signed to press a month after the United States began bombing North Vietnam—that "at the present time there exist no territorial [or] economic disputes and conflicts between [the United States and the Soviet Union], their national interests do not collide either globally or regionally."[32]

Toward a New Realism?

The works conceived during the Khrushchev era and signed to press during 1965 constituted the high mark in the evolution of Soviet perspectives on American foreign policy. From approximately September, 1965, the modernist tide seems to have ebbed, primarily, it would seem, as a result of the Vietnam war. On all scores there was evidence, to be found especially in *International Affairs* and the central newspapers, of a resurgence of more traditionalist modes of analyzing American foreign policy. Articles appeared explaining why big business had picked Johnson over Goldwater and intimating that Johnson's election campaign had been little more than a deception.[33] Many public utterances in 1965-66 were replete with references to (undifferentiated) imperialists, and statements appeared stressing the essential homogeneity of views within the American ruling group.[34]

[30] *Dvizhushchie sily,* especially pp. 12-13.

[31] *Dvizhushchie sily,* p. 507.

[32] *Ibid.*

[33] See, in particular, the articles by "A. Sovetov," "The Aggressive Policy of U.S. Imperialism," *International Affairs,* No. 9 (September, 1965), p. 67; and "The Soviet Union and Present International Relations," *International Affairs,* No. 1 (January, 1966), pp. 3-9.

[34] Sovetov, "The Aggressive Policy . . .": "It is important to bear in mind that, although there was a contest between two tendencies in U.S. foreign policy, there was, in the final analysis, no fundamental difference between them." See, too, M. Marinin, "Sotsialisticheskii internatsionalizm i politika voinstviushchego im-

Even publications of the Institute of World Economy and International Relations intimated that the "two tendencies" in American foreign policy were not as clearly defined as previously claimed and warned that events had demonstrated that it was wrong to assume that the forces of reason in bourgeois states would "automatically" be in the majority.[35]

Similarly, since September, 1965, there has been a more vigorous public expression of the view that not even strategic parity with the United States would be enough for the USSR. One military commentator, Colonel Rybkin, declared that there were ways of countering an enemy's nuclear attack. An even more intransigent stance was adopted by one Colonel Grudinin, who labeled as "mistaken and even harmful" the views of Talensky and others who "deny any possibility of victory in a world-wide nuclear-rocket conflict."[36]

The American intervention in Vietnam brought out another divergence in perspective relating to American capabilities. It, too, had important policy-relevant consequences, since it bore greatly on Moscow's proclivity to risk a confrontation with the United States. In this instance, there was little doubt that the divergence of perspectives extended to the ruling group—as the Supreme Soviet election speeches in June, 1966, made clear. In interpreting the events in Vietnam, Kosygin (along with Brezhnev and Podgorny) adopted a stance consonant with the low-risk, Khrushchevian posture of emphasizing United States might. "It would be incorrect," Kosygin stressed, "in conditions of the strengthening of the danger of aggression to minimize the possibilities and potential of the United States; we do not belong in the number of those who are inclined to draw such conclusions from the contemporary situation."[37] G. I. Voronov, by contrast, evidently *was* among those who did draw such a conclusion (and thus was presumably more inclined to risk-taking than Kosygin), for he declared, apropos Vietnam, that "the growing aggressiveness of imperialism is by no means a sign of its strength."[38] So, too, apparently, was A. N. Shelepin: "The events and facts of recent years," he asserted, "show that the American imperialists are conduct-

perializma," *Mirovaia ekonomika i mezhdunarodnye otnosheniia*, No. 6 (June, 1966), p. 8.

[35] *Mezhdunarodnye otnosheniia*, III, 61. This volume was signed to press September 16, 1965.

[36] See above, pp. 116-17. If Rybkin is a "Red hawk," then Grudinin is a pterodactyl, for he even attacked Rybkin for taking into account the impact of technology on the nature of war.

[37] *Pravda*, June 9, 1966. For Brezhnev's and Podgorny's statements, see, respectively, *Pravda*, June 11 and 10, 1966.

[38] *Pravda*, June 4, 1966.

ing themselves increasingly irrationally . . . first of all because their positions have been shaken." [39]

The most strident and vigorous resurgence[40] of traditionalist characterizations of American foreign policy related to American motives and behavior. A bevy of articles and brochures appeared condemning the United States' role as world gendarme and asserting that the United States had by no means abandoned its goal of world domination. The influential spokesman who hides behind the *nom de plume* "A. Sovetov" went so far as to declare that "even [the United States'] membership in the anti-Hitler coalition in the Second [World War was] determined by its drive for world domination." [41] Soviet commentators professed to see American moves in Vietnam, the Dominican Republic, and elsewhere as part of a single pattern. The United States was bracketed with West Germany as countries, unlike "many capitalist countries," wishing to continue the Cold War.[42] In view of all the foregoing, especially the attacks on American goals, it was not surprising, therefore, that the XXIII CPSU Congress, in its resolutions, explicitly rejected the thesis which had provided much of the rationale for de-emphasizing American hostility; i.e., that under conditions of mutual deterrence the United States was moving away from its prior reliance on the instruments of violence.[43]

[39] *Pravda*, June 3, 1966.
[40] A particularly vivid illustration of the return to the old phrases is contained in I. Ivashin, "The October Revolution and International Relations," *International Affairs*, No. 11 (November, 1966), pp. 48-52.
[41] "The Aggressive Policy," p. 63.
[42] A. Yermonsky and O. Nakropin, "General Line of Soviet Foreign Policy," *International Affairs*, No. 9 (September, 1966), p. 77. The authors hedged their attack by noting: "Although aggressive sentiments are now obviously dominant in Washington, it is well known that other, sounder tendencies exist in the U.S. capital. The strengthening of these tendencies will meet with due understanding on the part of the Soviet Union." Similar remarks have appeared in more authoritative statements. For instance, A. P. Kirilenko in a speech commemorating the 97th anniversary of Lenin's birth emphasized that "the Government of the Soviet Union has more than once declared we are prepared to work together with all capitalist countries on the basis of the principles of peaceful coexistence in the task of strengthening peace, in the development of mutually beneficial economic relations. This would apply equally to the United States if the government of that country would take the path of observing the norms of international law and would cease its involvement in the internal affairs of other countries and peoples." (*Pravda*, April 23, 1967.)
[43] It appears that members of the Institute of World Economics and International Relations were reluctant to abandon their position on this issue. A lead article in *Mirovaia ekonomika i mezhdunarodnye otnosheniia* a month before the XXIII CPSU Congress continued to affirm the view that "the possibilities of using [prior] methods have significantly contracted (although they have not fully disappeared) as a result of the sharp changes in the political situation and political

Thus, in 1966, scarcely a year and a half after Khrushchev's removal, it appeared that the trend in Soviet commentary of the latter years of the Khrushchev era had been reversed.[44] But the reappearance of traditional characterizations may have represented a tactical —and transitory—response to the American involvement in Vietnam, as the Chinese purport to believe. Books like *Motive Forces,* they declared in 1966, express views which "are the very ones the new leaders of the CPSU would make themselves" [45] in circumstances more conducive to expressing a somewhat benevolent view of American foreign policy. Certainly, the Soviet ruling group's reluctance to express a charitable appraisal of American motives at a time when the United States was waging war against a socialist country is readily understandable. Whatever else the members of the Politburo are, they are not masochists; to give vent to favorable views about American foreign policy at such a time would only expose them further to such vitriolic attacks from the pro-Chinese elements in the world Communist movement as the following:

> Today, every man, woman or child killed by U.S. imperialist bombs, bullets and poison gas—in Vietnam, the Dominican Republic or anywhere else—is a victim not only of U.S. neo-fascism but also of those who preach the traitorous doctrine of "peaceful coexistence" with imperialism, the "reasonableness" of U.S. imperialist leaders, and the "changed nature" of imperialism.[46]

Moreover, the dominant Soviet leaders have taken pains to make clear that the war in Vietnam is the primary obstacle to improved Soviet-American relations, suggesting that the new line may last only as long as the war lasts.

There are, however, several important difficulties with such an interpretation. It assumes a control over the communications channels which over-simplifies Soviet reality, ascribes a misleading homogeneity

---

climate in the world." (N. Kolikov, "Osnovnye sily sovremennogo mirovogo revoliutsionnogo protsessa," *Mirovaia ekonomika i mezhdunarodnye otnosheniia,* No. 3 [March, 1966], p. 6.)

[44] Soviet commentary had not gone full circle. The emphasis continues largely to be on Washington, not Wall Street, as the locus of decision-making; there are intermittent references to the "two tendencies"; political controversy over foreign policy as a fundamental feature of contemporary America continues to be stressed.

[45] "Confessions . . .," p. 8.

[46] The passage is taken from an article entitled "Victory Over Fascism—Stalin's Leadership," which appeared in the *Malayan Monitor,* published in London, and reprinted in *Global Digest,* II (1965), No. 11, 49. Although Chinese and pro-Chinese Communists usually quote Soviet statements accurately, the present author knows of no instance in Soviet commentary where, in so many words, the "changed nature" of imperialism has been asserted.

to Soviet perspectives about American foreign policy, and fails to consider the impact of external events on Soviet internal politics. (It is also possible that, in any event, a temporary conservative turn in policy would have followed Khrushchev's removal simply because the key Soviet power bases to which a person attempting to consolidate his power would appeal would be attracted by conservative symbols.) The record suggests that the return to old symbols has proceeded at differential rates—which is most plausibly explained as indicating a reluctance on the part of some to abandon previous positions. Moreover, there are those for whom the traditional Leninist characterizations have considerably more operational significance than they do for a Kosygin, for instance, at least in the sense that these symbols correspond to the intensity of animosity to the United States. Persons who fit this description appear to be drawn largely from three groups. They include military men (e.g., the now deceased Marshal Malinovsky, who termed the United States "worse than Hitler") with a stake in continued heavy military spending, old ideologues who during the past decade have been shunted into positions of relatively low status and little influence (like Ivashin and Deborin), and persons whose career patterns suggest a favorable disposition to domestic reactionary policies (like Shelepin, who also finds the Hitler analogy attractive). For them, the war in Vietnam is not an isolated event but evidence that the United States confronts Soviet interest in revolution in every corner of the globe.

An explanation emphasizing the manipulative character of the reappearance of old symbols, furthermore, probably fails to take into account the extent to which for all Soviet observers American foreign policy from 1965 cast doubt on new hypotheses and rekindled old fears. Even if the resurgence is a function largely of the perturbations in Soviet-American relations, it seems unlikely that at any time in the near future Soviet perspectives on American foreign policy will be as favorably disposed to the United States as was the fashion in 1963-65. Out of the clash of the "two tendencies" in Soviet perspectives on the United States—represented by the mode of Soviet commentary in 1963-65 on the one hand, and 1965-67 on the other—there will probably emerge a new perspective on American foreign policy. This would include the more sophisticated analysis of the way in which internal political processes affect American foreign policy, as exemplified by the work of the specialists in the Institute of World Economy and International Relations, but would be characterized by a more jaundiced view of American foreign policy goals and behavior than was the mode in 1963-65. There are already some indications of this "new realism." Soviet observers—partly as a result of projection—seem increasingly to be attracted to rather cynical, national-interest explanations of the behavior of states (including the United States) in which transnational class ties play an insignificant role. Examples of this new cynicism were already apparent in the specialized international relations literature in 1965-66. Thus, in N. N. Iakovlev's study, Franklin Roosevelt is much less the "progressive" figure he has usually been made out to be in recent Soviet historiography and much more the conservative realist calculatingly preparing the nation for war.[47] Similarly, in Baryshnikov's analysis of the United States, China, and the Taiwan question, he speculates about a time when—Taiwan having lost its military significance—the United States will abandon the Chinese Nationalists in order to secure a rapprochement with Communist China.[48] Moreover, by 1967 evidence of such thinking began to be found in the central press as well. *Krasnaia zvezda*, for example, in February, 1967, purported to detect "a Red China lobby" in the United States and to note "open talk" in Washington that "the ruling circles of the United States are interested in the retention of power by Mao Tse-tung." [49]

This new trend, if such in fact it turns out to be, may provide a more stable basis for a durable American-Soviet relationship than either the orthodox *kto-kogo* perspective or the dominant trend in Soviet commentary in the last years of the Khrushchev era. Khrushchev, perhaps to discredit the traditionalist perspective, did to a certain extent "prettify American imperialism"; the fact is that the interests of the United States and the Soviet Union, as perceived by key elites within the two countries, do and will clash. The new realism will facilitate an American-Soviet relationship in which peaceful coexistence, in precisely the Khrushchevian formulation, is possible: namely, a limited-adversary relationship involving both struggle and cooperation.

[47] N. N. Iakovlev, *Franklin Ruzvelt: chelovek i politik* (Moscow: Izdatelstvo "Mezhdunarodnye Otnosheniia," 1965).

[48] Baryshnikov, *op. cit.*

[49] E.g., *Krasnaia zvezda*, February 21, 1967. See also Chapter 6 above.

Glossary

Agitprop	Department of Agitation and Propaganda
CCP	Chinese Communist Party
CP	Communist Party
CPR	Chinese People's Republic
CPSU	Communist Party of the Soviet Union
gorkom	city committee
ispolkom	executive committee
kolkhoz	collective farm
MTS	machine tractor station
obkom	regional committee
oblispolkom	regional executive committee
raiispolkom	district executive committee
raikom	district Party committee
RSFSR	Russian Soviet Federated Socialist Republic
Soiuzselkhoztekhnika	All-Union Farm Machine Agency
sovkhoz	state farm
sovnarkhoz	economic council

y at the end of a Russian word is the plural equivalent of s in English

DATE DUE

11/15 MAR 17 1970			
MAY 3 1 1973			
GAYLORD			PRINTED IN U.S.A.